THE VISION QUEST

A GUIDE'S TRAINING MANUAL

TEACHINGS & TOOLS FROM
40 YEARS OF FIELD EXPERIENCE

SPARROW HART

The Vision Quest: A Guide's Training Manual —
Teachings & Tools From 40 Years of Field Experience

Sparrow Hart

Drawings and Illustrations: Anja Timm
Cover Photo: Joshua Earle on Unsplash.com
Author Photo: Willie Allison
Cover Design and Interior Layout: Blend Creations Design

Dedicated to the Earth
to the hawks
and to the bears.

PREFACE

To the vision quest guides of the present and those to come...

I wrote this book to help guides become well-versed in the art of leading contemporary vision quests and the skills required to do so. You will need to be familiar with both traditional ritual forms as well as psychological perspectives and practices that speak to the concerns and issues facing people today. I hope this manual proves useful. I expect it will be edited and expanded over the years. Suggestions or feedback to make this manual more helpful to those carrying on this tradition in the future are welcome.

We're living in times of great change on the planet and in culture and society. Though the number and effects of these changes will be vast, most don't need to be elaborated here, and many are still unknown. But some of them will affect how vision quests are led in the future. A couple of small examples: In the late 1980s, leading quests in Vermont, when I was asked about ticks, I'd reply, "There are no ticks in Vermont." Unfortunately, this is no longer true. Before the mid-1990s I had never met a transgender person. Now I've met many.

Traditional, stable cultures were adapted to stable times; their rituals and processes were practiced and refined over centuries. In our times, we're challenged to find a working balance between the old and the new, between honoring and applying what is ancient and essential while incorporating new perspectives and tools relevant to novel and changing circumstances.

Themes and processes that are archetypal and integral to the human experience need to remain. Some situations — like ticks in Vermont — can and will change. But the sentence "There is no oxygen in Vermont" will never be spoken, since oxygen is necessary for life and any possibility of vision quests. Similarly, certain foundational elements of the vision quest process — like rites of passage or the archetypal Heroic Journey myth — are fundamental to the human psyche, and guides must learn and know them well. But how these are translated and applied to the conditions of today must evolve as changes in ecosystems, societies, and social roles continue to happen.

Five hundred years ago, a medicine person knew the landscape and its inhabitants well. She would be well-versed in traditional tools to interpret dreams and access the spirit world, and she would be able to give instruction and guidance to those who were ready to follow this well-worn and familiar path. Yet those elders, wise in their time, would know little or nothing about

- Child abuse, foster children, neglect and abandonment, sexual abuse;
- Addiction, alcoholism, eating disorders, ADHD, workaholism, pornography, PTSD;
- Poverty, homelessness, racism, prostitution, pollution;
- Depression, anxiety, co-dependence, self-hatred, lack of self-esteem, mental illness; or
- Gay, lesbian, bi-sexual, and transgender issues.

Some of these concerns and their effects are likely to be present among participants in every small group coming for a modern-day vision quest. Because of this, guides of today and tomorrow — while not acting in the role of therapist — must have a basic familiarity with these conditions, a language for speaking about them, and a comfortable access to their own experience, along with useful perspectives and tools to share with those seeking guidance and help.

This is no small order. It asks a lot. But for those called, it is a path with heart that will never grow old. The chance to grow and learn, especially in times of change, will be a constant companion as you journey toward that mysterious Unknown, that great Mystery. This path can acquaint you with Nature, as well as your own nature; introduce you to kindred spirits; inspire you to learn about wisdom traditions, culture, and the human soul; and, of course, teach you how to put up your tarp in a storm.

— Sparrow Hart

THE BEGINNING — MY FIRST QUEST

In the 1970s, I'd found refuge in a commune in Vermont. I'd had a seemingly successful academic career: Phi Beta Kappa at Stanford, a full fellowship to the New School for Social Research. But even after leaving academia and hiking the Pacific Crest Trail, something was missing. At the core, I felt damaged and disheartened.

Was it the residue of an abusive childhood in which I was shamed, humiliated, and hit? Was it my experience at a high-end prep school, where my working-class background brought ridicule because of my clothes and manners? The times themselves? I'd been in college in the late '60s, the era of Vietnam, protests, racial unrest, and a widespread search for alternative ways to live. The whole system felt corrupt and phony; what was normal and expected felt like the problem. To put on a coat and tie and join the establishment felt like spiritual death.

In the commune, I learned how to grow food in an organic garden, repair a car, and manage a woodlot — activities that brought me closer to the earth in a visceral way. Sharing a home and meals with other people forced me to communicate, a skill I'd barely learned in my childhood or the decade after.

The commune helped, but — good company aside — with passion and desperation, I still yearned for a way to live more connected to my heart and soul, more connected to Earth and Spirit. I'd searched but found no elders or sages to show me another way. I knew what I wanted to leave behind, but I had no path or clear direction toward where I wanted to go.

In the winter of 1979, I read *Black Elk Speaks*, the story of a Lakota holy man born in the 1860s, transcribed by John Neihardt. One of the first books about Native American vision quests, it struck a deep chord in me. I felt a call and said, "I have to do this." When summer finally came, I hitchhiked to Harney Peak with little preparation other than my hope and enthusiasm.

It was the top of this mountain — in the Black Hills of South Dakota and since renamed Black Elk Peak — where Black Elk had been transported on his great vision.

I began to hike a little before sundown, and soon all light was gone. I was in the forest, clouds covered the stars, and I knew there were drop-offs along the trail. My pace became halting and tentative, my feet probing the ground ahead, trying to make sure it was solid before I took the next step. At times I squatted to feel the earth and locate the trail with my hands. I had no idea how far I had to go before I arrived at the top of the sacred mountain.

I felt the first drop of rain, then another and another. Finally, the sky let loose. My clothes — blue jeans, shirt, light denim jacket... all cotton — were soon soaked. I had no choice but to continue, driven by a headstrong will to "do a vision quest." I was woefully unprepared for rain and — from my perspective today — totally ignorant of what doing a vision quest actually meant.

The clouds cleared as I finally reached the summit of Harney Peak. An almost-full moon bathed the rocky landscape in silver. I had little idea what to do beyond the sketchy guidance of *Black Elk Speaks*. I hoped for a sign, a vision, a direction. I sat and prayed, staying awake through the wee hours, shivering in my wet clothes. It was one of the longest and most difficult nights of my life. But I sat, prayed, walked in a circle, and didn't leave.

I continued through the next day and night, and the day and night after that, without food, water, or sleep. I was nothing if not stubborn. Toward the end of the third night, as dawn brightened the eastern sky, something happened. I entered an altered state of consciousness as my awareness flowed out from my body and merged with the mountain. It was not an "out-of-body" experience because my body was very much part of it. My physical form, my "self," my being, included the mountain. I felt the rocks as if they were part of my back, and, feeling a shiver, I turned to see a squirrel scamper across the stony surface and disappear into a fissure. My boundaries dissolved as I became the mountain, and soon I was part of everything.

I don't know how long I stayed that way, but when I returned, I knew I'd been given something. I didn't know what to call it, but it felt alive and real. Later that morning I prayed, gave thanks, and prepared to end my sojourn on the summit. As I put away my pipe and told the mountain goodbye, a flock of birds crested the ridge and, in a spinning column, wheeled and whirled around me before flying off to the east.

I began the hike down, slowly making my way back to the world. I didn't know what that experience meant, or if it had been a "vision." I knew Spirit had spoken to me in some language I didn't understand, and, deep in my being, I was sure that understanding it was crucial to my life. And I strongly sensed that the process of going on visions quests, and perhaps leading them, would be a major part of my journey.

....

The book you're about to read is a result of the path I've taken since that summer. I'm much older and, I hope, wiser. I've now undertaken over 35 quests of my own, and I've led hundreds. As I gaze back at that first quest, I see how little I knew, how foolish I was, and how fortunate I was to not die of exposure or exhaustion. And I also feel blessed by the calling that drew me there, that resulted in a vision (and many a task) that I've followed, with a quiet joy, for decades.

I've learned a lot about fasting, safety, and how to do the whole process with little danger. I've learned about ritual and ceremony, developmental processes, medicine wheel teachings, psychological archetypes, and many other things. But the path began there, on Harney Peak, with that longing to connect with something deeper, wider, stronger, and more eternal than what I knew. It was there I first recognized the seeds the Great Spirit or Mystery had planted in me, and I began to explore ways to nurture, sustain, and cultivate them so they might grow and bear fruit I could give to "my people."

I hope to offer you some fruit from the seeds germinated in those summer days of 1980. I hope you find something useful, nourishing, and of substance. For me, the taste has been sweet. As I left that morning and began my journey from South Dakota back to Vermont, I realized I'd been given another gift. Like those sparrows who whirled around me and flew off to the east, I've also traveled a path toward the rising sun, filled with faith and gratitude for the beauty and possibilities inherent in each new day. And I took on the name Sparrow, determined to sing my song faithfully, and have treasured it ever since.

HOW TO USE THIS BOOK

This book is divided into eight sections designed to guide you through learning about the vision quest process: its whole and its parts, its broad brush strokes and its specific details.

Section I: "The Vision Quest" (pages 6–35) starts with a basic overview of the vision quest experience — its core elements and the broader historical context in which it appears. It then explains and comments on its actual presentation, beginning with an outline of an 11-day vision quest program, followed by a session-by-session, day-by-day elaboration and fleshing out of that outline. This refinement and fleshing out contains references to other teachings, resources, and supporting material. These are described in the sections that follow.

Section II: The Four Shields medicine wheel teachings (pages 36–65), or some version of them, are part of the preparation provided by most quest organizations. Modified or adapted by various organizations and teachers, they provide a framework where the usual polarities of physical and spiritual, oneness and diversity, doing and being, individual and community, etc., are joined in ways that make sense. This allows participants to see their struggles and conflicts — as well as their purposes and intentions for the quest — in a larger context that can bring understanding and offer a path toward resolution.

Section III (pages 66–79): Though most people undertake a vision quest for spiritual or psychological growth and healing, it also has a powerful effect on the body. Fasting, solitude, and being in nature is an intimate encounter with physical-sensual reality. This chapter, "**Physical-Plane Concerns**," addresses the issues of fasting, safety, and the landscape, flora, and fauna that — if left unaddressed — can seriously impact the experience and outcomes of the quest process.

Section IV (pages 80–111): The vision quest is often a life-changing ritual that contains many other powerful rituals within it — fasting, purpose circles, death lodges, etc. Understanding **Ritual and Ceremony** — how ritual works, what it is and isn't, what the traditional practices were, and what options exist for individually tailored processes — results in a strong foundation for guides tasked with giving those in their care tools to translate purpose into practice and intent into action.

Section V (pages 112–137): The vision quest is archetypal. It is always a heroic adventure, often a rite of passage, and within its confines many other important processes — praying, the visitation of dreams, creating sacred space, engaging in council, etc. — may prove significant. "**Themes Within a Vision Quest**" provides an overview and explanation of these classic patterns and paradigms that can be crucial parts of the experience.

Section VI (pages 138–151): In each quest, a group of unique individuals engages in an archetypal, universal practice. This section — **"Other Rituals and Exercises"** — offers a selection of processes and practices that, while not universally applicable, may appeal to some participants.

Section VII (pages 152–161): A modern-day vision quest differs from those that took place in indigenous communities throughout the centuries. The most fundamental difference may be the context. Today, people undertaking quests join small, intimate communities that are unrelated to those they live in, and will return to, after the quest is completed. This issue, usually unavoidable, must be addressed at the end of a vision quest program, and this section, **"The Return**," offers tools, options, and strategies for doing so.

Section VIII (pages 162–185): Behind the rich and evocative experience of every quest lies a wealth of knowledge, skills, and attention to detail — work — that makes that experience possible. This section, "**Requirements and Resources**," is a compendium of information, documents, and necessary skills and knowledge that help form the foundation for those leading quests. It includes suggested readings, information about wilderness ethics, a description of useful skills, and examples of documents (equipment lists, preparation letters, etc.) for participants.

Section IX (pages 186–190): This section is to show some appreciation, gratitude, and **Final Words** for those heading down their own path.

SECTION I:
THE VISION QUEST

Overview **7**
What is a Vision Quest? 7
Reasons People Go 7
Today's Quests Versus "Traditional" Quests 8
Guides Versus Therapists 9

Basic Form of a Modern Vision Quest **11**
Program Length 11
Group Size as It Relates to the Integration Process 11
General Outline (11-day Quest) 12

Before People Arrive **13**

Days 1–4: Preparation **14**
Day 1 — Morning: Logistics and Introduction 14
Day 1 — Afternoon: Participant Introductions 16
Day 2 — Morning: Four Shields Teachings 16
Day 2 — Afternoon: Physical-Plane Issues And Concerns 17
Day 3 — Morning: Ritual And Ceremony, General Introduction 21
Day 3 — Afternoon: Self-Created Ritual And Ceremony 22
Day 4 — Finding Spots and Establishing Stone Piles 23

Days 5–8: The Solo **26**

Days 9–11: Return and Integration **27**
Day 9 — Morning: Returning from Solo 27
Day 9 — Afternoon: Weaving the Sacred and Daily Together 28
Day 10 — Morning: Story Time Continued 30
Day 10 — Afternoon: Mirroring And Feedback 30
Day 11 — The Return 32

SECTION I:
THE VISION QUEST

OVERVIEW

Before immersing ourselves in the wide-ranging subject of vision quests — whose concerns range from emergency procedures to connecting with an ultimate Source — it may be useful to begin with a few basics about what a vision quest is, who goes on one and why, and the differences (and their implications) between a vision quest today and those in the past that we may have heard or read about.

WHAT IS A VISION QUEST?

The solo experience at the core of a vision quest includes three elements: fasting, solitude, and nature, usually wilderness. With pre-solo preparation and instruction, along with a process for integration afterward, a quest is designed to create a deep change in the bodies, emotions, minds, and imaginations of participants.

FASTING

Fasting creates a change in consciousness. Going without food during the solo causes focus to become more broad-based, attention more dream-like and less riveted on rational thought. The internal dialogue slows down; other thoughts and ways of perceiving bubble up to the surface. We find ourselves thinking about people or things we've not considered for decades. As the mind quiets and the surface static dies down, that "still small voice" and our deeper longings can emerge and be heard.

SOLITUDE

A person on a vision quest is alone, removed from social conversations, cultural roles, routines, habits, and expectations. To discover your authentic purpose or voice and become the author and creator of your own story requires listening deeply to yourself while saying goodbye to other authorities — parents, teachers, priests, peer groups — as well as the stories about the world and ourselves that we've inherited. These stories influence us, mostly unconsciously, and arise from the time and culture of our childhood.

NATURE

A vision quest happens in nature, usually wilderness. There we live within a larger ecosystem. If "my home is my castle," then leaving that home removes my usual sense of power and self-centeredness. The world no longer revolves around "me." In nature, we immerse ourselves in something larger, become a strand in the web, not the ruler nor the purpose of the web itself.

We can't "meet our Maker" by staying inside a world that we have made. To leave behind roads, houses, televisions — the human-created world — requires entering the much older world — Nature — that created us. As a species, we've evolved through millions of years of interactions with this living earth. Returning to intimate contact with it awakens forgotten senses and atrophied ways of perceiving. Our wild, authentic, and natural selves can emerge and be reclaimed only through a reconnection with nature herself.

Though often associated with Native Americans, vision quests have been undertaken by people in diverse cultures for millennia. In 500 BC, Buddha entered the forest to fast in search of enlightenment. Christ and Biblical prophets went without food in the desert. Moses climbed Mt. Sinai; Mohammed retired to a cave. These founders of religions, as well as innumerable Native Americans, mystics, ascetics, and seekers of spiritual truth, have undertaken vision quests through the centuries. Their reasons were many — to find their direction and purpose; to come close to God or Spirit, or to have a profound encounter with the Source of life in order to guide themselves or their people through the challenges of their times.

REASONS PEOPLE GO ON VISION QUESTS

Although there exist many variations, there are a few core reasons why people undertake vision quests.

AS A RITE OF PASSAGE

A rite of passage implies a movement from the end of one thing to the beginning of something else. For example, in tribal societies, puberty rituals marked the end of childhood and an initiation into adulthood. Many beginnings and endings in outer life can become more compelling and real when consciously undertaken as an act of power. Parenthood, retirement, choosing (or ending) a career or path; marriage, divorce, and coming of age... These are important beginnings and endings, and they can be ritualized, marked, and experienced more deeply in order to provide insight and result in changes on a soul level far beyond any of their social consequences.

A vision quest can also be used to catalyze or cause an inner change: the end of living as a victim, a decision to no longer play small and avoid risks, a commitment to leave behind guilt or shame and love oneself, the choice to become a healer, etc. These and many other internal changes can be effected, powerfully experienced, and made real through a vision quest.

TO DISCOVER THEIR DIRECTION, PURPOSE, OR "MEDICINE."

TO HAVE A "VISIONARY EXPERIENCE."

Vision refers to an opening and engagement with a presence and energy larger than the ego and socially conditioned self. Many well-known examples in the quest tradition — Buddha's illumination, Black Elk's grand vision — describe powerful experiences within another order of reality. Some come to a quest seeking a similar experience, a confirmation of a "spiritual reality" they have sensed but never fully realized.

Those who seek an extraordinary experience usually find it. A vision quest is, by definition, non-ordinary. Leaving behind our familiar lives, habits, routines, and comforts while alone in nature is not ordinary life. Plus, fasting influences our awareness to be more expansive and dream-like, resulting in feelings of union, oneness, and connection. With help and guidance, it is almost impossible to *not* connect with more expansive perspectives and considerations.

Opening to this transcendent energy and larger universe, along with developing a relationship to it, can form a conduit that brings meaning and direction to one's life. Understanding "what I'm here for" brings passion and a profound sense of purpose to people who then become a vehicle for bringing this larger energy to their communities. Realizing and claiming your calling — as a poet, teacher, shaman, healer, or musician, for example — gives a direction and a compelling path for bringing your gifts to the world.

Vision quests are experienced as both spiritual and deeply soulful, and the resultant changes are among the major reasons why people choose to undertake them.

RENEWAL OR RECONNECTION

The passage of time and demands of daily life often result in a loss. This could be the loss of the sense of wonder experienced as a child, the loss of dreams once so important, or the lapse of a commitment to a path, purpose, or practice that formerly was meaningful. On vision quests, all the rules, roles, and routines of normal life are left behind, and (in both simple and profound ways) we can reset our internal compass, refreshing and renewing those core truths and commitments to guide us through life.

TODAY'S QUESTS VERSUS "TRADITIONAL" QUESTS

Vision quests and rites of passage have taken many different forms in cultures through the millennia. They've included entombment underground or in the dark; confinement to a small circle on high ridges; or months-long walkabouts through the landscape. And they could take many forms today. It would be impossible to describe every possible form or what might be important in each of those contexts. But I've come to believe that it's important to *not* try to model your vision quest after a culture, religion, or spiritual path you're not part of.

Over the years, I've heard many people say, "I want to do a traditional quest, not some new-age, watered-down version of a quest." People who express this may not have thought it through. The obvious response, "traditional to whom?" usually elicits the reply, "You know, a Native American vision quest."

In the year 1500 AD, 15 to 20 million people in North America lived in 200 separate nations with a wide range of languages, traditions, and cultural practices. Given that diversity, it's unclear to what tradition the idea of a "traditional" vision quest would actually refer. And beyond the differences in ritual forms, it's important to ask whether any "traditional vision quest" is useful and a good fit for someone without knowledge of or experience within the culture from which that particular tradition arose.

Today we tend to think of primal peoples as being closer to nature and more connected to realms of "spiritual experiences" than those who have grown up in a secular, materialistic world. In some ways, this might be true. But, as I've said to many, *"your vision quest needs to fit and speak to you,"* with your beliefs, ways of perception, and personal history, as well as the myriad attitudes, ideas, and opinions about the world and who you are that follow from that.

If we rewound time several centuries to a small village somewhere in North America, most everyone there would share the same stories, creation myths, and tales of adventure. They'd have similar values and outlooks, be intimately familiar with the landscape and its inhabitants, and be versed in the meanings of terms like "butterfly medicine." They'd be conversant with seasonal rituals and ceremonies because they had been instructed in them since they were toddlers. In a culture where everyone shares the same mythology, prays to the same gods, and agrees on a cosmology and their people's place in it, there could easily be a traditional vision quest that would fit everyone.

Modern people don't grow up in that world. In hundreds of small-group vision quests, I've frequently seen a few people in one little circle having greater differences among them than warring nations did in the past. Today's small group might contain someone with a terminal diagnosis who seeks to release feelings of victimhood and live her final days with grace and power. A man, fresh from betrayal and divorce, searches for a way to move past that crisis and look to the future with hope. Another might be transgender, while a fourth has a history of abusive and destructive relationships, her intention to learn to love herself and no longer allow people to treat her poorly. Others may have spent their whole lives trying to please parents or partners, and they come to find their voice, true direction, and the work and gifts that are uniquely theirs to bring into the world.

It's important for people to make their vision quest their own. If they're not from a tribe on the plains or a pueblo in the Southwest, the rituals and traditions of those places and people will likely not fit them. Traditional quests arose to meet the needs of traditional cultures in traditional situations. Helping people make this quest their own requires finding rituals and ceremonies, and *creating forms of connecting to Spirit, that speak to where they are in their lives*, with their unique histories, belief systems, challenges, and sources of support.

GUIDES VERSUS THERAPISTS

From the previous section comparing a modern quest to traditional quests of centuries ago, it's obvious that the range of individuals and their attendant issues is far greater today than in the small, tight-knit communities of the past. Communities of the past were relatively homogenous, lacking wide diversities of:

- Wealth, class, and economic status;
- Racial, ethnic, and gender identities; or
- Family dynamics, upbringing, and personal history.

In a small village on the plains, over a whole lifetime, one might know, interact with, or depend on a total of a 150 people. One identified with the village or the tribe. Today, social media and telecommunications have completely changed the categories in which we think. People now identify with issues or "imaginary communities" (for example, vegans, progressives, libertarians, or animal rights activists), and they've never met even a fraction of those they claim to feel connected to. A modern person is generally aware of seven billion people, views news and video footage shot all over the globe, and, though having a thousand "friends" on Facebook, may actually be close to or intimate with no one.

Also, primal peoples lived in physical and psychic landscapes where the human world — perhaps a village in the jungle or encampment on the savannah — was small, dwarfed by an immense natural world whose forces — storms, extremes of temperature, large animals — could nurture or destroy life.

Today, most of that is reversed. Human settlements sprawl across the globe; urban areas are inhabited by millions; and the forests, rivers, and sky have been cut down, dammed, paved over, and crisscrossed by electric lines and jet trails. The natural world shrinks away, restricted to managed forests and parks set aside and protected from the onslaught of the human. An adolescent today recognizes over 2000 corporate logos and fewer than ten native plants. All of this has consequences.

In the past, vision quests were more likely focused on "vision," on opening to forces beyond the human, beyond the self. Who would go to nature in search of renewal if a normal day included tracking deer through the forest, fishing in the pool where the river bends, or gathering mushrooms in shady spots under the hemlocks? How many would quest for healing if they'd never been hit or humiliated or felt alone and unwanted? Vision quests of the distant past took place within a sensuous, nurturing, and intimate daily life, and in that context were focused on creating personal connections with spirit guides and the "more-than-human" world, whether that be labeled Wakan-Tanka, Dreamtime, Nierika, or the ancestral realm.

In the twenty-first century, most who "go to" nature experience "normal" life as a left-brained reality of reason, logic, and material reality. Many seek relief or freedom from today's "cultural consensus," a set of assumptions that are dismissive of and disconnected from nature. This consensus also separates us from our bodies, emotions, and each other, and it's a primary contributor to much of the pain, suffering, and spiritual crisis — personal and collective — we face today. Whether or not in actual pain and crisis themselves (and many are), most sense something's wrong or missing in daily life. They long for some connection to other modes of perception and being, an awareness that feels deeper, more profound, and "real." And they're curious about other worlds, including those referenced in myth, experienced in dreams, and spoken of in spiritual texts and by saints and sages over the millennia.

Guides today need to have a range of familiarity with the dysfunctions and dis-eases of modern life that's far wider than anything required in the past. They should also have a language to speak about these conditions and be able to offer a broad palette of processes and perspectives relevant to the spectrum as well as the specifics of those who seek their guidance.

But a guide is not, and shouldn't try to be, a therapist. That role is too limited and too immersed in the paradigms behind the problems themselves, for therapy:

- Assumes (and focuses on) pathology and illness in the particular individual, ignoring the collective pathology in which those individuals develop;
- An adjustment to normality is desirable;
- Is hierarchical — the one seeking help has problems; the therapist has answers;
- Is specialized and limited — the therapist is Jungian, Freudian, somatic, cognitive, psychiatric, etc., and therefore the "problem" (and answer) are viewed through that discipline's myopic lens.

A guide accepts the presence of something larger, an elusive force or mystery referenced through the millennia, whatever name might be applied to it. Accepting this is humbling. In the face of this unknown, he realizes he has few, if any, of the answers. At the same time, it's liberating, for one's role becomes to simply assist those who seek to develop *their own relationship* to that greater force beyond what they know now, and in so doing, to find their own truth and answers.

Today these formerly separate realms (temporal and eternal, known and unknown, left brain and right) need to be woven together and balanced if we're to bring hope and a sense of grand adventure to the practical tasks of living well in challenging times. Vision quest guides are explorers on a journey, committed to that grand task of "connecting heaven and earth." They've learned much, and they recognize the end is limitless, there are no experts, and all who come seeking assistance are companions on the path.

BASIC FORM OF A MODERN VISION QUEST

I'll begin with a simple model of a vision quest that's the basis for many programs offered today. This model, also used by Circles of Air and Stone, is a multi-day program that takes place in a wilderness or camp-out environment. It consists of preparation beforehand, a solo (usually four days and nights), and a period of integration to assist people to return to their communities.

PROGRAM LENGTH AND TIME ISSUES

The vision quest described in this outline takes place over 11 days. It includes four days devoted to preparation (which includes travel to the solo site and participants finding their spots); a four-day—four-night solo; and three days for integrating the quest and preparing to go back to daily life. Most quests today follow this basic format, though some organizations offer programs as short as nine days or as long as twelve.

Those who use a different format will still find much here that's valuable and applicable to their programs. Some of the variations in program length — shorter preparation or shorter solo — may be related to the different content an organization chooses to offer, but most of the variation relates to issues of group size. I'll mention some of those concerns here.

GROUP SIZE AS IT RELATES TO THE INTEGRATION PROCESS

The size of a quest group usually has minimal effect on preparation. For most of this time, the guides provide information, teachings, or perspectives, and, other than personal introductions, councils, and questions people might have, whether there are four or fourteen people listening has limited impact on the time required. Likewise, group size is unrelated to the length of the solo, assuming the landscape can easily provide privacy for everyone in the group.

However, once the solo is finished and people return, the stories of the quest experience begin. This involves telling, listening, mirroring, and feedback. Here, the number of people and the time required can be causes for concern, and various programs address this in different ways. Here are three options:

- **Add extra days.** If your quest program is 12 days as opposed to 11, you've increased your incorporation time by 30 percent, and this allows for a greater number of participants.
- **Limit the stories and feedback.** In most quest programs I'm aware of (Circles of Air and Stone is the exception), the telling of the solo-time story is limited, usually to 30 minutes or less, and mirroring and feedback are given only by the guides, and thus also limited, to about twenty minutes.
- **Limit the group size.** At Circles of Air and Stone, the group size is limited to eight to allow for community feedback. Everyone — having prepared for and undergone a solo together — is part of the mirroring and feedback process. People are not just observers while the guide or guides mirror. People fully participate in all aspects of the quest, and this results in strong feelings of cohesion and camaraderie. But it has consequences in terms of time. Telling eight stories takes twice the time as four, but during the mirroring process, the time expands exponentially. Four people mirroring four stories is 16 conversations, but eight mirroring eight is 64.

GENERAL OUTLINE (11 DAY QUEST)

DAY 1:
Morning: Logistics and Introduction
Afternoon: Participant Introductions

DAY 2:
Morning: Four Shields Teachings
Afternoon: Physical-Plane Issues And Concerns

DAY 3:
Morning: Ritual And Ceremony, General Introduction
Afternoon: Self-Created Ritual And Ceremony

DAY 4: Finding Spots and Establishing Stone Piles

DAYS 5–8: The Solo

DAY 9:
Morning: Returning from Solo
Afternoon: Weaving the Sacred and Daily Together

DAY 10:
Morning: Story Time Continued
Afternoon: Mirroring And Feedback

DAY 11:
Morning: The Return

BEFORE PEOPLE ARRIVE

Groups do not just arrive and begin, and preparation doesn't start when the group first sits in a circle. Much needs to happen just to make the gathering, usually far from home, possible. Pre-quest logistics, both for the guides and the group, need to be researched and attended to. For guides, they could involve knowing the times of sunrise and sunset; the openness and conditions of roads to the camping area and wilderness; weather reports (ten-day forecast); reservations, permits, and requirements for campground use; etc. In addition, flights get delayed, baggage gets lost, people miscalculate, and roads wash out. It's good to have thought about how to proceed with "plan B" in case something unforeseen happens.

Some logistical information needs to be sent to the group beforehand. This can vary in different locations, but it usually includes the following:

- **Travel information:** nearby airports, rental cars, driving directions and time, food and/or lodging possibilities en route.
- **Contact lists:** giving participants options for communicating beforehand. This could be for sharing rides and/or rental cars, as well as for the possibility of traveling, camping, sharing motels, or simply getting to know one another while getting there.
- **An equipment list that describes what's necessary** for the solo, as well as what might be useful for the time in camp before and after.

But preparing includes more than just info on travel and equipment. Are people ready psychologically, spiritually, emotionally? Someone emotionally unprepared or out of balance can affect the whole group. Ultimately, it's impossible to screen out everyone who might not be ready, but it's helpful to have requirements in place that attempt to do so. Some of these are:

- **Health questionnaires and liability releases.** A liability release protects (somewhat) the guides and organization. A good health questionnaire will alert you to issues that may appear or need to be addressed on the fast, such as
  - Diabetes or hypoglycemia;
  - Medications — can they be suspended or taken on an empty stomach?
  - A person's ability to hike in to and out of whatever wilderness area is being accessed; and
  - Emotional state: questions related to psychiatric hospitalizations, current care, anxiety, medications, etc. can reveal cautionary flags that need to be followed up.
- **Deposits and balances.** There are wide variations in income and how financially easy or difficult it may be for someone to schedule or undertake a quest. But lax behavior with respect to submitting money, letters, and required forms can be a sign of stress and overwhelm, an inability to keep agreements, or a person's resistance to responsibility or accountability.
- **Letters of intention.** This can be an important requirement. For some, hearing about vision quest can stimulate an "I want that" response, a response that doesn't see the shadow and the light, that doesn't acknowledge the work or difficulty involved. Some might imagine or want altered states, to chill by a river, to have an awesome experience, or to just say they "did it." Some might think of a quest like a tourist, take it lightly, and pack at the last minute.
  - *A quest is not for tourists.* It's not about achieving highs or "being awesome." A vision quest is virtually always a journey outside the comfort zone, and making people aware of the challenges, possible difficulties, and work involved is important. Providing prompts — questions to answer in their letters — is helpful. "What are you willing to say goodbye to?" "What will you sacrifice to realize this?"
  - *A letter of intent is often revealing.* How people reply — what and how much or how little they say — can give a good indication of their assumptions and how deeply they know themselves. Letters can be full of clichés or

catchphrases, or state the obvious, like, "I want to become closer to spirit... " Well, sure. Who doesn't? But what are you willing to let go of or face, and how do you plan for that to happen?

- **Tasks**. Reading a preparation manual, taking nature or medicine walks, keeping a journal, recording dreams, making dietary or lifestyle changes, cutting out drugs or alcohol, etc., can all be helpful for those preparing. These tasks can be required or suggested. As a rule, those who put more thought into and focus on their preparation tend to have more confirmatory experiences on their solos. Since their work has been started and engaged with beforehand, the solo becomes a time of confirmation — a process of grounding, completing, and claiming the results and consequences of the commitments and work already begun.

People who choose to become guides do so because the vision quest process has been important in their lives. It's natural to want everyone to take it as seriously as you. Not everyone does. It's a joy working with people who are ready and willing to give it their all, explore their depths, and approach their edges. And, knowing the benefits and possibilities of the process, it can be frustrating seeing someone treat it lightly. Try not to judge or take it personally. "I didn't have the time to fully prepare" says something about the participant and his or her commitments in life.

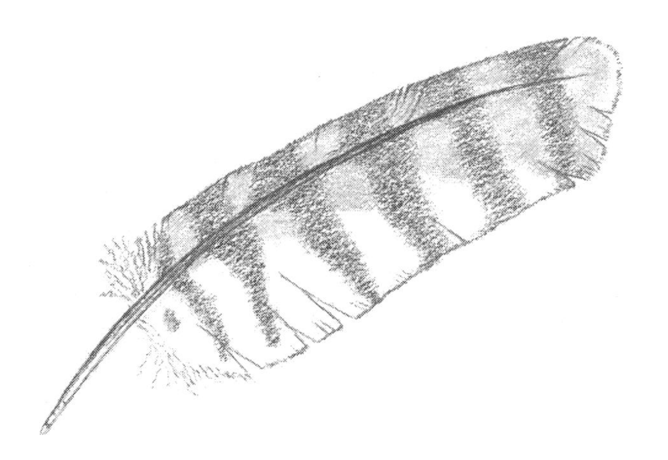

DAYS 1–4: PREPARATION

DAY 1 – MORNING: LOGISTICS AND INTRODUCTION

It's best to cover certain basics before the group sits down and begins to focus on what they — and we — are here for. People are far readier to share their hearts and souls when they know where they'll sleep, when and where their next and future meals will come from, and where the bathroom is. Depending on location, weather, and organization of the program, physically setting up tents, shelters, and a meeting circle — the basic structure of the preparation camp — may be the first order of business.

When that's done, and the group is formed into a circle, it's useful to get the rest of the logistics out of the way first thing. This can include information about the following:

- Bathrooms, nearby towns, stores, markets, water sources, hot springs, etc. These will obviously vary by location. Some general information about the proximity of town and food options needs to be communicated beforehand, since it affects what people bring, but the specifics can now be described.
- How will people wash? Showers, hot springs, rivers?
- Are there laundromats, places with camping equipment, or stores selling warm clothes nearby?
- Environmental concerns, also varying by location and time of year.
    - Altitude and its effects: low energy, shortness of breath, headaches, harsher sun exposure.
    - Dehydration and its effects: headaches, drying of mucous membranes, chapped lips, nosebleeds, the lack of obvious perspiration in low-humidity environments, the need to drink water.
- Group and individual time and needs.
- Schedule for the 11 days.

When the practical and logistical concerns of the earthly dimension have been adequately addressed (allow time for questions), it's time to move into the heart and soul of the quest process. I like to ritually mark this transition with smudging, but other opening rituals can be equally effective. (For more information, see "smudging" in Section VI.)

Some people may be unfamiliar with this practice, so it's useful to ask, and if needed, give a brief description or background before describing how smudging will happen during the program. Here is an example:

1. Describe the simple physical act: waving the smoke over yourself before passing it (sun-wise) to the left.
2. Invite people to speak, to say something from their hearts (prayer, gratitude, feelings of the moment), when the smudge bowl is in their hands.
3. Assure them speaking is not required.
4. Explain the process will be complete when the smudge has made it around the circle.
5. Announce the group will begin each day with this ritual.

A ritual opening accomplishes several things. It makes and marks a transition from social to sacred time, and it focuses the group's energy and attention. It introduces ritual (smudging is a ritual), which will be a major part of the teaching and preparation process to follow. And it asks, invites, or challenges people to begin speaking from their hearts, which, for some more than others, may usher them out of their comfort zones.

INTRODUCTION TO THE VISION QUEST

Topics

- The need to make this *your own* quest
    - You don't have to be good. "The Wild Geese... "
    - "Singing Images of Fire... "
- The heroic journey archetype as related to rites of passage.
- The symbolism of "leaving home"
    - Literally leaving home (houses and homes, showers, beds, family, friends, work, etc.)
    - Metaphorically leaving home (habits, routines, cultural inheritance, ways of seeing the world)
    - Home as representative of both our personal and cultural download
- Cultural download #1 — Christianity and "God in heaven"
- Cultural download #2 — Scientific thought: the primacy of reason and objectivity
- Download #3 — The English language and its world of separate objects
- Dreaming — we're always dreaming — dreams as a loss of separation, loss of ego-centeredness, merging with the world; becoming awake

THE ROLE OF COMMUNITY

- Traditionally quest was not done alone; give examples of support
- The return as the weak link in a modern quest
- What gifts do you have to give to *your people*?
- Being present in the community while here

REASONS FOR QUESTING (OPTIONAL)

- Visionary experience
- Rite of passage
- Renewal
- Direction, personal growth

DAY 1 - AFTERNOON: PARTICIPANT INTRODUCTIONS

After introducing the quest process, it's important for people to introduce themselves. Some of the themes of the Heroic Journey or rites of passage — severance, monsters, the gift, leaving home, etc. — may be suggested or used in this introduction. A metaphor I've found useful, usually stated in the first session, is that an introduction to the quest happens in two parts. First, the parts and process of the quest are introduced, and the form of the quest (wilderness, fasting, the return, etc.) creates the *container* that our time together takes place in.

But a container, though necessary, like a pot or a pan on a stove, does not predict what will be cooked in it. Therefore, to complete our introduction, each person introduces himself or herself, telling us what ingredients he is bringing to this pot as well as the intended or hoped-for outcome of this process will be.

To facilitate this sharing, it's often useful to provide the group with a list of relevant questions to address, the answers to which will provide structure and focus to their introductions. It may also help to have people write the questions down and take 10 to 15 minutes to reflect on them before they begin. You may need to intervene and redirect. This introduction is about their *choice and intention* to quest, not an opportunity for people to tell their life story. Some relevant questions:

- What brings you here? (question of intention or purpose).
- What are you ready to say goodbye to?
- What one thing would you most want to leave with, 11 days from now?
- What are your monsters (fears)? What, for you, seems most challenging about this process?
- How can we, this group, best support you?

Be aware of time and the number of people who will be speaking. You can let others in the group ask further or clarifying questions *if time allows*. Questions, but not advice. This is not therapy.

DAY 2 - MORNING: FOUR SHIELDS TEACHINGS

(As a visual aid, it's helpful to collect and place four stones in the cardinal directions.)

The four shields medicine wheel teachings (see "Four Shields" in Section II) have been described as helpful by almost every person I've guided on a vision quest. This usefulness is probably a result of two factors:

- It's one of the primary mythic themes of humanity. The first, the heroic journey, (used in the morning's introduction) helps deepen people's awareness and appreciation of what brought them to the quest and introduces them to the larger, archetypal nature of their calling.
- The four shields is a powerful and useful example of the myth of the eternal return. Simply put, the myth of the eternal return illustrates the cyclical nature of things. It states that every journey brings us back where we started after we've gained experience and the ability to see the ends and beginning with new eyes. In this cycle of return, spring leads to summer, to fall, to winter, and back again to spring. Morning becomes midday, transforms into the evening, then night, and back to morning. Birth leads into childhood, adolescence, adulthood, eldership, and eventually, death and/or rebirth.

Seeds germinate, grow tall, flower, and fruit, and new seeds are dropped on the ground to start again. The Four shields teachings affirm and honor the twin poles of unity and diversity and provide a model where people can look at their issues — fears, judgments, and assorted "dysfunctions" that may have brought them to the quest — in a framework that

a. Makes sense,
b. Provides an image or model of wholeness and balance, and
c. Provides images and consequences of imbalance (not failure or pathology) and how those might be re-framed and addressed (lessons that need to be learned) within the quest and beyond.

The model is useful for other reasons as well.

- For those infected with the disease of disconnection and separation (most of us), this teaching connects the powers and qualities of nature — the cycles of the seasons and cycles of the day; the medicine animals and their powers — to the human psyche and its development through childhood, adolescence, adulthood, and eldership.
- It defines health and wholeness as learning and embodying a series of lessons, describes what those lessons consist of, and explains how the presence or absence of this knowledge may play out in one's life.
- Perhaps most importantly, it provides a useful definition of adulthood. Modern culture is predominantly childish — self-centered, competitive, materialistic, and narcissistic — and playing victim is a national pastime. Meanwhile, people long for community and ways to make meaningful contributions, while simultaneously feeling at a loss for where to find this community or discover what they have to give. The twin teachings of wisdom and the giveaway in the north (adult) shield tackle that head-on.

You might need to allow up to an hour per direction. Sharing and explaining the teaching, including the shadow or "stuck" side of the shield, takes time. Allowing space for people to speak about how the teaching applies to them and their quest adds to that. Throw in a pee or snack break between each direction, and this session may bleed into the afternoon.

DAY 2 – AFTERNOON: PHYSICAL-PLANE ISSUES AND INSTRUCTIONS

The afternoon of the second day is a good time for talking about physical-plane issues and concerns.

A vision quest is a unique engagement with two factors called *set* and *setting*. *Set* refers to the constellation of internal factors that motivates a person to quest. This can include a desire to put an end to some behavior, a need to reconnect with oneself, a longing to know one's purpose or direction, etc. Set would likely remain the same in whatever landscape or environment the quest occurred. *Setting* refers to the physical place where the quest is happening — mountains, canyons, desert, and forests, with all their qualities... wet, dry, cold, high-altitude, buggy... Setting has a major impact on the experience. It strongly shapes how a person's set is manifested and plays out within physical, sensual reality.

When the group first arrives, issues of setting relevant to the start of the program are immediately addressed: tents, food, bathrooms, showers, etc. This allows the group to feel safe and grounded enough to immerse themselves in the learning community. This is followed by more information on the schedule and various concerns — altitude, dehydration, etc. — to assure a minimum level of comfort so that the deeper issues of the set — why people are here — can be addressed.

After those initial and important concerns of setting are attended to, the next 24 hours are mostly devoted to set. This begins with the ritual of smudging and prayer and is followed by a description of the heroic journey, an examination of what "leaving home" could mean, and teachings about the traditional role and importance of community. Then, participant introductions, where questions about set — motivations, fears, deepest hopes and desires, and relationships to the community — are directly addressed. After this, the Four Shields teachings provide a different lens for viewing those individual issues and concerns (each person's set) and an examination of the foundations on which those individual stories may have been built.

All this is good and wonderful, but after 24 hours focused on set, it's a welcome relief to move back to setting, where the questions, concerns, and answers are simpler and more direct. "What do I do about the lack of trust in my life?" may be a complicated question. "How do I deal with a cactus?" is not. And at this point, we are now almost halfway through our preparation time. The initial concerns about food, shelter, and bathrooms are behind us; concerns about comfort during this preparation period have been answered. But the time alone in the wilderness is rapidly approaching, and fears related to that time — going without food, being cold or wet, getting lost, encountering animals, etc. — have yet to be spoken of.

The outline below lists topics that need to be covered to adequately prepare a group for a four-day solo quest in the wilderness. Some, like fasting, stone pile, emergency procedures, staying dry, and miscellaneous, will remain consistent regardless of location, while others vary considerably in different environments. Some of those variations are as follows:

Water. In the desert, all water may need to be carried in. Other locations may have springs, streams, or lakes. In those, information about filters, pumps, Steri-pens, water treatment, and containers may need to be given.

Animals. The conversation should be about animals that inhabit the specific environment of the quest and could present a danger. It should include a reality check about what those dangers are and how to minimize them. You may need to speak to the difference between actual and perceived threats. Many people come to quests afraid of "being eaten by a bear," something that never happens, but have little or no fear of slipping on a wet rock and hurting themselves, which is a hundred times more likely. For a sample description of concerns about flora and fauna, see Section VIII, Resources: Flora and Fauna.

Tarp. Setting up a tarp in areas containing trees is straightforward, but nearly always needs to be demonstrated so people understand good placement, basic knots, and options for tying. Putting up a tarp in the desert without plants taller than two to three feet is a challenge, and a demonstration, using rocks, roots, and bushes, becomes even more important.

Handouts can be useful and may be more or less valuable in different locations. At Circles of Air and Stone, participants are always given lists of emergency and first aid procedures to have with them. Other handouts may include:

- **Maps of an area.** These are probably unnecessary in a desert where you can see 10 miles in all directions but may be very helpful in canyons or heavily wooded environments.
- **Information on fasting (what to expect) and/or the flora and fauna of an area.** If these are given (or sent) out to be read beforehand, less time in camp may need to be devoted to them.
- **Equipment list.** Always send out beforehand.

The outline that follows lists what needs to be addressed and conveyed to a group about to go on a vision quest. But a guide's experience and knowledge of nature, wilderness, equipment, first aid, etc. should be much greater than what is listed in the outline. People often ask questions that are unexpected (and sometimes irrelevant) and being able to answer them will help give the group confidence both in their guides and in their own safety.

If you do this long enough, unanticipated situations will arise: hurricanes sweeping through, snow in June, equipment failures, heavy rains with flash floods, forest closings because of fire danger, roads or trails getting washed out, etc. One can't plan for all the possibilities — although with the weather, getting a ten-day forecast helps — and sometimes the resources you need are internal, such as creativity to go off script, adapt, and find alternative solutions to conditions that can't be predicted.

For a broader and more detailed discussion of some of the topics below, see Section III: Physical-Plane Concerns.

BASIC PHYSICAL-PLANE OUTLINE

FASTING

Side effects

- Slow energy
- Dizziness
- Headache
- Nausea (antacids)

Drinking water

- How much? (Urine color)
- Logistics: springs, filters, containers, etc.
- Electrolytes
- Miscellaneous: bring toothbrush

STONE PILE

- How it works
- Two- and three-person stone piles
- Making changes obvious and permanent
- Minimalist vs. artistic
- Stone-piling from base camp

EMERGENCY PROCEDURES

- Miscommunications
- Getting lost
- Injury
- Leaving time (afternoon shift)

FLORA AND FAUNA IN THE QUEST SITES

Plants

- Cacti
- Poison ivy/oak

Animals

- Predator/prey relations — never run!
- Snakes, scorpions, ants
- Coyotes, bobcats, mountain lions
- Javelinas
- Bears
- Moose
- Other people

STAYING WARM AND DRY

Clothes

- Synthetic vs. cotton or wool
- Layering
- Chimney effect (closing loose openings)
- Hat (for cold and sun)

Other equipment

- Sleeping bag rating
- Ground insulation (sleeping pad)
- Rain gear
- Ground cloth (garbage bags)

TARP-TYING INSTRUCTIONS

- Equipment
  - Rope
  - Tarp
  - Plastic or nylon
  - Size
- Principles: look up, look down
  - Drainage — ground and off tarp
- Practice
  - Knots
  - Tie-downs — rocks, logs, trees, roots
  - Grommet reinforcement

MISCELLANEOUS

- Coming in early
  - Quest continues at camp
  - Stone pile responsibility
  - Conversation limited
- Bathroom etiquette
- Fires
- Leave no trace

HANDOUTS

- First aid/emergency procedures
- Maps, if useful or required

NOTES ON THE OUTLINE

The outline above lists the subjects that need to be addressed in most presentations on the physical-plane aspects of a quest. The location will influence how simple or extensive the conversations on certain subjects are, specifically flora and fauna, water issues, and, to a lesser degree, tying a tarp.

(Items 1–5 below are presented in more detail in the appendices listed.)

1. Fasting, side effects and drinking water: Section III: Physical-Plane Concerns
2. Stone pile: Section III: Physical-Plane Concerns
3. Flora and fauna: differs relative to each landscape. A sample list and description of flora and fauna in one wilderness area is provided in Section VIII: Resources.
4. Equipment and clothes: see sample equipment list in Section VIII: Resources
5. "Leave no trace" camping and wilderness practices are described in the "Wilderness Ethics Statement," also included in Section VIII: Resources.

TARP-TYING

It's important to demonstrate putting up a tarp (a picture is worth a thousand words) in the area where people will be fasting. People will want to see (and perhaps practice) tying the knots and learn how to adjust the tension in the ropes to get a tight and stable structure that will shed rain. In most circumstances, I demonstrate this soon after arriving at base camp.

BATHROOM ETIQUETTE

Digging a poop hole: Feces should be disposed of in a hole, 6 to 8 inches deep, at least 200 feet (about 80 paces) away from any water source (rivers, streams, springs, etc.). A trowel for digging is usually required. Toilet tissue should be either packed out (a Ziploc bag works fine) or burned. Unburned toilet tissue should not be put in the hole or left on the ground.

Coming in early

The intention is for participants to enter the wilderness and not return until four days and nights have passed. But the plan may not be the reality. In all guided quests, there should be someone at base camp for safety and support. Sometimes people on solo come in to "visit" because they need something. It could be a Band-Aid, moleskin for blisters, or more water because they have spilled theirs in an accident. Sometimes a question or issue comes up and, unable to move through it alone, they need to talk with someone. In those cases, we sit, hold council, and address the need, and the participant heads back out. But sometimes a person comes in to stay.

Spirit moves in mysterious ways. Coming in early can be absolutely right for various reasons, and the most important realizations of the quest could happen after, or because, someone comes in. An early return may require facing our demons — wrestling with voices that accuse us of failure, that compare ourselves with others and fear what they'll think. Given this, it might take more courage to come back than stay out.

For anyone returning early on vision quests at Circles of Air and Stone, we take the point of view that the vision quest is still happening, its last chapter unexpectedly taking place near base camp. The returning quester is expected to fulfill his or her stone pile duties. Though the participant has returned from solo and may be eating, we contend that a sacred process is still happening, and therefore the time is not social. We do not chat about movies or sports. We may hold council on issues, struggles, dreams, or challenges related to the intent of the vision quest, but this time is not for "hanging out." Later, when everyone shares stories of their solo experiences, the early returnee does the same, his or her story including the time spent at base camp.

There can be good, profound, and even courageous reasons to come in early, but boredom is not one of them. At base camp, we do not entertain, and boredom will just happen in a different place.

DAY 3 – MORNING: RITUAL AND CEREMONY, GENERAL INTRODUCTION

(For a detailed and more comprehensive overview of ritual and ceremony, see Section IV: Ritual and Ceremony.)

After the morning opening — this could include smudging and prayers, a check-in or community time of some sort, an invitation for dreams, or an inquiry about anything unaddressed or pending — we announce we'll be addressing the theme of ritual and ceremony.

This subject may be easy and natural for some participants, edgy for others. For people with a strict Catholic or religious upbringing, ritual may denote arcane, meaningless mumbo-jumbo without relevance to what feels important and alive. For someone else, ritual may be associated with something dark or scary, like voodoo or Satanism. Given this — plus the fact that a vision quest *is* a ritual — I've found it useful to give some simple background and introduction about what ritual is and is not.

An outline of the morning session follows:

GENERAL CONCEPTS
(all described in more detail in Section IV)

- Ritual as language of the old brain
- The difference between "ritual" and "ceremony": transformation vs. confirmation
- Creating or choosing ritual forms that fit you

RITUAL ACTS THAT EVERYONE WILL BE DOING
(described in more detail in Section IV)

- The quest itself
- Finding the solo spot
- Fasting
- Stone pile

COMMON RITUALS ON A VISION QUEST
(described in more detail in Section IV)

- Threshold ritual
- Death lodge
- Purpose circle
- Calling in the dark

OTHER COMMON QUEST EVENTS
(described in more detail in Section IV)

- Medicine names
- Medicine songs
- Animal encounters

DAY 3 – AFTERNOON: SELF-CREATED RITUAL AND CEREMONY

The morning session began with an introduction to ritual and ceremony, which included:

- A general overview of what ritual and ceremony are;
- Three activities — fasting, stone pile, finding a spot — that contained symbolic or ritual aspects;
- A description of some major rituals people might choose to do, with instructions for doing them; and
- Instruction and core concepts around medicine names, animals, and songs.

The afternoon is meant to provide teachings, tools, and ideas to inspire and help people create their own rituals and ceremonies — acts of power that speak to them deeply and personally — and address some of the core concerns they've brought with them to the quest process.

As with the previous outline, the subjects will be listed and organized below and treated in far more detail in Section IV. Since there are so many ritual forms and acts, it's useful to create structure by organizing them into:

- Rituals of severance, designed to leave behind and be done with relationships, situations, and investments of energy that no longer serve us and inhibit living a larger dream;
- Rituals of incorporation (the opposite), designed to call in, welcome, and embrace those investments of energy that serve one's growth and higher good; and
- Rituals of attunement, which are focused on the present; designed to neither bring in nor leave behind, they explore ways to engage with inner and outer nature in ways that are deeper and more profound.

Seen as a list, the rituals seem dry and lifeless, but they come to life when you have examples and stories to tell. Some of those stories are shared and told in Section IV. Feel free to use them; over time, you'll develop a repertoire of your own.

RITUALS OF SEVERANCE
(described in more detail in Section IV)

- Burning
- Burying
- Casting away
- Cutting
- Expelling/vomiting
- Retiring
- Smashing, breaking...
- Washing off, removing...
- Leaving behind

RITUALS OF INCORPORATION
(described in more detail in Section IV; there are multiple overlapping categories, as might be expected with rituals of "joining")

- Entering: caves, groves, thresholds; immersion, baptism
- Ingestion: drinking — placing a medicine or power object in a water bottle; breathing in
- Carrying: rocks, staffs, scepters, power or medicine objects; bringing with
- Creating/building: altars; walls; ritual, symbolic, or ceremonial spaces
- Planting
- Burning: offering prayer; using smoke as messenger (for example, smudge or pipe)
- Weaving together, gathering, collecting
- Putting on, wearing: clothes, medicine objects (crowns, rings, bracelets, pouches, pendants, jewelry), tattoos, paint or designs
- Embellishing: carving, creating power objects (sticks, staffs, prayer arrows)
- Embodying: postures, asanas, walks, dances
- Cutting/growing hair (severance and incorporation of old and new appearance)

RITUALS OF THE THRESHOLD, OR ATTUNEMENT (described in more detail in Section IV)

- Speaking to:
  - Conversations with trees, stones, rivers, sky
  - Prayer
- Speaking — from the known to the unknown... as gift of energy to parallel worlds
- Offerings:
  - Songs, gratitude, praise, tobacco, cornmeal, gifts, commitments, promises
  - As sacrifice, or "making sacred"
- Listening
  - Meditation
  - Recognition of signs, omens
  - Working with dreams
- Walkabouts, being guided, intentional "medicine walks"
- Exploring perception or sensing
  - Eyes
- Gazing exercises
- Adopting different points of view (example: snake)
- Long views (staring at bark, candle, fire, mandalas, one square foot of ground)
- Walks without focusing
  - Ears
- Rattling, drumming, chanting, medicine songs,singing with or to wind
  - Touch and smell
- Exploring an area without using eyes
- Taking off shoes, clothes; being naked
- Exploring mud, water, sun
- Exploring feelings
  - Truth mandala
  - Presenting ego to tree
- Exploring imagination — working with dreams
  - Energy flows where attention goes
- Setting out paper, pen, light
- Asking for a dream (general)
- Asking for specific information
- Use of images in dream requests
  - Telling dream story from point of view of other "character"
  - Returning to dream to dialogue with other entities (active imagination)
  - Bringing dream images into this world; for the day; to stone pile

At the finish of the pre-quest instructions, we've arrived at the last evening in preparation camp. Ask about any needs, concerns, questions, or unaddressed issues that want to be spoken about before leaving for the solo area in the morning. Announce the logistics for the next day.

DAY 4 – FINDING SPOTS AND ESTABLISHING STONE PILES

It's the fourth day, the work of preparation has been completed, and it's time to travel to the area where the solo will take place. Usually, this involves driving to a trailhead, leaving the cars, and hiking into the wilderness to a base camp. Questions and concerns about vehicles and security at the trailhead may vary by area. In planning for this move, guides need to take into account how long the drive is; how long the hike is, generally; and how long the hike is for people who may not be in good physical shape.

BEFORE LEAVING

In the morning (or perhaps the evening before) you'll need to give appropriate information about packing and moving issues. Those pre-caravan conversations could include the following:

- **Taking and leaving cars.** Can rides be consolidated and some vehicles left behind? Will people have to stop for gas or get anything on the way? (It's better to have this done beforehand). Are there concerns about the security of vehicles (and valuables) at the trailhead?

- **Storage**. May tents or other things can be left at the preparation camp, and if so, where and how?
- **Water.** Does it need to be carried in, or is it available at base camp? Do people have adequate filters and containers?
- **Packs and readiness to hike.** Some people may not have ever carried a pack (or packed one). Advice on how to pack — what to keep or jettison, the importance of getting the weight on hips instead of shoulders — and help in tightening straps may all be needed. Finish packing before getting in vehicles. Most packing should be done *before* you're at the trailhead.
- **Permits, low profile, and/or legal issues.** Are there issues regarding where you can and can't park, or boundaries of National Forest, state, or private land that need to be attended to in some way? If so, have the conversation (and questions) before getting in the vehicles.

TRAILHEAD ISSUES

Trailhead issues could include the following:

- Reminders about water and/or food for the day,
- Appropriate footwear and/or hiking poles if the trail is steep or rocky,
- Hiking: pacing, trail junctions, stopping and waiting for people, etc., and
- Pointing out relevant features of the landscape (especially at overlooks if hiking down).

ARRIVING AT BASE CAMP

Rest is often the first order of business when arriving at base camp. People may be tired, especially those who don't exercise or aren't used to carrying a pack. And, depending on altitude and the length or steepness of the hike, that could include almost everyone. Taking off packs, drinking water, and eating snacks will help rejuvenate those who need it.

BASE CAMP TASKS AND ACTIVITIES

The highest priority of the day is each person finding a "spot" — a home base for the four-day solo. The next-most-important goal is determining buddy and stone pile assignments. Stone pile assignments could, if necessary, be addressed in the morning, though this is not ideal. There are other issues and concerns that should be addressed at base camp, but guides must be sure those other things don't take attention, or too much time, away from the primary reason for being there. These other activities or focuses might be the following:

- Demonstrating how to set up a tarp: In most circumstances, I demonstrate this soon after arriving at base camp. Having just carried in their packs, people usually want a short rest before heading out in search of their fasting sites. Observing a demonstration is a good use of time. Also, base camp is where the guides will stay for the duration (four to five days) and putting up a tarp for shelter is a task that needs to be done anyway.
- Orienting and pointing out landscape features, such as streams, water sources, side canyons, trail locations and river crossings; the location of sunrise and sunsets; and possible dangers (mine shafts, etc.) or other concerns (poison ivy, archaeological sites, people in boats on a lake, etc.). Providing this information helps fill in the details for those with some sense or picture of what they want and are looking for.
- Setting up tarps/shelter for the night if sky and clouds look ominous.

Before people leave base camp in search of their solo spots, encourage them to announce where they're drawn to go. Often there are major and fairly immediate choices to make — the east or west side of the lake, upstream or down, this canyon or that. Announcing one's intention and direction allows participants to leave base camp with those drawn in the same direction who might be their stone pile buddies. As they head out together and then separate, they can make plans to meet sometime later at a specific landmark. Then, if they've found places for their solos, they can show each other those places and establish a stone pile without having to return to base camp and figure out logistics from there.

Generally, people come back to base camp within two to four hours, but for some, it takes six or more. Occasionally, someone returns, frustrated, having not found an area or spot that works or feels right. These are difficult situations. If you know the area well and have used it many times before, you may be able to suggest a spot or two, taking the person to it right away or early in the morning.

EVENING

As the sun settles toward the west, certain things need to be taken care of to get ready for the evening. These include the following:

- Everyone setting up their sleeping arrangements for the night.
- Eating/dinner plans, which can be loose or organized
- Some ritual or activity that brings the group together, takes inventory, and addresses where each individual is and asks how he or she is doing. This can be done in many ways, simple or elaborate.

At Circles of Air and Stone, whether or not the group has planned to share a meal together, we make sure the group sits together while eating. Once people have their food prepared, a talking stick is passed around, and each person reports on how looking for a solo site affected him or her. This can include a report of the search itself — rituals performed, prayers spoken, omens and signs, what happened and where it led — as well as feelings about the process and the result, including whether the process is complete or needs to be finished in the morning.

After people speak about their search for a spot, we move into the subject of prayer. The morning's send-off ritual is described (see "Departure" under "Days 5–8: The Solo"). We inform the group that one way the guides "hold space" for those on solo is by coming to that departure circle at least twice a day — morning and evening — and praying for each of them. After they're informed of this, we ask, "Since you now know that people will be praying for you while you're out, what would you like them to pray for?" (It's useful to announce that safety and protection are always part of the prayers, so that doesn't need to be mentioned. Saying this helps them focus on their longing and intent, rather than on their fears.)

This always feels like sacred time. People speak slowly. It may take a few minutes before the first person speaks, and there are many pauses between speakers. Generally, people don't seem to ask for much, perhaps because during the days of preparation and sharing they have honed their focus and intention down to what truly matters. There are few long lists, and most requests are simple. It helps to have a small notebook to write down what people ask for. Ask if there's anything more. Let them know you've heard them and will follow through on their requests.

Before people settle in for the night, remind them of the protocol for the following morning — packing, smudge, and blessings. And if they haven't already been told — for example, earlier in the evening or while describing the purpose circle — what time they're expected back on the ninth morning this should be announced now.

We give guidelines (between 8:00 and 10:00 a.m.) for returning to base camp and emphasize there's no need to rush in at dawn when the quest is over. We encourage them to finish the time well. There are things to be done on that last day. Some are practical, like packing clothes and dismantling the purpose circle, but there are matters of the heart that also require completion. Connections and relationships have been developed with trees, rocks, or special spots that protected, taught, or welcomed them during those four days. Remind them to give time and attention to saying goodbye in an appropriate way and to feel complete before they return. "Don't rush and don't dally" is good advice.

DAYS 5–8: THE SOLO

DEPARTURE

Sunrise marks the beginning of the four-day solo, the vision quest proper. This is a time of excitement, anxiety, a quickening of the soul. The guides have researched the time of literal sunrise, and, hoping to send the group out as the sun crests the horizon, rouse those still sleeping about 30 minutes (longer if needed) before then, giving people time to pee and pack. Some will be much faster than others.

Leaving is best done with a ritual and heartfelt send-off. While the group attends to packing, the guides can attend to the ritual space. This may be simple or elaborate, but it's important. As stated previously, ritual marks and creates a change, and leaving base camp is a great change: from the community to solitude; from familiar comforts to their absence; from the known to the unknown. Departure says goodbye to the human and social world and initiates an entry into a sacred time and relationship between oneself and the Earth, oneself and that which has created us.

At Circles of Air and Stone, we construct a circle of stones, 10 to 12 feet in diameter, made from 8 to 12 rocks. We begin by placing stones in the four cardinal directions, praying that the powers of each shield be with the people during their time on the land. The remaining stones are then placed to fill in the circle. Sometimes meaningful or decorative elements — pine cones, flowers, or bones — are added.

When people are packed and the space for departure created, everyone is called together (not in the ritual area) and offered a final chance to speak to their companions before departure. Some are silent, but most affirm their intentions or offer some form of gratitude, encouragement, or prayers to their fellows. After this, the group proceeds to the ritual space.[1]

The rite of departure should be something that's meaningful and to the point, acknowledging the change that's about to take place. It should also be something you, as a guide, are comfortable with. There are many possibilities — smudging, prayers, smoking a medicine pipe, songs, calling in spirits, sprinkling cornmeal or tobacco, etc. — but it shouldn't be forced. It needs to be real, genuine, and not too long. We didn't get up before sunrise just to stand around the circle for an hour.

In our quests, people arrange themselves around the outside of the departure circle. The guides produce a bowl (abalone shell) and proceed to fill it with smudge (usually crushed sage, sometimes with cedar added). While the smudge is being ignited and stoked, they instruct the group to think about what they are leaving behind and what they are heading toward as they prepare to walk out of base camp, and tell them that when the smudge is fully lit and ready, whoever is first moved can step into the circle to begin that journey.[2]

The person stepping in first is smudged and receives a prayer/blessing. When finished, he or she steps out of the circle and walks into the wilderness while the next person steps in. This proceeds until everyone has left and quiet descends on camp.

HOLDING SPACE

The group has departed. The camp is empty and feels spacious. The guides relax and boil water for coffee or tea. The days spent around base camp while people are out on solos are mostly rich and wonderful, especially in good weather. After days of preparation — days filled with emotion, information to present and tasks to accomplish, and almost constant social interaction and being "on" — time off is very welcome. In addition, four days alone in a beautiful place with no emails, calls to answer, or anything that needs to be done: how often do we experience that in daily life?

Most guides look forward to, even need, this time, and during it, they might take walks, read a book, or simply gaze at the clouds and river.

Though there are some constraints — guides need to be present, or not away for too long, in case someone returns — this can also be a sacred time for those in camp. Most wilderness guides "have the bug." They've chosen to become guides because of their deep connection with the land and this sacred process. They've been taught, touched, held, and healed by the living Earth, and they long to nurture, reconnect, and renew this relationship. The time at camp while the group is on solo offers that possibility.

In the days before the solo, participants sometimes ask, "What will you be doing while we're out fasting?" They ask this question partly out of curiosity — facing their own challenge of how they'll spend their time — but they're also looking for support and assurance, a comforting sense of community from knowing the guides are somehow with them. ("I'm doing something very frightening and difficult. It helps to know you care.")

Most guides do care. The people out on the land are often on their mind, and they find ways to "hold space" for those out. This could be as simple as sending good energy, but it helps to formalize and make it a practice. I make a point to come to the blessings circle (the circle from which the group left) in the mornings and evenings to pray for each person who is out. I speak whatever comes into my heart, but I've also asked what they want me to pray for, and I do that, as requested. I might also sing to the mountains or desert, chant, smudge, or walk or dance around the circle, and sometimes get carried away. Find what works for you, what brings you present and alive, and a way to share that energy with the land and those who are out upon it.

DAYS 9–11: RETURN AND INTEGRATION

DAY 9 – MORNING: RETURNING FROM SOLO

Some basic time and logistical issues:

The return process: If you've instructed people to be back from their solo by 10:00 a.m., how will you proceed if they're not? What is the impact of being late? For example, in the Chama Wilderness, the hike out is an easy, fairly level 1.25 miles. Being a little late back to base camp means very little. But in the Gila Wilderness, the hike out is rugged, with a thousand-foot rise. Doing that hike in the bright sun in the middle of the day is hard, especially after a fast, so getting back to base camp on time matters. In addition, a person in good shape can easily do that hike in less than an hour. Others, in poor condition and after a fast, might barely make it in four. These possibilities can have big impacts on how much time you have and what you can do later in the day. Be aware of your parameters, constraints, and options.

When people return, they should be enthusiastically welcomed. Help them with their pack, if needed. Congratulate them and give them a warm hug. Have food ready, usually something simple and easy to digest, like fruit salad or oatmeal. Prepare for this before they come in.

Gently engage, but don't push. Let them speak and share at their own pace. They have been in intimate contact with nature, immersed in the silence. They don't need a barrage of words or interrogation: "Did you do a purpose circle? What animals did you see?" For the first person in, you may need to restrain your curiosity. Be cognizant of what they need and let your conversation respond to their cues. If five people have returned already, they will make up the welcoming party and you can let them carry the tempo of the conversation. Be observant of what you see. Be supportive. Your needs and curiosity can be satisfied later.

When everyone has come back and taken in food, discuss the game plan for the rest of the day. This can vary depending on the length and difficulty of the hike out, time for the drive back, and what's left to be done and its relation to the size of the group. (Smaller groups require less time for incorporation.)

When everyone has eaten and understands the game plan, create a ritual closing — a time for saying goodbye and expressing gratitude for the time on the land — before starting the hike out. On Circles of Air and Stone quests, we return to the circle of stones where people left for their solos and do a ritual that is similar to but slightly different than the one done four days before.

Again, while people stand around the circle and the smudge is being lit and stoked, the guides ask them to think about what they're leaving behind as they get ready to leave this natural place, and what they'll be stepping into as they return to the human world — both the joys (restaurants, ice cream) and the sorrows and ugliness of what they will soon be immersed in. As before, when the smudge has been lit and smoldering and people feel the commitment to take all that on, they step into the circle. When everyone has stepped in and all are standing in the circle together, the prayers and blessings commence.

When finished, dismantle the circle of stones before the hike out. If the hike is long or difficult, you might hand out granola or energy bars that will provide glycogen (blood sugar) on the trip out. Any relevant or useful advice about hiking ("take your time, find your own pace, keep hydrated") should be shared. At the vehicles, it's good to remind the drivers to go slow and stay focused. If you are leading the caravan, you can set the speed.

DAY 9 – AFTERNOON: WEAVING THE SACRED AND DAILY TOGETHER

The hour when you gather to begin the process of integration and incorporation can be affected by many factors:

- The time of year: Around the summer solstice, sunrise might be 5:30 a.m., and you could find yourself hiking out by 10:00 a.m. At the fall equinox, sunrise will be hours later.
- The return (hike and drive) from the solo area could take anywhere from one to four hours on average.
- Time needs to be budgeted for showers, cleaning up, setting up tents at camp, food, etc. Depending on group size and the length of the journey back, more (or less) time can be allotted for this.
- In very small groups, allowing extensive free time and beginning the mirroring process the next morning (or beginning sooner and finishing the whole program early) may be an option. In larger groups, with an 11-day program, the telling of stories should begin this afternoon.
- Sometimes, for various reasons, participants haven't allowed enough time to finish the whole process; for example, someone announces they need to leave by 10:00 a.m. on the last day to get to an airport. Decisions about how to proceed (by guides or the whole group) may need to be made.

Your job as a guide is to lead a vision quest.

Often when people return from their solos, they feel proud, excited, and connected to all those who shared the experience with them. Naturally, they may want to celebrate, and in most instances, this is good. It's a chance to create more community and is easily accommodated. But sometimes the desire to celebrate and connect comes into conflict with the need to complete the vision quest with integrity and impeccability.

As a guide, your commitment is to the quest process, not to the social needs or desires of the group. Going out to dinner or for ice cream is fine, sometimes wonderful, but when people write their letter of intent, dinner and ice cream are never part of it. Location makes a difference. In some places, a good restaurant (or a hot spring, or...) is five minutes away. At another location, the nearest town or restaurant is an hour over winding mountain roads with no center stripe. As a guide, your commitment to the vision quest process may be important in keeping a group on track as they return to the rich and tempting world of socializing and "civilization."

When the group is refreshed, fed, cleaned, and finally gathers, the time for sharing stories of the quest has arrived. This process needs to be introduced and framed. As previously mentioned, some quest organizations, usually those who take larger groups, put time limits on the solo story and limit the mirroring to the guides. If that's the case, it should be stated at the beginning, with boundaries and directions clearly described. (This is not the case with Circles of Air and Stone, and our protocol is shared below.)

Since this group circle is the first since before the solo, we begin with smudging, followed by announcing the game plan for the remaining time. We let the group know there will be three separate processes (see below) and, to the best of our knowledge, when they'll happen:

1. Telling and sharing stories. In this first part, each person speaks and shares his or her quest experience, while all the rest listen.
2. Situation reversed (usually afternoon of day 10): Each person listens while the rest of the group speaks about "what they heard in the teller's story." Let them know that instructions and guidelines will be given when that time arrives.
3. Addressing the return (usually on the last morning) — suggestions and descriptions of the challenges and tasks of "bringing your vision back to your people."

After sharing the game plan, introduce this session with some general remarks about story-telling.

- The importance of the task. The story of your vision quest is not the same as your quest. Creating (and telling) a story is a creative act, not a report. This isn't "what happened." (Thousands of things happened that were never noticed; thousands barely affected us. But these things — what we speak of in our story — did!) The story you tell is *what spoke to you*. Your story allows the mystery, the unknown, to find its way into the known. It is a conduit for bringing your sacred time alone back into the human world.
- Each story is different. Your story is about *your* conversation with the mystery. Don't compare! Every person in the group went into the same wilderness, slept under the same sky, and encountered the same weather, yet everyone comes back with a vastly different tale of what that was about.
- Each story is a myth (or dream) that teaches, provides answers, and can be lived into. Coming to a vision quest with intention and purpose is like asking that unknown or mystery for a dream. Your story represents the dream that arrived in response to your longing and request.
- Telling stories is a fundamental human gift. What's unique about the human animal is our imagination. It allows us to create stories that bring an encounter in the moment, an experience or memory from the past, and the collective wisdom of millennia into a narrative that connects and weaves them into a single tapestry. This is magic, and it's a power. If this telling of stories is a uniquely human gift, we ought to tell some good ones, ones that connect us to the depth, breadth, and miracle of existence.

This is followed by guidelines and instructions for the storyteller:

- Encourage them to tell it in *their own way* what feels right and genuine to them. This could mean there are parts they want to keep private (for whatever reason), to stay between themselves and Spirit. Give them permission.
- This is not a contest about who saw the most animals or cried the most tears. Remind them that this is a narrative about their meeting with Spirit and the encounter and conversation that they, and the mystery, needed to have. Love the story, whatever it is!

- In the spirit of "this is your story," it can be useful to mention options:
    - They could tell the whole narrative chronologically, beginning when they walked out of base camp, or organize their telling by subjects and themes, such as "my battle to become an adult" or "creating healing with the spirit of my mother."
    - Some speak extemporaneously, completely off-the-cuff, while others do the opposite, just reading from their journals. Many do some combination of the two.
    - Most people speak in the first person, from the "I," while occasionally someone speaks in the third person, as in a legend or fairy tale: "This young prince went out to face the dragon of worthlessness, and here's what he found... "
    - Guidelines of time (helpful to share.) Let people know that 30 to 45 minutes is standard, and though they won't be cut off, if they appear to be wandering and unfocused, they'll be called back to the task.

And finally, some simple guidelines for the listeners:

- No interruptions. The teller has the floor, and it's his or her decision about what is shared and how. Those listening may be curious, want more, etc., but those are the needs of the listener, not the storyteller.
- Taking notes is useful. There's a lot to take in and, as with dreams, if it's not noted it may quickly disappear.
- Encourage people to listen with their own ears. Each person will hear the story through their own filters and may be struck by something no one else catches. Invite people to honor that and write it down. Affirm that what strikes them may be important (or not) and sharing it may help the storyteller see things he or she might have otherwise missed.

Begin the stories. Ask for a volunteer. Before starting, read or recite *"Praises of this Place"* by T. Griffin (in the resources section).

DAY 10 – MORNING: STORY TIME CONTINUED

The plan for this morning is to finish the telling and sharing of stories. Much of how that takes place will depend on time and logistical decisions made the previous afternoon. If you have a small group, and seemingly plenty of time, the telling of stories could begin now.

DAY 10 – AFTERNOON: MIRRORING AND FEEDBACK

In quests with Circles of Air and Stone, sharing and reflecting on the stories of the vision quest takes place in two parts. In the first, now completed, each person was given time to tell his or her tale of insight or adventure while everyone else listened. In part two, the structure is reversed: Each participant listens, while the rest of the group has a chance to speak about what they heard, observed, thought about, or concluded from witnessing that person's journey.

There are many possible ways to do this. In Circles of Air and Stone quests, the following is our choice.

STRUCTURE OF THE PROCESS

1. The order in which the various stories are addressed is random. Names could be chosen out of a hat; written on a piece of paper with numbers assigned to each, the numbers then chosen by members of the group; or chosen by any number of other methods.
2. After that person is chosen, approximately five to ten minutes are allowed for the other group members to review and evaluate what they've previously noted about the participant and/or his or her narrative; or simply meditate or think about the person in question and what they're moved to say.
3. After this time is up, and people acknowledge they're ready, whoever is in the seat of honor is asked if he or she has any special requests (explained below) and if he or she would like someone to take notes of the feedback.

4. Then, whoever is first moved picks up the talking stick — placed in the center of the circle — and offers mirroring and feedback to the person whose story is currently being attended to.
5. After the first person finishes their mirroring, the talking stick is passed to the person on their left (sun-wise), until everyone in the circle (other than the listener) has spoken.
6. When the mirroring circle has been completed, the listener is then asked if there's anything he or she would like to share in response. Usually, this is just a simple "thank you" or expression of appreciation for the process. The guides need to make sure that it remains simple and doesn't slide into commentaries or rebuttals of the mirroring that's just happened.
7. Make sure everyone understands the process before moving on to instructions for mirroring and listening.

INSTRUCTIONS FOR THOSE MIRRORING OR OFFERING FEEDBACK

- Emphasize the essential and unavoidable subjectivity of the process. We all hear a story through our unique filters and lenses. These lenses come from our background, culture, family, and personal history as well as the particular intentions that brought us here. Because of this, when we listen to a quest story, something that strikes us as crucial or important could be important to the teller, or it may seem crucial because it's a big issue in the listener's life (but not in the teller's). Therefore, offer it in the hope of the former, but accept the latter if it's not picked up.
- Those who mirror the story are not giving advice or assuming they know what events in a story ultimately mean. To remind ourselves of this inherent subjectivity, it's good to speak of it by using phrases such as:
  - "If I had that dream (or experience), what it would say to me is... "
  - "If that had happened to me, what I'd be thinking or want to look into is... "
  - "When those things have come to me, I've found it useful to... "
- Remind people to keep the focus on the listener and not go into their own narratives. Something the listener said may seem powerful to someone else because of their personal history, but that personal history doesn't need to be shared.
- For the sake of making good use of time (refer to the number of people in the circle):
  - Encourage people, especially those whose turn comes early, to focus on the three or four most important reflections and share those. Someone may have consulted their notes and highlighted 15 different things they could speak about, but...
    - Some are more important, and some are less.
    - Other people will speak after them. Trust that someone else will say what you don't.
    - If there are things that, as a result, don't get mentioned and still seem important, these can be shared "off-line," around dinner or on a break.
  - Encourage people to not repeat what others have already said. If they think it was important and want to emphasize, a simple "ditto that" will suffice. Having eight people say the same thing is not useful.
  - If everything you would have said has already been commented on, announcing that and then passing the stick is fine and appropriate.
- The mirroring and feedback can include elements that are not part of "the story." What was shared about the quest by the person currently being attended to will likely be in the forefront of what the rest of the group responds to, but sometimes others, to greater and lesser degrees, have shared time with that person on breaks, driving to the quest site from the airport, talking over dinner or around the campfire, taking walks, etc. Important or significant conversations may have happened during any of these occasions. Or experiences may have been shared that weren't witnessed by the whole group, and these may provide context for and/or be included in the mirroring process.

INSTRUCTIONS FOR THE LISTENER, THE ONE WHOSE STORY IS BEING MIRRORED

- Encourage the listener to just listen; to focus on what's being offered and shared.
- If the listener would like extra attention or insight into a part of the story (an important dream, for example), he or she can request it.
- If the listener wants a record of what's being said, suggest that he or she ask someone else to take notes, or a voice recorder that's simple to operate could be an option. The point is for the listener to stay present, to not have his or her attention taken away from the moment by the need to write things down or focus on the technology of a recording device.
- Remind the person of honor to "take what you need and leave the rest," that the subjectivity of peoples' responses is both unavoidable and previously noted. Invite the listener to consider the implications of what seems to fit or be useful, and to let go of, and not take personally, whatever doesn't resonate or seem relevant.
- If there is a follow-up that needs to happen, this can happen "off-line," during a break, around dinner or the campfire, etc. This might be clarification with whoever took notes or further dialogue about a point someone mentioned in the mirroring. These conversations don't need to immediately happen and take up time in the circle.

DAY 11 — THE RETURN

Whatever the length of the vision quests you're guiding, eventually you'll arrive at the last day and the final circle before parting. There may be a particular set of teachings, rituals, or things you want to share or accomplish before this parting happens, so it's important to know, as best you can, when you need to be finished.

As mentioned, factors such as group size and how much time was involved in transitioning between the solo and incorporation sites will affect the amount of time you have available. But circumstances you haven't planned on sometimes arise. A participant says, "I need to leave by 10:00 a.m. on Sunday." This could be a need, like having a flight at 6:00 that evening, or a want, such as making the drive back during the daylight. One can judge these wants or needs harshly or benignly, and you could choose to try to accommodate them or not, but it's good to know about them beforehand and not be surprised and trying to adjust at the end. As soon as the group reconvenes, post-solo, I suggest asking if anyone has to leave early (and if so, by what time and for what reason).

OVERVIEW

In earlier eras, when people rejoined close-knit communities familiar with and committed to the vision quest process, the incorporation process might continue indefinitely after the returnee was welcomed back and celebrated. Meetings with allies and elders, inductions into medicine societies, sharing of further dreams, and reminders to enact one's vision might continue through months (and years) to come, as the sacred dream experience is slowly woven into the fabric of daily life.

In today's small groups, the brief time after the solo is important to celebrate and integrate the experiences and lessons of the quest. But this time is short, a pale shadow of the support and reweaving into a community that once was common. Once the stories of the quest have been told, celebrated, unpacked, and examined, most of the incorporation work that can be done has been accomplished. This witnessing, mirroring, and affirmation, important as it is, comes to an end, and participants soon head back to a home and community and a daily life likely to be, at best, partially supportive, and, at worst, nonexistent or actively hostile.

Since ongoing incorporation and integration is largely unavailable within small, temporary groups that quest together, the concluding sessions are both a warning about and preparation for a coming period (the return home) mostly deficient in the qualities and assistance traditionally critical to completing a vision quest. Going home without the presence of a welcoming community may be far more challenging and difficult than four days alone without food.

Those guiding modern-day quests must address and allow for this fact. The issues of return and reintegration are extremely important for people without access to the traditions and support common in indigenous tribes and villages (most of us today). After the rich time of sharing with the group is over, suggestions, teachings, and tools for going back to daily life need to be provided. The final meetings offer the last opportunity to affirm and anchor the gains that have been made as well as provide perspectives, practical advice, and resources to continue the journey "on the other side of the mountains," in one's home community and social life.

This final circle usually includes:

- Speaking about the return, with its potential and challenges;
- Sharing tools, processes, and resources to help in the transition; and
- Affirming and grounding the changes and commitments of the quest time.

SPEAKING ABOUT THE RETURN

If the group's preparation included teachings about the traditional three phases of a rite of passage or archetypes of the heroic journey, this could be a time for completion of those lessons. Now we face the return phase of the heroic journey or incorporation phase of the vision quest. The situation is similar for any other teachings used to "frame" and introduce the vision quest process.

In the heroic journey archetype, the realm of primal forces was described as an entry into a far different landscape than the one from which the hero departed. Coming back, the task of the return is to bridge these two worlds, to bring something from the imaginal, liminal, soul-filled realm back to the world of daily life. In primal, earth-based cultures, this might not be difficult; there would be a plethora of support. But western culture is "mythologically challenged" and suffers a split and disconnection between above and below, matter and spirit, the practical world and a spiritual, soul-based life.

Many myths of the heroic journey show the return to be dangerous. *The Odyssey* is a prime example. Danger means there are outer forces (people, vested interests, situations) and inner investments of energy (habits, beliefs, ways of seeing the world) that oppose any major change of orientation. People may feel threatened, frightened, or simply not want to give up the comfort and familiarity of the way things have been. For further elaboration of the symbolism in the theme of the return and its relevance to coming back from a quest, see Section VII: The Return.

Planting a seed can be a useful metaphor to illustrate the tasks and challenges of coming back. The seed contains the future and new life. It is the egg, the germ, the beginning. It must be planted and grow if that future is to unfold, if the new life is to fulfill its promise and renew the old. This seed contains the potentials within the soul and is synonymous with vision, whether expressed as speaking the truth, finding one's voice, being authentic, or living one's dream. It must be planted in daily life, in the world of work, relationships, and community. This metaphor of planting a seed is more fully unpacked in "The Promise: Finding Fertile Soil," which is part of Section VII: The Return.

SHARING TOOLS, PROCESSES, AND RESOURCES TO HELP IN GOING BACK

Many tools and tasks are listed and described in "Practical Steps on the Path Home," also a part of Section VII. Some of these, like calling a council of allies and making physical changes to one's living space, can only happen after the group has departed. Others, such as writing a letter of intent for going back, could be done while the group is still in camp. A strong focus on intention could be emphasized by having participants read these letters to the circle along with making commitments and establishing some form of accountability process before leaving.

There are many options if you want the final sessions to contain a "work component" as well as providing information for the journey ahead. Here are some possibilities:

- Having people write letters of intent (as stated above).
- Having people write letters to themselves. These could be letters of commitments; letters of love, validation, or support; or letters about "things I want to remember (or not forget) upon returning home." These letters could then be put in envelopes, addressed, and collected by the guides (or given to someone else in the circle) to be mailed at some later time.
- Making commitments and establishing accountability around any number of other acts, such as
    - Beginning the stone pile letter;
    - Participating in group conference or follow-up calls;
    - Writing a letter of intent (at home) and sharing it with the group within a certain time; or
    - Following through with any number of stated commitments.

AFFIRMING AND GROUNDING THE CHANGES AND COMMITMENTS OF THE QUEST TIME

As the time for departure approaches, people find it hard to stay in the present. The call of the future, exciting or upsetting, may make people want to get on the road or dread leaving. The power of the past dozen days can fill people with sadness or fear of losing something. Without the intimate communities of the distant past, these feelings are common and mostly unavoidable. It's important to have an ending, a closing ceremony of some sort (severance), and for people to feel they're leaving with something (incorporation).

Leaving with something (incorporation): Some of this may have already been addressed with plans for a stone pile letter, letters of intent, or statements of commitment and/or accountability. A few more specific tools that guides sometimes offer are:

- Offering to host group conference calls for updates and check-ins, either once, or at some predetermined interval;
- Ongoing or follow-up counseling, coaching, or mentoring;
- Possible follow-up programs available only to those who've completed a quest (these could be reunions, shorter "advanced" workshops, or the possibility of apprenticeship in some fashion);
- Enrollment in various closed vision quest communities (Google+ groups, Facebook groups, etc.); or
- Subscriptions to newsletters, discounts on repeat quests, or other perks.

Closing ceremonies can be simple or elaborate. A guide should find something he or she is comfortable with and use that. A short list of possibilities, neither exclusive nor exhaustive, is

- Some version of the final council (everyone speaks once);
- Group prayers, passing around the smudge or talking stick;
- Group celebrations: feasts; going out to dinner; soaking in a hot spring together, etc.;
- Circles of affirmation, validation, or blessings (many possibilities); or
- Handing out talismans: some object (stones, crystals, medicine pouches, arrowheads, T-shirts, group photos, etc.) they can carry home to remind them of their shared time and connection.

As the participants head homeward, in a similar but different way, the guides return to "normal life" as well. This return may be longed for, a time where one no longer has to be "on" and always available, helpful, or intelligent. But letting go of this focused and intentional community is also a loss (loss of community) for those guiding it.

In the sacred space of vision quests, we cultivate a fierce openness to our inner lives and each other. That openness is rare "on the other side of the mountains." In general, guides miss the depth and soulfulness of the community but welcome the downtime of not being a leader, and it's important for them to find their own closing rituals. After the closing with the whole group, there's still the need to make closure with the guide role. If guides have worked together, part of that usually involves debriefing — speaking about the program, participants, and each other about what worked and went well and what was difficult. Sharing about what it was like working together; honoring the path and the work; and affirming, honoring, and blessing each other are important.

Being a quest guide is itself a seed that needs to be planted, watered, and cultivated; a passion that's unusual and out of step with much of today's mass culture. Feeling oneself as part of a larger context — the community of quest guides, a keeper of wisdom and tradition, a member of the family (friends and protectors) of the beautiful living earth, and so on — can help us maintain our direction and remain on solid ground while we tend and nurture this calling as it grows, flowers, and bears fruit to help feed and heal our hungry world.

SECTION II:
FOUR SHIELDS TEACHINGS

Overview: Models and Maps of Reality ... 37
- Medicine Wheels ... 37
- Teachings of the Wheel — Wholeness; Sacredness; Inclusiveness ... 37
- Medicine ... 38
- Division by Four ... 38
- The Four Shields ... 39

The South Shield: Childhood ... 40
- Medicine Animals of the South ... 43
- Shadow as It Appears in the Medicine Wheel ... 43
- The Shadow South: Stuck in Childhood ... 44
- Mirroring in Relation to the South Shield ... 45

The West Shield: Adolescence ... 46
- Who am I? Creating the Separate Self ... 46
- Soul ... 48
- The Shadow West: Stuck in Adolescence ... 49

The North Shield: Adulthood ... 52
- The Adult Self ... 52
- Wisdom ... 53
- The Giveaway ... 54
- The Inner Community ... 56
- Buffalo, Medicine Animal of the North ... 56
- The Shadow North: Stuck in Adulthood ... 57

The East Shield: Sage or Elder ... 58
- The Way ... 58
- Toward the Unknown ... 59
- Images of the Formless ... 60
- Going Wild: Dancers, Mystics, and Clowns ... 60
- The Self of the Sage or Shaman ... 62
- Stuck in the East: Spiritual Unreality ... 62

The Circle and the Cross ... 64

Notes on Medicine Animals ... 65
- Bear, Medicine Animal of the West ... 65
- Eagle, Medicine Animal of the East ... 65

SECTION II:
FOUR SHIELDS TEACHINGS

OVERVIEW: MODELS AND MAPS OF REALITY

MEDICINE WHEELS

We begin our exploration of the medicine wheel with a simple definition, courtesy of Wikipedia:

"Medicine wheels, or sacred hoops, are either a symbol of indigenous North American culture and religion or stone monuments related to this symbol."

As stone monuments, medicine wheels can range from large, megalithic structures like Stonehenge to many smaller circles of stone, thousands of which have been found through the northern plains of North America. The most well-known is located at Medicine Wheel National Monument in Bighorn National Forest. These stone circles were built and used by a wide range of indigenous peoples for religious, ritual, healing, and teaching purposes. In most, the center was marked by a large stone or fire ring and then connected to the outer ring by lines of stones, or "spokes," usually marking the four cardinal directions. These medicine wheels were used as altars, places for ritual and ceremony, or spaces for centering one's energy and awareness. Labyrinths, forms of which have been found all over the globe, can be thought of as specialized versions of the medicine wheel.

While the actual structures built throughout history were undoubtedly related to the particular culture's cosmology, myths, and ceremonial uses, there are certain themes and teachings inherent in the medicine wheel that are universal.

TEACHINGS OF THE WHEEL — WHOLENESS; SACREDNESS; INCLUSIVENESS

The circle represents oneness — the whole, the universe, everything. Among native people of the plains, this wholeness was called *Wakan-Tanka* (literally "The Great Everything") and it referred to both the outer cosmos and one's personal universe. Many Native American teachers refer to the ubiquity of the circle and its manifestation all throughout nature, expressed in weather patterns, the shape of birds' nests, and the orbits and movements of the moon, seasons, and stars. The medicine wheel teaches that everything is sacred. The circle, or sacred hoop, embraces everything. We are all included; there is nothing outside it. There are no "bad" people, forms of life, or points of view; no hell or place of excommunication to which rats, spiders, or the unwanted are banished.

EQUALITY

The medicine wheel teaches that we are all equal. Mathematically, a circle is a series of points *equidistant from the center.* We occupy our place in the circle, and no one is closer to that center (God or Spirit) than anyone else. There are no priests or holy people better or higher than the rest. Faster, stronger, richer, smarter — there's no quality that makes me any more important, special, or sacred than you. This is true for both individuals and groups. I am no better for being white, a man, an American, or even human. We — man, woman, Iraqi, deer, dragonfly, socialist, shaman, piranha, Pope, and pimp — are all in the circle. Each of us is one point, one perspective, a component of the whole. All of life — every form — is in the circle. Each is sacred; each is important; each is equal.

RELATEDNESS

As members and parts of the circle, everything is interconnected, a piece of a larger whole. Awareness of that larger whole leads to the realization that we are all related. Native peoples saw other forms of life as relatives, part of the family, and prayed for "all my relations" upon entering the sweat lodge. "Grandmother Moon, Brother Wind, Sister Brook, Father Sky..." — nature in its many forms was a friend, ally, teacher, and beloved. To realize and live in harmony with these intimate connections, this Great Mystery, was to follow our "original instructions," and following the good road led back to the garden, to our home, this heaven on earth.

HUMILITY AND RESPONSE-ABILITY

Just as no one in the circle is more important than any other, no one is less important either. With everyone equal, equidistant from the center, and part of a larger, sacred whole, there's no reason or place for either shame or self-importance. Everyone has a response-ability — like the raven, thrush, loon, or sparrow — to sing his or her song, to speak his or her truth, to share his or her unique perspective and point of view. You stand in the south and face north — those standing in the north can't and don't see what you see. Man, woman, elder, child, African, mother; blind, bereaved, rich, exploited, Hindu, abused — your perspective is different and unique. Wisdom can only be found through the ability to hear the Larger Story, the symphony of the whole sacred hoop. You are not the whole story. And yet, you have your note to sing and a part to play.

MEDICINE

What is meant by medicine? In today's world, *medicine* has come to be associated with surgical procedures and a wide array of pharmacological agents. But in a much older lineage, medicine is anything that moves us toward health, a word derived from an older English word *hale*, which means to be whole. So, in this larger, more traditional sense, medicine is conceived as anything that helps you to be or become whole. And help on that journey to wholeness can arrive through different avenues and appear in many guises.

Ultimately, becoming whole involves realizing our connection and interrelationship with all that we are; our larger selves. This "larger self" can include the many dimensions of reality — inner and outer, physical, emotional, and spiritual. Using this broader definition, medicine could be a substance, whether comfrey, Tylenol, psilocybin mushrooms, or holy water, if those "medicines" help ease dis-ease, bring us back into harmony, or introduce us to larger frames of reference or expressions of our being. But medicine could just as well be a story if it teaches and tells us something that broadens our perspectives and makes us more well-rounded or complete. It could also be a parable, a meeting or encounter with an animal, taking on a new or "medicine" name, or receiving a spirit or power song. All these could contain medicine.

We have been talking about the wheel, the circle, and the sacred hoop as symbols of wholeness. "Medicine wheel teachings" make up a set of images, symbols, lessons, and tools that can help us move toward and realize that wholeness. They can help us understand ourselves as well as life itself. They provide a map of the territory, a definition of and guide to the journey the soul longs to take as we search for direction in life. They can connect heaven and earth; orient us in aligning our physical, mental, emotional, and spiritual realities; and help us find solid ground in our heroic, shamanic, and ultimately human journey.

DIVISION BY FOUR

The fundamental mystical "event" is the experience of union, and at the core of all spiritual systems lies the insight that there's a oneness behind all the "illusions" of form and of separateness. And yet, we live in a world of radical diversity. There are approximately 10 million species of living things. And within each species — whether moose or maple trees or six billion people — no two are alike.

Between these two polarities — "we're all one" and "we're all different" — we live out our lives and try to make sense of our experience. To understand ourselves and the universe we live in with any depth, we need tools and teachings to join together these seemingly opposed, but very real, orders of perception. All throughout history, humans have created maps and models of reality — conceptual systems that could be scientific, psychological, religious, or visionary — in order to explain, elaborate on, or emphasize the various facets of our existential landscape.

These models may emphasize mind, matter, psyche, or spirit to help us navigate through a life that is ultimately mysterious and multidimensional. To be useful, they must bring together and integrate the different experiences of change and constancy, mind and matter, dream and waking, life and death, millennia and moment in a way that makes sense.

Many maps of reality start by dividing the universe into a few great or basic powers. The symbol of oneness is the circle. One of the oldest and most common models divides this circle into four:

- **Four directions.** North - South - East - West
- **Four elements.** Earth - Air - Fire - Water
- **Four seasons.** Spring - Summer - Fall - Winter
- **Four energies.** Body - Psyche - Mind - Spirit
- **Four perceptions.** Sensing - Thinking - Feeling - Imagining

In the pages to follow, one of these models, the four shields, will be described. It starts as a map of the directions, includes and resonates with many of the other "divisions by four," and has proved helpful to many preparing for a vision quest.

THE FOUR SHIELDS

In the four shields teachings,[3] these grand "powers" or elements reside both within us and in the outer world. Since we are creations and representations of the living earth, it should be natural that the constellations of energies within humans should reflect the structures and energies of the universe, and vice versa. The assumed separation between self and world is a cultural artifact related to language. Definitions and boundaries are essential for creating a noun, whether that boundary exists "in reality" or not. The polarities that "make sense" in language are often not part of the sensuous landscape of life. For example, we cannot speak about *left* except in contrast to *right*. There's no *up* unrelated to *down*, no *within* that lacks a *without*. Like *within* and *without*, there's no *self* except in relation to *world*. Each direction associated with the cycles of the sun and earth, the seasons and stars in the "outer" world, is reflected inwardly in a corresponding quality in our lives and psyches.

The east is associated with morning, the rising sun, and the emergence of light. As time moves onward, the sun climbs higher in the sky, firmly entrenched in the south by midday. From there it continues westward, ushering in the evening; finally setting, bringing us to the north and the darkness of night. This daily cycle is reflected in the larger cycle of the seasons. East evokes springtime, brimming with the energy of the new and rising sun. The sun moves south, climbing higher into the sky, bringing us summer, its heat bearing down on us from directly overhead. As the sun travels west, the abating heat and fading light of evening are reflected in shorter days and cooler temperatures of the fall. Finally, the sun sets, ushering in the cold, dark nights representative of the north shield and the season of winter.

In our human or inner world, each direction, or shield, is seen to reflect a stage or energy in the cycle of a person's life as well. East, home of the rising sun, represents beginnings. It's the birth of the day, an opening and a time of transition. But "every beginning is also an ending" (T.S. Eliot), and this door leading in can also be an exit, an end. The east shield, where the day starts, signifies the energy of birth or creation. But in every transformation or creation of something new, some form is left behind. This time of transition and new light is intimately connected to, and born out of, the dark, fertile soil of death. The east shield represents those moments and movements of transitions — between the spirit world and the physical, the past and the future, one form and another. It's the gateway, that liminal zone between this cycle and another. In a human life, times of transformation, including the many other beginnings and endings between our literal birth and death, are associated with the east.

When the sun climbs high in the summer sky, things expand and grow rapidly. In a human life, this time of growth and expansion describes, and the south shield represents, the energy of childhood. Later, during the time of the descending sun — evening and fall in the outer world — the rapid growth and expansion of summer slows down, ceases, and reverses. The rising sap that produced new shoots, branches, and leaves through spring and summer starts to pull back. The grasses and leaves turn yellow, become brittle, and fall to the earth as the sap retreats from the periphery and migrates underground. This pulling back and turning within, the west shield, is associated with adolescence, the heightened self-consciousness that lies between childhood and adulthood.

In winter, we enter a time of making choices. The carefree ease of warm weather has ended. There's no fruit to be picked off the earth or plucked from the tree, and we have to live on what we've grown and harvested. The necessity of making good decisions about our resources and clear determinations about the situations we're in can govern if (or how well) we survive. Immediate gratification may need to wait. Cold temperatures and a barren landscape require us to learn planning, wisdom, detachment — the north shield lessons of adulthood.

In the following pages, the directions will be presented one at a time. But remember, this is a circle. Though we must speak of them individually, as we do seasons in a year, they happen within a larger context and are all connected. Each shield can be conceived of as representing qualities we need to possess or lessons we need to learn as we face different situations or seasons in our lives. Each is a constellation of energies that, if they remain unintegrated, will leave us incomplete, out of balance, or dysfunctional.

THE SOUTH SHIELD: CHILDHOOD

South is the shield of childhood. It's noontime of the day and summer in the yearly cycle, a time when children, like grass, grow rapidly. This rapid growth expresses the fertility and productivity of the earth. Summer's warm, moist energy is like a tropical rainforest, fecundity filled with sensuality and desire, a creative chaos where things copulate and devour each other.

In the four shields teachings, the lessons required to have a whole and healthy childhood experience are those of *Trust* and *Innocence*. Trust is the sense that this body, this life, this earth, is a good place to be. The feeling "It's good to be alive! I love this world!" expresses the knowledge, experience, and belief that this physical incarnation is positive and pleasurable. This lesson is basic and pre-verbal, the security of knowing that I belong, that I am safe. Being here is good.

Humans are different than most other species. We arrive in the world undeveloped. Many other mammals, though small, can quickly walk, eat, and fend for themselves within hours of birth. Humans, perhaps due to the coexistence of large heads with small pelvic passageways, are helpless for years. Therefore, we must develop and grow within a "second womb," our community of people.

Children acquire their sense of trust when — after they arrive in this life — the community around them (mother, father, sister, brother, aunt, uncle, village) welcomes them into the world. They are held, fed, protected, touched, played with, and sung to. When they are hungry, someone is there to feed them. When they hurt, they are picked up and soothed. If this happens consistently, children develop a sense that they can trust this world. They arrive here with needs, longings, and vulnerabilities, and the human community responds to those needs positively and lovingly.

In Bali, there's a custom that when a child enters the world, it is held constantly for the first six months of its life. Its feet barely touch the ground. Someone is always there, carrying, singing, speaking to, playing with, and touching it. It experiences almost uninterrupted physical and sensual contact and feels a constant connection to others and the communion of village life, the melody of voice, beating hearts, pulse, and skin.

Compare this to a typical Western hospital birth. Sometimes the mother is drugged, anesthetized against pain, so the child, who shares the same blood, is drugged also. It may be pulled out of the birth canal by a pair of pliers (forceps) gripping the head; held upside down; slapped until it screams. After a short stay with the mother, the child is whisked away to spend most of its first days in a nursery, alone in a plastic bassinet under fluorescent lights. If it is a male child, he will soon have the most sensitive part of his body torn off without an anesthetic. When our child finally gets "home," most of its time will be spent in a crib, isolated from contact, perhaps even in its own room. This "welcoming" of pain, isolation, and disconnection is the typical experience of a modern Western child, a child that will have no experience with which to conceive of or imagine the level of trust developed by its counterpart in Bali.

And all this assumes a "good" home, a "good" birth, with "good" parents. But many children in our society are hit, beaten, abandoned, abused, violated, or neglected in basic and horrible ways. To be healthy and whole, a child has to learn the lesson of trust that this is a good place to be. We must ask ourselves, "How much of this lesson of trust have I learned? Do I feel, unequivocally, that this is a good place to be? Do I really experience joy in being alive?" If the answer is not an unequivocal yes, there is work we need to do, and you may be on this vision quest to do that work, to learn or complete the basic lesson of trust.

The second lesson of our south shield is the lesson of *innocence*. Trust and innocence are complementary. Trust is about the world; innocence about the self. Trust declares, "The world is good!" while innocence announces, "I am good!" Innocence is a basic sense and conviction that I — with all my impulses, desires, wants, acts, expressions, feelings — am good; who I am is valued and welcomed. Again, our child comes into the "second womb" and does what it does. He yells and screams, poops in his pants, crawls into the cupboard and pulls everything out. She puts everything in her mouth, wallows in the mud, sings, throws a temper tantrum, and does all of the things that children do. The child will learn that she is good when the response from the world says "This is great! You are so cute and adorable! We love your childishness, your curiosity, your wondrous enthusiasm!"

The lesson of innocence can be learned if children and their behaviors are met with consistent, positive responses. The adults or community may not want many of those behaviors, like dragging everything out of the cupboard, in a 200-pound adult, but in the child, they are lovingly accepted, even welcomed. The word *enthusiasm* contains, at its center, *theos*, or god, and healthy adults recognize something sacred in a child's boisterous enthusiasm. The child may need to be guided or limited for its own protection, but a healthy, functional adult or community recognizes that this child embodies nature or spirit itself — still unformed, yet expressed in all of the child's wild lunacy, passions, and appetites. If this child is met with consistent love and welcoming, he learns that his impulses and who he is are okay. She learns, "I am good."

How well have you learned the lesson of innocence? Most modern men and women, if they are honest, admit to being wounded, their sense of worth partly or greatly compromised. Many children have been routinely told they are bad or stupid, or that they have ruined the parent's life. Many have been threatened with abandonment, criticized or ignored, told to shut up and go away, or met with silence. These situations may seem extreme, but they are far more common than we admit publicly. Guilt and shame are issues most everyone in modern life faces.

Even in "good homes," there are personal and cultural shadows that affect children. Families always have definitions of what is "good" and what is not, and these messages teach a child, "This part of you is valued, but that part is bad." In one house expressing anger is punished; in another, loudness will get you sent to your room. Many have grown up with the admonition, "Don't talk back!" and the repressive injunction that "children should be seen and not heard." As a result, a child learns that its thoughts, feelings, and opinions are not welcome.

In most homes, the child's sexual and erotic nature will be repressed and labeled unacceptable. There are "bad" words and "dirty" areas of the body. Each home may have its particular rules or flavor, a set of values where some part of the child is not welcomed. Children take these messages personally. Adults are large, powerful, more experienced, and seemingly all-knowing. Nearly every child will take these judgments — no matter how irrational, ignorant, or dysfunctional they are — as a sign of personal failing.

In addition, some cultural messages fracture innocence. For millennia, the Western world has lived under the doctrine of original sin, which implies we have been flawed from the beginning. How can one start from original sin and ever arrive at innocence? For generations, it's been unacceptable for women to be assertive or intelligent, while boys are shamed as sissies if they are sensitive, cry, or play with dolls. Schools train children to focus and pay attention, while the body's desire to run around, the emotional and social needs that drive us to whisper to friends, and the imaginative dream realm that pulls our attention out the window and away from the blackboard have all been considered disobedience, a behavior problem, or a flaw.

"Have I learned the lesson of innocence?" It's important to ask. Do you feel that some part of yourself is not okay, not good enough? Is it part of your intention on your quest to know you belong here and are valued; to find a certainty, a trust and faith in yourself that's like a rock, a foundation that everything else can start from? Are you hoping to relearn or complete the lessons of trust and innocence in your vision fast?

If we truly learn the lessons of trust and innocence, the gifts that follow are many. The south shield is associated with emotion and expression, the capacity to manifest a wide range of joy, sorrow, grief, anger, etc. "E-motion" means motion or movement "out of." A healthy child easily expresses its internal states. If our south shield is healthy and functioning, we can do the same.

Physical, sensual life is associated with the south shield. One sees this in children. They fully inhabit their bodies; they experience things viscerally. They pull things apart, put them in their mouths, and rub them all over their bodies. They explore the world in tactile ways; they look at mud as something to get into. The core of our erotic life is centered in this shield, whether expressed in sexual relationships, appreciation of nature, or love of painting, touch, food, or music.

If we trust the world, we will want to know it. If the world and who I am are both good, well, let me jump into it! Curiosity, the fascination with and openness toward the expressions of the world, is part of this complex. The sense of wonder — the child's desire to explore its environment, pull it apart, play with and understand it, and find out how things work — is a healthy quality that can express itself in more complex ways as adults, whether in science, art, or spirituality. People of genius, like Einstein, or with spiritual gifts, like the Dalai Lama, are notoriously curious. They possess a childlike openness to experience. That openness combined with later mathematical training may produce a brilliant and creative theoretical physicist; with different training, serene and peaceful wisdom that giggles much of the time.

A well-functioning south shield results in a passionate zest for life. If I truly trust the world, know it as a good place to be, and realize my own goodness, then I will want to engage life fully. I'll want to explore what's unknown, participate in life's adventures and offerings, jumping into the fray to experience its chaos and creativity, its miraculous and messy beauty. The child self, or south shield, is the foundation upon which we build our stance toward and motivation for living. When well-developed, it brings forth a cornucopia of rich and positive gifts that are a blessing to the self and to others.

MEDICINE ANIMALS OF THE SOUTH

Mouse is the animal most often associated with the south. The mouse is focused on physical things: safety, pleasure, eating, and security — lower chakra concerns. His attention is on what's immediate and close by; he does not see the big picture. He exists at ground level, burrows underground or hides in the grass, and reacts to what is right before his nose and in the moment.

Coyote is also sometimes placed in this shield. There are numerous Native American stories about coyote's egotistical and self-centered exploits which — driven by desire, lust, and curiosity — are alternatively (or simultaneously) comical, crazy, or creative. He represents the sacred clown, the child run rampant, and he usually manifests something wildly original or initiates outright disaster.

SHADOW AS IT APPEARS IN THE MEDICINE WHEEL

In the four shields teachings, the term *shadow* has a different meaning or emphasis than its common psychological connotation. In its usual form, *shadow* refers to those parts of the self, judged as bad (ranging from simply unattractive to downright evil), that the ego attempts to eradicate or hide from the world. These qualities, concealed or denied, eventually become invisible to the ego itself, and their still-active energies are then expressed in unconscious (usually dysfunctional or destructive) ways. In a more broad-based view, the shadow can sometimes mean all those qualities, impulses, and energies of the self that the ego is unaware of.

But the four shields teachings are located within a circle, outside of the usual polarities — good-evil, heaven-hell, inner-outer, right-wrong — of our modern, linear mythology. Within a sacred hoop that embraces everything, what is the meaning of *shadow*?

In these medicine wheel teachings, the shadow is more an expression of imbalance. For example, if a healthy diet includes some combination of protein, carbohydrates, and fats, and your diet is 98 percent fats, then fat consumption casts a shadow on your overall health. Fats themselves are not bad — they're even necessary — but their dominance or imbalance is unhealthy.

When considering the shields — south, west, north, and east... and the energies of childhood, adolescence, adulthood, and elder — visualize a stool with four legs. If this stool has four strong legs of equal length, the stool is functional. It works well. It's solid and in balance. But if one (or two or three) of the legs are much shorter than the others, or the opposite — one (or two, etc.) — are much longer than all the rest, it functions poorly or not at all. You'll always be out of balance or lacking adequate support. You may even collapse or topple.

Take the south, for example. If you haven't learned the lessons of trust and innocence — the lessons of the south shield — you will not fully realize the gifts of passion, curiosity, vitality, expressiveness, physicality, etc. that are natural byproducts of this realization. This condition — a lack of access to, embodiment of, or full embrace of these energies — is analogous to the south leg of the stool being too short.

The opposite condition, the south leg of the stool being too long, could be called being "stuck" in the south or the shadow of the south. South shield or child energy dominates the other shields, and one habitually responds to situations through the child's lens or impulses, rather than with other, more appropriate responses, such as might come from someone grounded in their separate identity (west) or a healthy adult (north).

Whether we describe the south shield as overdeveloped or see the other three shields as underdeveloped is irrelevant. The point is that we enter the shadow, are "stuck" in the south, when this shield dominates and is overdeveloped *in relation to* the other shields, and thus our responses are habitually mired in child-centered reactions. The resolution of this shadow energy does not come from condemning or attempting to repress "the child." We seek balance, and the remedy for too much south-child energy may well be more adult (north), the development of greater access, awareness, or skills in the arenas and energies of other, complementary shields.

THE SHADOW SOUTH: STUCK IN CHILDHOOD

Our south shield expresses a shadow aspect when we become stuck there and respond only from the child self, without access to the capacities of the north, west, or east. This can take several forms, a few of which are described below.

One expression of this shadow is materialism. Becoming stuck in the south, we do not develop an appreciation for and relationship to the other, non-material, aspects of human experience. The positive love of physical life gets fixated on and becomes an obsession with things.

Here we might see a certain stereotypical male, driving a Porsche, Lexus, or monstrous four-wheel-drive pickup truck. The back contains a snowmobile or all-terrain vehicle, and the bumper sticker reads, "Whoever dies with the most toys wins." This stereotype is a larger version of the little boy in the sandbox, only with bigger toys and bigger trucks. Materialism as a female stereotype might play out as an obsession with clothes or shopping, a closet containing a hundred pairs of shoes. The little girl who played dress up with her Barbie takes on the same pattern in her relationship with herself. Spending a small fortune on cosmetics, she becomes an object to be manicured, permed, painted, perfumed, dressed up, and decorated.

On a larger, cultural scale, our society measures its well-being in terms of a growing economy, and it equates success with more money and more stuff. Cars, houses, appliances, vacations — the more you can purchase the better off and more successful you are. Our overall health is measured in goods and services; our national product is gross. This is materialism, and, purely and simply, it is childish.

Self-centeredness is another expression of being stuck in the south. Self-centeredness is a mark of the child, and is appropriate to its stage of growth. Developmental psychologists say the child, at first, does not distinguish between inner and outer experience. There is no self-and-other, no self-and-world. Everything is "me" to the infant. Gradually it learns to distinguish "me" from mother, father, sister, dog, and other. The psychology of the child is centered in the self; it defines the whole world in terms of "me." A child thinks, "If you give me what I want, you're my friend. But if you don't, you're mean, and I hate you!" Any "other" — people, situations, environment — is totally defined by what it does for "me." Child-like thinking involves a world centered and revolving around "me."

Think of foreign policy, and the words "our national self-interest." Our enemies are defined as those who do not give us what we want, and our friends are those who do, no matter how authoritarian or oppressive they are. As long as they satisfy our (mostly materialistic) desires — access to their resources, rights to their waters, and land for military bases — they are our allies and friends. The United States is often attracted to leaders who epitomize the childlike president and the politics of the sandbox: "If you take my truck, I'll grab it back and hit you over the head with it." Grenada, Panama, Nicaragua, Iraq, Iran... "If we dislike what you do, bullets and bombs will fly." Defining Central America as "our backyard" or Afghanistan as vital to "our national security interests," we are at times unable to conceive of other nations as autonomous and independent countries.

In domestic affairs, we have an almost-unquestioned faith in the politics of the marketplace, an assumption that the greatest common good will arise from a process where separate interest groups fight and compete for their own share of the pie. This viewpoint about the sanctity of competition, individual rights, and the marketplace has disastrous consequences for the common good, yet it is rarely challenged. It is essentially mired in the south, "me first," childlike thinking.

On the personal stage, all unconscious, reactive, or addictive emotions can be seen as shadow aspects of the south. For example, eroticism is a great gift. A rich and whole relationship would suffer without it. But when relationships are defined by or fixated only on that energy — sexuality as lust — they generally end negatively. The woman who is "promiscuous," the man who is "a player" or needs to prove himself by jumping bed to bed, secret or inappropriate liaisons that damage others... when our interest is limited to our organs or our own pleasure, when it does not consider the heart, the partner, or the wider community, we are acting as a child whose focus is only on "me." And others will often feel used, devalued, or ultimately diminished by that interest.

A passion for life and a joyful optimism toward the process of living is the reward if we've truly learned the lessons of the south. But childhood has the potential for many possible wounds, and the limitations, imbalances, or lack of wholeness we inherit may signify either that we are stuck — the leg of the stool too long — or unable to embrace the lessons of trust and innocence with their attendant gifts of desire, motivation, and expression — the leg is too short. On vision quests, we always ask, "Is part of my reason for being here to learn, complete, or reclaim those capacities, lessons, and gifts of the south?"

People often inquire, "If I haven't learned the lessons of the south, what do I do about it?" This is a good question. One avenue of healing is to learn to "feed the child," to embrace our south shield needs and desires. This could involve exploring our sensual, instinctual, or animal self, or practicing the expression of all those emotions that have been held back. It may require a commitment or kinder attitude to the body, a greater valuation of pleasure, play, or relaxation in relation to work or productivity, or a willing engagement with creativity and expression. And, of course, any "therapy" or guidance in addressing our wounds and releasing blocked energy can be useful. Making changes like these in our habitual attitudes are direct, sometimes obvious (though not always easy), and often necessary remedies for a diminished south shield capacity.

But a more complex and deeper answer to this question says that we may have difficulty experiencing trust and innocence because we received the message, usually from the adults in our lives, that we were inadequate and no good, and who we were and what we did was wrong and bad. To heal those wounds requires being free of those messages and replacing them may necessitate creating a loving adult voice within ourselves, a voice we've never had. As long as there are judges and critics within us announcing that we are stupid or a failure, our "inner child" will never be truly happy. An important, core part of ourselves will always feel deadened, hurt, rebellious, or deeply sad. The long-term solution will not come from attacking the critic — for it is the critic who thrives in the attack. Instead, one may need to create a healthy and loving adult voice (the north shield) that can consistently show and tell the child self that she is valued and welcomed, so that the child can finally feel trust and experience innocence.

MIRRORING IN RELATION TO THE SOUTH SHIELD

The topic of mirroring is broad and deep and could be the subject of a whole book. But I want to mention it in the context of a child's development and its relevance to issues of the south shield.

A child comes into the world with no boundaries, no differentiation between self and world. As mentioned, when the infant first contacts the breast, he has no sense of other, and the experience is absorbed by the sponge later called "me." The child's sense of self only develops as he perceives himself in a mirror, as he is reflected by the world and others around him.

When a baby is first born, she is hard-wired to gaze out into the world with openness and wonder, and her biology/neurology expects or needs to meet a similar gaze coming back. This gaze is usually provided by the mother. When the openness of the child meets and connects with the open presence of mother, a host of neural connections start to form in the child's limbic system that wouldn't be made otherwise. Through this process of bonding through eye contact, the child begins to learn to regulate herself, absorbing the mother's comfort when distressed, modulating and gaining some mastery over the surges of sensations and emotions coursing through the infant body.

For an infant, this "mirroring" is essential in the evolution of its biology, affecting its ability to self-soothe and self-regulate. And it stimulates neural development in the subconscious that affects the ability to harmonize, connect, and, as time passes, to love.

Later, as the child becomes more mobile, social, and adept in its environment, it still depends on this mirroring for his emergent sense of self. This child will gurgle, pull things apart, scream in rage, and test its will and the world's limits. It will wallow in the mud, sing in joy, or wail in grief or frustration. Aside from its innate experience of these states, it will still "see himself" through the eyes of mother, and later, father, siblings, and friends.

If mother's mirror projects back an image, an energy, of "my precious and adorable child," this youngster will develop a confidence and trust in his urges, actions, and impulses that will serve him well through most of his later life. But an adult's reaction to his expressions may send back a message or image that conveys "bad (unacceptable), stupid (defective), burden (unwanted), etc." Or if the child is ignored and not responded to (invisible... I don't exist), these mirroring experiences produce immense distress in his inner world and can set him up for all sorts of internal conflict. Rebellion, people-pleasing, anxiety, inauthenticity, avoidance, timidity, lying, sneaking around, and anger projected outward onto others make up just a small sample of potential distress and dysfunction.

In a functional culture, it is the job of healthy adults to hold up a mirror to the child. This mirror (their responses) should reflect back acceptance and belonging. Through these reflections, children learn of their value, potential, and beauty. They learn they are loved and have an important place and role in the community.

Modern culture, where many people wrestle with feelings of inadequacy, not being good enough, or deep feelings of shame (like they are a mistake), suffers from an epidemic of inadequate or destructive mirroring. The distorted mirrors through which children learn to see and know themselves nearly always produce damaged self-images that may take a lifetime to heal.

THE WEST SHIELD: ADOLESCENCE

The day passes, and the sun moves from south to west, from midday to evening. Seasons change from summer to fall. Our child is ushered into the shield of adolescence, that constellation of issues, commitments, and concerns that lie between childhood and adulthood. The lesson awaiting us in the west is introspection, where we learn the requirements and harvest the fruits of the art of looking within.

This is partly a natural process, the result of growth and development. The child is expressive, totally centered in himself. He does not look within. But as he becomes older, he is faced with the increasing realization that there are others in the world with different ideas, needs, and wants. The universe is no longer just about "me" and my judgments, desires, and dislikes. As our adolescent looks out at the world, the awareness that there are others looking back grows within him, and the budding youth is moved to recognize and grapple with "looking at himself" as well.

At first, the response may be superficial. In fifth or sixth grade, the gaze looking at oneself may merely result in time spent in front of the mirror. The adolescent wonders, "How do I look?" The concern with what others see may emphasize hair, clothes, or complexion. But as the years advance, the examination — hopefully — moves beyond the surface.

WHO AM I? CREATING THE SEPARATE SELF

The task of adolescence is the creation of the separate self. This was not a part of childhood. The self of childhood is embodied and embedded in the world. Creating a separate self is difficult: how does one become separate and yet remain connected? The imperatives of this task pull in different directions — separation and belonging, differentiation and communion. Harmonizing, balancing, and finding that "sweet spot" or middle ground can be difficult, and it can influence our character through later life. Too much separation and we become detached — isolated, distant, disconnected. If there is not enough separation, we become co-dependent, caretakers, approval seekers, or people-pleasers.

With these conflicting forces of separation and belonging swirling around, adolescence is often a time of high drama. The first push and pull may be felt at home, with parents. "You can't tell me what to do [or wear, listen to, watch, read, smoke, or when to go to bed]. This is *my* life! Is dinner ready yet?" But then it migrates to school and neighborhood. Cliques and circles of friends form and become important. We want so much to belong. But then our friends do things we are uncomfortable with — driving drunk and out of control, stealing, being cruel to those less fortunate — and we feel the distance; start to pull away.

Introspection waits, always available to open and explore the inner life, as issues with peer groups and pressure raise the question, "Who am I?" Our friends want to party; they're all going out drinking. "Is this okay with me? Am I a prude or a coward, or are they jerks?" We engage in the struggle to decide whether we can be different, and if so, how. These years are often chaotic and emotional. Alliances form and break as we vacillate, trying to differentiate and create a separate self while not cutting all bonds because we need to stay connected. We struggle with the dilemma of whether we can be separate, but not be excommunicated.

The work of self-exploration takes time and is challenging. Looking within is essential to this process. Introspection is both cause and effect: it's the result of differences and conflict, and it marks, creates, and solidifies uniqueness and individuality. This introspection initiates and facilitates the formation of a self that did not exist before. As we grapple with strong, sometimes extreme, feelings, the sweep of these emotional tides is just the visible effect of deeper questions: "What are my values? What is important and meaningful to me? What are my feelings?" Though born of conflict and crisis, as we commit to this deepening investigation, we begin to develop an inventory, a separate identity that wasn't present in the child. Something new — the separate self or personality — is birthed through the process of looking in.

This sense of self and identity arises along with an awareness of the "other." The task of differentiation, if done well, results in an ability to relate to others as "other," not just as an extension of oneself and one's needs. The ability and capacities necessary to do this — empathy, forgiveness, ability to listen, and compassion — are birthed out of the same process of introspection.

For example, if I meet you and ask, "How are you doing?" and you reply, "I'm feeling lost and like a failure because my lover left me," I can empathize. Because I have done my own work — looked within myself and been present with my own inner experience — I can remember the feelings of hurt, rejection, and abandonment. I can respond (the true meaning of response-ability), meeting you where you are, in your pain. I can reply, "I know how you feel; it hurts so much." I allow you to be *other* — my lover hasn't left me — and yet I can meet you *in your space*, the place of grief and sorrow.

If I haven't done my inner work, I will be unable to meet you there. I will be unfamiliar with and uncomfortable in my inner landscape. I won't have access to the depths of my own emotions. I won't know what feelings of deep sadness are like. I may reply as a child — "Gee, sorry to hear that; want to get a beer?" — but I will be out of my league, unable to connect with you over your feelings. I will avoid or try to change your experience, pull you out of your space so you can engage and join with mine. Empathy, the ability to join with another across the bridge of separateness, is beyond the capacity of the child. It rests on a foundation of introspection and an access to and familiarity with the landscape of one's inner life.

Two other capacities that can bridge and create bonds across the gulf of separateness are compassion and forgiveness. Compassion means literally "to suffer with" (*com* = with, and *pathos* = suffering). To suffer along with another, to meet them within their grief and loss, requires that we have plumbed the well of our own hurt. And forgiveness for those who have hurt us requires a recognition and acknowledgment of our own failings within the larger embrace that affirms our essential goodness. In forgiveness, we extend this stance of loving kindness, practiced on ourselves, to another. These capacities, essential to the creation of mature and healthy interdependence, require a foundation of well-developed and healthy introspection.

SOUL

If we do this work of the west well, we will harvest the rich gifts of self-acceptance, self-love, self-respect, self-confidence, and self-care. This process of self-examination, though midwived in tension and conflict, creates not only the separate self, our "personality," but a depth of character, a quality, we call "soul." If we are successful, we will become solid like an oak: grounded, rooted in our self, with an ability to relate, reaching across the gulf of separateness to the other, with empathy, compassion, and gifts to give.

We can conceive of the west shield of our medicine wheel as the place, or arena, where *soul* is developed or created. *Soul* speaks to a depth of character that requires facing and grappling with the challenges, joys, and sorrows of life. When we speak of soul, in music or in life, we think of those who have wrestled with addiction, suffered the pain of racism, struggled with the dark nights of self-doubt and emptiness, and yet found a way to bring light, serenity, and a connection to something larger into those dark and painful places. The work of the west involves plumbing the depths of one's being, seeing and accepting the darkness and light, and lovingly embracing the strengths, gifts, and limitations of one's unique identity and its response to the world.

Spirit and soul are not tangible, but they can be conceived of as movements, complementary directions energy takes within "the tree of life." The spiritual urge is analogous to the rising sap, whose impetus travels up from the roots and out toward the infinite sky. This movement begins in spring (east). It seeks higher states, elevated consciousness; it longs to open and flower. It wants to transcend; break free of the bounds of space, time, and the forms we find ourselves in; experience oneness, the source of all that manifests. Spirit spreads out, diffuses, radiates, finds rapture in the heights. Spirit moves beyond, breaks free of form, and dissolves into light... enlightenment, illumination.

Soul stirs in the opposite direction. Soul brings the energy of the heavens down to earth. As the leaves gather sunshine, they harvest this sky-sourced radiance. They fix and concentrate it in saps and sugar compounds that are stored in the roots over winter. The tree turns light into carbon-based substances. We develop our souls — become more soulful — when we bring the grand and universal vision (sky) down into the nitty-gritty limitations, struggles, and darkness of the lives we lead.

Soul is earthy; it seeks depth. It grounds, establishes a foundation, creates an underpinning. It generates reliability, steadfastness, and character. Soul embodies, concentrates, transforms radiance into reality. It creates structure, mechanism, conduits, and channels through which the transcendent, compassionate, and non-dual perspective can manifest in the theatre of everyday life with all its difficulties, limitations, and conflicts.

Rare among animals, humans, like trees, stand erect, our spines aligned along the vertical dimension. The human vertebrae and the tree's wooden trunk symbolically represent the staff, whose vertical thrust joins earth and sky, matter and spirit, temporal and eternal life. By opening a conduit upward and down, the trunk/staff/spine creates an axis, a pivot and center point around which the horizontal dimension, the temporal circle of our lives, revolves.

Heaven and earth, above and below... In the World Tree, the poles are joined, balanced, although in different seasons of the year the movement in one direction or the other becomes more dominant. The sap rises in springtime, and the growth of summer moves upward and out, beyond what was there before. Budding, leafing, unfurling, and flowering, the barren earth of late winter explodes in a riot of new forms and color.

Come autumn, the trajectory reverses; the elevator descends. We enter the west shield, and the direction is downward. The photosynthesis that peaked amidst summer's expansive greenery has created food that must be stored in the root system beneath. The energy of life becomes concentrated and migrates underground. The blossoms of spring culminate in fall's fruiting; seeds drop to earth to await springtime's resurrection. Outward existence contracts. Branches grow bare as leaves flutter downward. The sap seeks out darkness and depth. The action moves inside, under the surface.

In healthy ecosystems, these opposing impulses sustain and feed each other. All the expansion above the ground must be supported by what's below. If the purchase of a tree's roots is limited, it can't grow tall without toppling. Similarly, when the canopy is constricted, the leaves will fashion little food into flesh, and root expansion will not take place. Our tree must develop in both dimensions, and to blossom and thrive, humans must do the same. Our branches and roots must be connected, above and below, outward and inward, spirit and flesh. Earthly and spiritual life must be in balance. "God" and earth need not, must not, be opposed. Our sacred and daily dreams were not meant to be separate.

But adolescence is a difficult time for most. Compelled to reconcile two seemingly contradictory things — the impulse toward individuation and an autonomous, independent self and the urge for communion, connection, and bonding — it can be a time of turmoil. Alienation, loneliness, and various forms of acting out are common.

This birthing is necessary, but modern culture offers few resources. There is little real community of men, women, or tribe to join or that could teach us. Rites of passage into adulthood do not exist, and few adults or elders know themselves and their gifts. (Even fewer shoulder their responsibility to mentor the young.) Adolescents are often told or expected to "get it together" on their own. In addition, we've inherited a Cartesian-Newtonian world in which the *self* has been divorced from earth, nature, spirit, and cosmos. As a result, even those adults who have navigated the confusing and uncharted channels of adolescence have inner landscapes that are limited, impoverished, and removed from the sources and great cycles of life.

In more primal cultures, the inner landscapes pointed to by the west shield are larger. The landscapes accessed by going within include vast shamanic and non-ordinary worlds. Ancient wisdom cultures recognized that we are far more than our personality or personal history, and exploring what lies within can include archetypal and ancestral knowledge. For example, a human embryo in the womb will retrace the evolutionary forms of our past. As the fetus develops, it forms little gills, fins, and a tail, all of which are later reabsorbed. Many older cultures developed techniques, skills, and methods of going within that tap into other dimensions, some accessing the "collective unconscious" or knowledge beyond the species boundary. In these cultures, it was not considered impossible or unusual to know or experience the world of fish, raven, coyote, or eagle.

In this larger perspective, the landscape of the west shield can include knowledge and initiation into "other forms of the self." The descent below the surface takes us into the fertile soil surrounding the roots of the Tree of Life. This soil is the foundation and sustenance of many primal wisdom traditions, whether the territory is described as Dreamtime, archetypal images, shamanic realities, morphogenetic fields, or the messages encoded in our DNA.

The metaphor of the west shield involves descending into the darkness and then returning, often with a gift, to the light of day. This dark zone could be the world of dreams, one's personal unconscious, or parallel universes, and these journeys can be inspiring, creative, terrifying, or soul-making. They can develop depth, courage, wisdom, and "powers," as can wrestling with our personal monsters and tracking them down to their roots. In North America, Bear is the traditional medicine animal of the west. Come late fall, bear enters the dark and the dreamtime, going deep into the labyrinth of the dream-cave before returning in spring.

THE SHADOW WEST: STUCK IN ADOLESCENCE

What does it mean to be stuck in the west? The core image of the west involves a journey into the cave and an eventual return with wisdom or gifts. To be stuck involves a movement within, with a delayed or detoured journey back out. Some versions of this include:

TOO MUCH EMPHASIS ON MEANING

In the creation of our personal identity, we discover or form a set of values: what we like and pay attention to; what is important or meaningful to us across a wide membrane of interactions and fields of endeavor. These values help us make choices and interact in ways that are satisfying. They create a context and a map that helps us set a course through life. But when this internal landscape of symbolically charged images gets in the way of engaging with and meeting the requirements of life, we have become stuck in the west. When we need to consult our spirit guides before ordering a meal, choose our clothing based on what chakras the colors represent, obsess over past lives at the expense of this one, or consult an astrologer before choosing a mate, we are mistaking feelings for reality, the map for the territory. When our astrological charts, guides, past lives, and Enneagram numbers become a description of who we are, actual life has become lost in the models we create of it.

Meaning is important, but an overemphasis on the meaning of things can be an avoidance of acting. If you're dissatisfied because your job is meaningless, that's important to know. But what can be changed? What needs to happen? Continuing to ask *why* you're dissatisfied (because you moved around a lot, had a bipolar mother, or have Pisces rising) doesn't change the fact. What can you do about it?

Meaning describes a resonance, or lack of it, between one's inner and outer world. It creates a context that, like a compass or a map, is necessary to allow us to orient, find direction, and stay on the path. If you sail the ocean staring at your charts, you've forgotten the real world where the journey must be made. A storm may be coming; the sails could rip; the hull leak. You must pay attention to now. You could spend months researching reports and reviews before buying a car and never actually make a decision. The constant search for meaning, or other realities and perspectives — whether on life, dreams, stars, or tea leaves — can be an escape from engagement with the world, from making choices and taking action in relation to the issues that face you.

TOO MUCH EMPHASIS ON FEELINGS

Being stuck in the west can appear as over-dependence on and overvaluing of feeling over other modes of perception. Many people begin sentences with, "I feel like... " They assume their inner landscape is data, a descriptive statement about an outer reality. Most often it's not. Images, thoughts, judgments, and sensations may be undifferentiated, all lumped together and assumed to be feelings. Feelings are fluid and always changing, and people who make decisions, statements, and agreements based on them will often appear "flaky" and unreliable to anyone not like them. They often find themselves stuck in major areas of life. They make little progress because they have not developed the detachment needed to discriminate among the mass of expressions — projections, fantasies, feelings, and judgments — that arise in their inner lives.

A cultural stereotype worth noting here is that women get stuck in the west, while men never go there. A woman asks her husband what he feels; he tells her what he thinks. Conversely, the husband says he can't talk to her because she's so irrational and emotional. He doesn't go into his feelings. She goes in, gets lost, and doesn't realize that she hasn't come out.

A person stuck in the west needs to get out. The solution is not to go farther in. If you've been avoiding looking within, your wholeness and healing will require serious self-examination and the practice of introspection. Getting in touch with your feelings is healing only for one who avoids them. For one who wallows in or is swamped by them, being in touch with feelings is part of the problem, and distance is called for. Conventional therapy virtually always promotes an introspective/feeling mode of perception, and it can be very useful or a complete waste of time, depending on your relationship to the landscapes denoted by the west shield.

TOO MUCH EMPHASIS ON SELF-CRITICISM

Self-criticism is another manifestation of being stuck in the west. Introspection results in the development of a self. But summer precedes autumn, and what is grown in the heat of summer is usually harvested in the fall. If the lessons of trust and innocence were nurtured and took root in the summer of your childhood, your likely harvest will be self-love. But if what was planted and cultivated in the south shield of youth was a mixed bag of wounds and ways in which you were wrong or "not enough," when fall arrives and you look within, the harvest may be bitter. You will see your cowardice, your fat, your ugliness, your stupidity. You will focus on all the ways in which you are lacking and carry a black duffel bag loaded with shame.

Self-criticism is a vicious cycle, and it removes us from the world. Our center is internal, "back behind the eyes." We restrain ourselves, observe, wonder what those "out there" are thinking of us. We feel bad about our fear, shyness, or cowardice — our holding back. If we notice that we are beating up on ourselves, we criticize ourselves for that. It is painful and relentless, and many people know it well. The focus always remains inside, on the self, but this focus is critical and unloving. This self-judgment can easily switch and lead to judgment and criticism of others. Feeling at fault, always "one down" and "less than," we attack, gossip, snipe, and put others down, knocking them off their perch so they are no longer above us.

DEPRESSION OR DETACHMENT

It's an oft-stated maxim that depression is anger turned within. Without addressing the "how" of anger — whether it's justified, expressed appropriately, etc. — we can say that anger is an energy that pushes out against the world, whether that's someone standing on your foot, a friend who has betrayed you, or a foreign army occupying your country. Anger helps create a boundary, a line between self and other, between in and out. When healthy, it's like having an immune system that says, "This is toxic and doesn't belong here." It acts to move what's damaging or unacceptable out. It defends the self.

But anger chronically directed inward destroys and diminishes the self, depleting its energy until one can barely get out of bed or perform any effective action in the world. The world becomes large, powerful, and overwhelming; the self shrinks away and moves far back into the cave. When advanced, this is extremely difficult to change, and it's no surprise that highly energetic actions in the world, such as physical exercise, are the most effective inoculation against depression.

Detachment (isolation, disconnection, etc.) describes someone who consistently stays on the separation end of the separate — self-in-the-world continuum. While clearly not as dangerous or debilitating as depression, its sufferers are people who are often socially awkward, emotionally flat or cold, and hard to get to know.

Humans, like all mammals, have been equipped with a complex set of physiological reactions — the fight-or-flight response — to handle danger. The storm of emotions and conflicts of childhood and adolescence can be painful and frightening. Many choose to flee, to withdraw into a safer, more detached world where those emotional storms are fewer and farther away. From mildly introspective to an outright hermit, this bear prefers his cave.

For those who learn and integrate the lesson of introspection, the gift of the *west* is self-love, along with a depth of character or soul that's rooted within community and the deep wellsprings of ancestral memory. This self is individual, differentiated, and unique, yet it has the ability to accept and bond with those who are different, or other. It has an inner life that is rich, compassionate, and connected to other forms and possibilities of perception. If our work in the west is successful, we'll gather a rich harvest. We'll be willing to feel and suffer our human condition, as well as others'. Blessed with a deep soulfulness rooted in kindness, compassion, and empathy, we will not be afraid of our emotions or ourselves.

The creation of the self and the development of the tools that resolve the tension of its separateness follows upon the south shield of childhood. But many people have childhood experiences that were incomplete or traumatic — too much or too little. They did not get the nurturing response that fosters trust and innocence. When autumn, the time for introspection, separation, and differentiation comes, they may separate too much, finding safety through disconnection (flight) that leaves them isolated and alone. Or, they may not separate enough. Hiding, staying below the radar and not making waves, they become caretakers, codependents, or approval seekers, unaware of or unable to commit to their own voice and path.

As children and adolescents, we're dependent on the world around us. The reality we inherit and inhabit is mostly determined by the choices of others — in our culture, by our parents. If we are still carrying unhealed wounds from childhood or have places of distortion and denial in our manner of looking within, there is still hope. Healing, though not easy, is still possible. It requires changes, choices, decisions, and action. Undertaking these tasks and developing the abilities to engage them brings us to the north shield, the threshold of adulthood.

THE NORTH SHIELD: ADULTHOOD

North represents the time of night, the energy of winter, the position of the adult. Most indigenous cultures had ritual forms, rites of passage, that moved a young person from adolescence to adulthood. This transition is not merely a natural progression, nor is it easy to make, especially for boys. In response to its difficulties, cultures developed ritual processes to assist them in breaking away from the parents — Mother in particular — and move out of childhood dependency into the community of men. For girls, lacking the need to dis-identify with woman/mother, the transition was usually smoother. Bodily changes were initiated and orchestrated by nature itself as girls became capable of childbearing, changes that were dramatic and obvious to the whole community.

Modern society lacks any real and effective processes for moving into adulthood. This has consequences. Most boys have a strong craving to "become a man," yet there is no community of men to join. There are no passage rituals and no one to even tell a boy what "becoming a man" entails. The adolescent boy feels immense pressure to be this "man," but without anything solid to move toward, he often defines himself by what he moves away from: anything considered feminine or identified with women. This creates fertile ground for attitudes of misogyny, which can include not only the denigration of women but any so-called feminine qualities he senses in his own makeup. His empathetic, nurturing, or feminine side is judged as weak or labeled sissy. He'll likely repress his emotions, dam up his tears, and fear any fondness for his brothers. The tragedy is not just that this strategy causes pain to himself and others. It also doesn't get him to where he wants to go.

THE ADULT SELF

North, the season of winter, is home to our adult shield. The lessons associated with this direction are *wisdom* and the *giveaway*. In any functional or sustainable culture, it is the adults who keep the community together. They hunt, teach, build houses, sew moccasins, take care of the children, and support the elderly. Adults must act, choose, and work, and their choices need to be wise if they're to "feed the people." Adults must be response-able. Many depend on them, and their choices and actions need to be not only capable, but also directed toward the welfare of something more than themselves.

Each movement, from one shield to the next, involves an expansion of self. The child sees the world filtered through the lens of "me." During adolescence, a differentiated and separate self is formed with an awareness of and ability to be in relationship to others. The self or identity associated with the adult expands again, an identity that includes "the people," the whole circle. This self is different from and larger than the separate self. This self is woven into the community (whatever one's community is). Adults see a larger context; grasp the interdependence of life; realize that no one can be happy, healthy, or fulfilled in isolation. Adults know the threads of health are woven into the fabric of relationships. If the community is unhealthy, everyone's well-being is compromised, If the ecology isn't flourishing, neither are they. The jaguar can't be king of the jungle if the rainforest is dying. If it dies, he dies as well.

The adult, aware of the larger context, enacts the *Giveaway* — embraces the role of contributor to the greater good. Among the Cheyenne, this was expressed through the tradition of "Sweet Medicine." In this teaching, the grass grows. The deer eat the grass, and the hunters kill and eat the deer. Thereby, the people live. The hunters pass away, and they're buried in the ground, which feeds the grass, which then feeds the deer again. In sweet medicine, each individual form contributes to a larger whole and participates in the cycle of giving away. Becoming adults, we learn to identify with the circle, the whole, the common good, and we give our energy to what is larger than ourselves.

WISDOM

In winter, we live on what we've grown and harvested during the summer and fall — our childhood and adolescent experiences. We must make decisions and choices about how to apply and use our resources. Wisdom, ultimately, is about the right use of energy. It begins with knowing where to invest your attention; where to commit your resources; what is useful and what is not. A good starting definition of wisdom is provided by the Serenity Prayer of Alcoholics Anonymous: "God, grant me the serenity to accept the things I cannot change, the courage to change the things I can, and the wisdom to know the difference." Clarity is important. Effective action requires *seeing reality as it is*, knowing where you are starting from, and knowing the difference between what can be changed and what cannot.

Imagine wintertime on the windswept prairie. We wait for spring, anxious for the relief and new life to come. We take inventory of how we're doing and notice we have no meat left. We have some corn, beans, a bit of squash, perhaps some salted fish. We initiate a conversation about what to do. Someone says, "Last year the snow was gone by the end of March, so we might be fine." But another replies, "Wait! Remember four years ago, when there was a blizzard in April, and the snow lasted until mid-May? What will we do if that happens again?"

We know how much food remains. We don't know when spring will come. We hold a council to consider the question, "What should we do?" The children would say, "Let's eat, we're hungry," for children are embedded in their senses, focused on themselves. They're hungry, case closed: it's time to eat. We turn to the adolescent, who speaks, "What does this mean? We still have a lot of corn. Since corn seems to work well for us, perhaps we should increase corn production by 50 percent. And remember the big wedding feast last fall? We consumed so much food then. We probably should scale back our weddings and harvest celebrations. And why do we have no meat? Maybe Harry Hunter is too old to successfully lead the elk ritual. Perhaps he needs to be replaced."

Our adults listen to the children and adolescents. They say to the children, "I know you are hungry. Do not worry, because we are here to take care of you." They turn to the adolescents and reply, "Perhaps you are right, and we should grow more corn, hunt less elk, and not have such big feasts in the fall. Those are good suggestions. We will consider them for next year, but we must turn our attention to what we're going to do now." The adult is responsive to the children and receptive to the larger meaning and ideas for change in the future. But there are difficult decisions that must not be avoided, that must be faced in this moment.

The relevant and important question is "What can we do now?" The village could ration food, children and elders eating full portions and healthy adults consuming less. The council could pray, perform a ceremony, or seek a shaman's advice, asking for a sign or direction to follow. They might consider organizing a winter hunt. Our adult entertains suggestions and considers options that focus on the present, *the situation as it is*. Energy flows where attention goes, and attention is not wasted on the past or any other things that cannot be changed.

Whenever we wish we had a different history or had taken different actions in the past, we are not inhabiting our north shield, our adult capability. We cannot change the parents we had, the choices we made, or the relationships we did or didn't pursue. We cannot change what we did (or did not) study in college. An adult understands that parents, relationships, and the choices and events of the past may have determined his resources, or lack of them, in a current dilemma. Our past may have created the full or empty baskets of corn — the gifts and the wounds we've inherited and deal with today. But our future can only be influenced by the choices, actions, and use of our resources in the present, and an adult must make a determination and act based on the situation as it is now. He starts from where he is, and that is where the dilemma, hope, distress, possibilities, and arena of choice are.

DETERMINATION

Wisdom begins with the ability to see the situation clearly: what is there and what is not, what can be changed and what cannot. To *make a determination* about the circumstances and the appropriate action, one must see clearly and determine the situation *as it is*. This seeing is detached, unemotional, and objective. We do not gaze through rose-colored glasses or the lens of how it "should be." We do not spout Pollyanna-ish pabulum like "everything will work out for the best." Whether the situation we're addressing is outer, inner, or both, we examine our strengths, vulnerabilities, resources, allies, opponents, wounds, gifts, and dysfunctional patterns. We conduct a searching and fearless inventory of the factors, outer and inner, that bear on the task at hand. After making that determination, we must then *have the determination* to follow through on our decisions. To consider, choose, and then act is required of an adult.

Many people avoid making choices and acting. Choices often do not work out perfectly the first time, and some people, rather than make an adjustment, get mired in self-criticism. They become "stuck in the west," and to avoid the painful self-accusations, they avoid acting altogether. There's often a learning curve, problems with our initial choices, and steps to address important issues. But as these roadblocks and false starts become apparent, we have more information than we did before, and this new information allows us to more clearly see the situation as it is, and as a result, make new decisions and adjustments.

Making mistakes and revising decisions does not have to be threatening to our self-image. For those who fully embrace their adult shield, concern with self-image may well be seen as a waste of energy. Thomas Edison performed over 900 experiments before the light bulb went on and stayed lit. He could have called himself a failure after five or ten attempts — certainly after 800 — but he didn't. He did not wallow in self-doubt and get stuck in the west. In every "failed" experiment he learned something new, examined what didn't work, and revised his next attempt. Eventually, the bulb stayed on, and potential "loser" became genius.

Some other examples: Colonel Sanders took his recipe for chicken to hundreds of investors before someone finally backed him. The book *Chicken Soup for the Soul*, which has sold 500 million copies, was rejected by over 150 publishers. Abraham Lincoln lost almost every election he ran in except the one for president. These "successful" men responded to failure or rejection with new actions, choices, and decisions. They considered what could be changed and what couldn't. And they had determination — they persevered with new initiatives until the world responded with a "Yes!"

THE GIVEAWAY

The self of the adult, sitting in council with the baskets of corn asking, "What do we do?" seeks what will benefit *all the people* — the children, youth, adults, and elders. Adults serve the greater community, the interdependence of life. They hunt, sew, repair the roof, defend the borders, and work to keep the structure of life safe and nurturing for the young and the old. The adults keep it together, providing the framework and container within which the community lives. They do the real work, molding their personal wants to serve something larger.

A traditional question asked during the vision quest is, "What gifts do you have to give to your people?" This is, in fact, two questions: "What are your gifts?" and "Who are your people?" The first question asks who you are: "What are you passionate about? What brings you alive?" Finding answers to these questions comes from, as Joseph Campbell reminds us, "following your bliss." The fulfillment of the giveaway does not come from giving up or sacrificing your passions for others. It comes from being yourself fully. If, in your soul, you are a singer, that is what you give to your people! If you are a teacher, that is what you give! If you are a shaman, a poet, a dancer, a healer, that is what you give! The giveaway is not about trying to be somebody you are not. It is about *being yourself fully... for your people*.

What is your gift? Imagine the universe has placed a seed inside you that needs to come forth and bear fruit, and, if you don't cultivate that seed, there is a hole in the fabric of the cosmos where something — you — should be. There is a poem by Rilke, "The Church in the East," that goes:

> *Sometimes a man stands up during supper and walks outside and keeps on walking because of a church that stands somewhere in the east. And his children say blessings on him as if he were dead. And another man stays inside, inside the glasses and the dishes, so that his children have to go far out into the world, towards that same church which he forgot.*[4]

There are hard choices in life. We wonder what we should do for our children and our families. How do we balance our individual needs with our moral or social responsibilities? This poem points to an answer. One man goes out and walks toward the church in the east, and there is a loss. His children have to deal with the consequences of his leaving. They feel sad and speak of him as if he were dead, gone from their world.

But the opposite choice is not without consequences. This man does not go out seeking his spirit, his church, his vision. And because of this, there is a loss of a different kind — a loss in the person. Having renounced his own journey, he remains in the house "with the glasses and dishes." But there's still a loss, a different emptiness. This emptiness takes residence in his children's world where a passionate man should be living. Because of this, they must fill this emptiness, seeking the church that — "far out into the world" — seems even more distant due to the lack of an elder whose inspiration could guide them.

This poem illustrates the trouble arising when we attempt to move into the role of adult — the man with children — without having done the work of the *west* (seeking the church and finding one's gift). The full expression of our north shield energy and abilities — the giveaway — depends on the work and foundation we've built in the south and the west. The task of the *west* involves creating an individual self with values, depth of character, meaningful commitments, and gifts. But you cannot give away what you have yet to find or realize. You must journey inside, know your inner landscape, and then come out. Some things can never be born if we've refused the call of our church.

Pain and loss are unavoidable. Any path you take leaves many untaken. The giveaway requires finding your gifts, your church — being who you are. When that has been found, you can carry the sacred flame home and bring your story *to your people*. If you're a singer, you must share your song. It is not enough to sing in the shower. Offer this gift. A person's full expression and flowering occurs in the context of community, and traditional rites of passage into adulthood were always *community rituals*.

Who are your people? The task of the *giveaway* requires finding and claiming your gifts, then giving them to "your people." Once upon a time, the definition of one's people was clear: those in your village or tribe. These people were in your immediate circle, involved in, and necessary for, your survival. But times have changed. The modern era is made up of multi-layered and complex social networks and an information overload that includes over 200 channels, shifting political affiliations, YouTube videos, Ted Talks, and hundreds of Facebook friends. This ocean of hazy, overlapping, and abstract affiliations can cloud our horizon and make answering this question "Who are your people?" difficult.

If we have a gift, where and to whom shall we give it? The question must be answered, for adults are woven into the larger circle of community, "the people." Lacking traditional answers that served us for millennia, we must answer this in our own way. One man or woman may answer, "My spouse and children. Those are my people." But that response will not serve everyone. Others might reply, "People in recovery" or "veterans" or "all the endangered species" or "those working for justice or peace." Adults today must define their "people" to make real their giveaway. Trying to give one's gift to the wrong people is a recipe for failure; the seed one needs to plant and nurture can die from barren soil and a lack of support.

THE INNER COMMUNITY

These teachings apply to the inner as well as the outer community. If we have serious wounds to the inner child (as most in modern culture do), a loving adult would ask, "What can I do now to heal this child?" The north shield, properly functioning, makes decisions for the whole of the self. If there are wounds or dysfunction in the shield of childhood, a lack of trust or innocence, this requires special attention. South, west, or east — feeding the child, satisfying our search for meaning, developing our spirituality — the adult asks, "What will best serve the *whole self*, the 'people?'"

Deep wounds to our south shields usually result from a lack of loving adult presences in our childhood. Healing these childhood wounds requires a real commitment to our adulthood, a commitment to making choices and acting to make a difference for that internal child. If a child within us has been put down or neglected for 20 or 50 years, a weekend vacation, though nice, will not restore trust that this world is a good place to be. Can we develop enough discipline and determination to follow through on our commitments — to keep promises, tell the truth, cherish and not criticize, and show up every day for that hurting child? If we can, the child within may begin to develop trust for being here.

Healing childhood wounds is not easy. It's hard to develop a loving "adult" voice or presence in our psyche if we've never had one in our life. But it's necessary. We must make a choice to become loving and seek the help, guidance, resources, and instruction we need to do so. Then we must practice, consistently, how to protect, nurture, guide, affirm, and tell the truth to the child within. We must, as an adult, make a decision to *learn* how to love, and then, with determination, follow through.

In our quest for wholeness, the adult part of our awareness has the capacity to look back and see the work we need to do in the other shields. Our rational, logical, and analytical mind is an ally here. We can examine our lives — "searching and fearless" or detached — and open ourselves to the real truth about our imbalances: the wounds inherited from childhood, the places we are stuck, our full and empty baskets. Perhaps we have not learned trust and innocence, or never explored the inner world of introspection. Or we did, and never fully reemerged. We must determine the situation and decide how to work on those areas and issues. Then we must follow through. If we can commit fully to these actions and processes, healing and becoming more whole is not beyond our reach.

....

Undertaking a vision quest always, on some level, involves movement into the north shield. One commits to the experience saying, "I come here to make a change in my life. I am choosing to act, to walk into the wilderness alone. I choose to face my fears. I'm willing to struggle, to sacrifice. I'm determined to heal. I am not a child."

Stepping into the north shield, standing in the place of decision and choice, moves us to the cause end of the cause-and-effect equation. There we experience a different sense of freedom, a "freedom to" rather than a "freedom from." We find a satisfaction that comes from giving rather than getting, being fully ourselves as we participate and contribute to life. This is an orientation very different from that of a child or adolescent, and it bears tremendous gifts.

This full expression of our north shield abilities rests on and incorporates the gifts and capacities of the other shields. As adults, we examine, choose, and act, but acting well depends on more than just clarity of mind. It also requires feeling, passion, embracing of one's values, and a sense of the larger story and meaning of things. A balanced stool or a well-functioning medicine wheel has all the directions working together.

BUFFALO, MEDICINE ANIMAL OF THE NORTH

In most instances, the medicine animal associated with the north shield is the large game animal of an area, the object of the hunt. This animal typifies the values of the *giveaway* by providing its flesh for food, fur and pelts for blankets or clothes, and bones for tools or musical instruments. It was a symbol of sacrifice, an object of reverence, and a source of ceremonial objects. On the

American Plains, this was the buffalo, but in other areas, it might be elk, salmon, bighorn sheep, bull, or deer.

THE SHADOW NORTH: STUCK IN ADULTHOOD

The north shield takes on a shadow nature — we become "stuck in the north" — when those attributes of analysis, reason, and cold clarity (so necessary for seeing situations exactly the way they are) come to dominate and suppress the sensuality and passions of the child, the realm of feeling and sense of meaning associated with the west, or the serenity resulting from the transcendent states of the east. One can then become a talking head, a cold fish who sees reality clearly but lacks an emotional or feeling response to it. The professor or bureaucrat reports in a monotone, "Yes, based on all projections and data, if we continue at the current pace of population growth and economic development, we should in 30 years see the extinction of 40 percent of the species living on the planet."

The facts are correct. But where is the feeling, the outrage, and passion? Herein lies the challenge of winter. In this time of cold, the air is crisp. It carries little moisture, and stars are bright in the night sky. The leaves of summer and autumn have fallen off the trees, and one can see deeply into the forest. The skeleton and structure of the woodland are visible. Winter is a time when vision is extremely clear, but this clarity — silent, still, almost lifeless — is very cold. This coldness represents the shadow side of north, an inability to access the realms of the body, heart, and imagination of the south, west, and east. It can manifest in various ways:

- Being detached, unemotional, and stuck in the head. This is fairly common, particularly among men. A familiar complaint of women is that their partners seem uncomfortable listening to or expressing feelings. Instead, they quickly offer ideas on how to fix the problem. Hiding out in the head where the rules are clear and "a fact is just a fact" avoids all those foggy vistas in the fluid swamp of emotions.
- Workaholism can also be viewed as a stuck-in-the-north phenomenon. A healthy adult who gives his gifts to his people connects to his passion and joy through his gift as a deep expression of himself. But sometimes this connection gets lost, and our adult forgets about himself. Or he loses himself in the tasks, details, and concerns for others, endlessly toiling for some end that brings him little benefit. Here is the martyr, a deadened soul going through the motions, becoming resentful as the needs for play, purpose, pleasure, rest, or recognition are prohibited by the Puritan code or given short shrift in the hallways of habitual busyness.
- Another shadow version of the north could be a preference for and overvaluing of "thought forms" at the expense of life forms. Here we find an obsession with rules, an allegiance to the letter of the law at the expense of the spirit of the law. A single mother is denied benefits because the form was filled out incorrectly. Property rights trump the rights of the streams, trees, and animals that live on the land. There's a lack of concern or empathy for anyone who gets labeled "enemy." In each case, an allegiance to some abstract category — illegal alien, unwed mother, Muslim, drug user, homeless person, nonwhite, unemployed person — becomes an excuse to block and deny our human responses of empathy, compassion, and a desire to help that connect us to other living beings.
- On a broader cultural scale, four centuries living in the age of science and the Newtonian-Cartesian world has led to a distinctly north, or reason-centric, model of knowledge. The western scientific method, with its insistence on objectivity and neutral, uninvolved observation, not only enshrines reason and rational thought as the highest and most worthwhile activity of the mind but also defines our natural human desires for connection and participation as impediments to the truth. Though quantum physics and relativity theory have shattered any notion of the possibility of detachment or neutrality, the power of the separate and static Newtonian universe still dominates our language and the way we see and engage with the world in much of "normal" life. Meanwhile, many of the process and relationship-oriented concepts and images of this new science can appear far-fetched or seem to contradict "common sense."

For those who are stuck in the north, seeing the situation the way it is could, ideally, result in a recognition of their stuck condition and lead to the question, "What am I going to do about it?" But "thinking about thinking less" generally doesn't work, and rather than trying to shorten this leg of the stool, the focus is better placed elsewhere. This focus could be shifted to the south, the body (via yoga or dance classes), the west (through psychology, therapy, or inner child work), or the east (by prayer, meditation, or other spiritual practice).

THE EAST SHIELD: SAGE OR ELDER

In most medicine wheel or four directions teachings, the entrance to (or exit from) the circle is located in the east. It's the direction of the rising sun, the season of spring. Morning and spring are the beginning of the day and the year. The east is the portal between this world and another, a movement between form and formlessness. Sunrise and spring are times of transformation, of sudden and unparalleled change. In the pitch darkness of night, we are blind. But dawn arrives. Vision multiplies, the world appears radically different, perception and possibilities proliferate. Winter is long and cold. Everything seems dead and brittle. But the snow melts away; the earth becomes muddy and brown. Suddenly — in a few short weeks, sometimes days — new life bursts forth in green and brilliant color. Forsythia, daffodils, and dandelions shock us with their radiance, and the landscape is transformed.

These times of transformation — morning and spring — represent the east shield with its lessons of illumination, or "enlightenment." But the lessons of illumination cannot be simply spoken about or put in an outline. For one who is blind or lives in the dark, the experience of sight will be far beyond any verbal description. If someone has always lived in winter (Antarctica, for example), understanding the color of an orchid, the taste of papaya, or the experience of Polynesia will be beyond her capacities. So too, the lessons of the east are beyond the reach of words, beyond the forms, definitions, or concepts we use to describe them.

Because of this, many of the world's spiritual teachings are cast in shapes — koans, parables, etc. — that are inaccessible to the linear, rational mind. The greatest story of illumination is the tale of the Buddha, or "awakened one." Following his enlightenment in the forest, he made his way back to the world. There, he was approached by gods and goddesses who beseeched him to teach humanity about his experience. Buddha's response was that illumination cannot be taught. So, he returned and taught "The Way."

THE WAY

You can't teach illumination. The experience is beyond words, outside the separations and limitations inherent in language. You cannot teach, and certainly can't talk about, what is beyond your concepts and definitions. But there *are* things you can teach. You can teach practices, postures, sutras, breathing exercises, and focusing techniques. You can teach many things that help free the mind, open the heart, or put people in accord with nature. All or any of these could make the possibility of illumination more likely. But they come with no guarantees. A Zen master once said, "Enlightenment is always an accident. And the purpose of practice is to make you accident prone."

One cannot force, teach, or achieve enlightenment. It is an accident, a gift, like springtime. Nothing you try to do will make it come any quicker, but trying too hard could slow it down. Another teaching states, "The last impediment to enlightenment is the desire for enlightenment." All those who seek enlightenment have desire; they're dissatisfied with where they are now. They think that there is some better place or way to be. Therefore, when you are searching and hoping for enlightenment, you are not here, now; you are not in the present. There is a restless self, wishing for something else. And that self has become an obstacle.

But then again, it is the desire for enlightenment that gets someone to sit on the cushion, to walk the path, "smoke the pipe," go to mass, attend a sun dance, do yoga, journey to Mecca, etc. — to engage in a practice in the first place. Paradox abounds. Effort is required. Desire fuels this effort but desiring then blocks the way. There is a longing for something beyond, unknown to you, something you cannot name and haven't experienced. This longing arises from the self — a dissatisfied self — that cannot exist if the transformation it seeks happens. Such a wonderful conundrum!

Joseph Campbell likened the spiritual path to crossing a river. Imagine you are standing on the island of Manhattan. All around you are the icons of civilized life: wealth, power, busyness, status, achievement. But in your heart, you long for something different. You want to feel free and natural, to return to an original innocence. You desire to return to "the garden state." But to get to this "Garden State" (New Jersey) requires crossing a wide river.

You come to the shore. You can see the obstacles. It's a long way to the other side, to where you want to be. It is daunting, but your longing is great as you stand at the edge and pace along the shore. Eventually, you come upon a rowboat. You realize this is the way, and you get in, push off, and begin to row.

This is your craft; rowing is your practice. It could be meditation, music, Tai Chi, painting, or something else, but your practice is to row, and row, and row. After a time, you think you must be getting close, but when you turn around the shore looks remote. You continue rowing. After another long while, you turn to look once more, but the goal is still far away. This happens again and again and again. Impatience, discouragement, frustration, even anger, set in. It appears that you're getting nowhere. Each time you look, the goal seems as distant as ever.

Finally, there comes a moment when you forget all about the garden state. You are just rowing. You feel your muscles, your rhythmic movements matching the sound of the oars. Your breath comes naturally; sunlight sparkles off the water; and you are totally immersed in this moment rich with water, boat, sun, light, and breath. Thump! You have arrived! You disembark, look about, astounded at how beautiful it is. With joy, you realize you are home, back in the garden state. You are happy to have arrived and thankful for the journey itself, even its dark and difficult moments. Blessed, fulfilled, and content, in wonder and gratitude you look back across the river at where you've come from, and — shocked — you discover that the "garden state" is back there too.

This is the paradox of enlightenment. It takes effort, purpose, and commitment to simply be where (and who) you are. A journey is called for when, in one sense, you never need to go anywhere. But if you do not go, you will never realize that. You have to undertake this journey; otherwise, you'll have no chance to discover that the journey was, in some ways, never necessary.

TOWARD THE UNKNOWN

The east is considered the direction or path to Spirit, but a direction is not a destination. Though sometimes given a name — Promised Land, Shambala, Nirvana, Dreamtime, Nierika — these nouns are symbols for what's formless and creates all form. We cannot speak of, know, or define the formless, but the landscape of the east shield can be thought of as the practices, processes, or tools that guide us toward, and open us to, that unknown. It also represents the human impulse toward ecstasy or trans-form-ative experiences — experiences in which the forms, stories, and categories we use to define ourselves and the world break down, and as they dissolve, allow a greater energy to flood in.

For example, prayer can be seen as an "offering to the unknown." Many people have difficulty with prayer because they associate it with a judgmental God, rigidity, and a repressive authority from their past. But at its core, prayer is merely an offering from what is known to what's beyond that, to the ultimate unknown and source of life.

When we pick up the smudge bowl, smoke the pipe, or fold our hands and speak, we use our native language. We're centered in, and speak from, our identity, the gestalt or circle of what we know — the ego, or "I." But what we are speaking to is beyond all that. Many names or descriptions have been created for what is beyond the self. Spirit, God, higher power, nature, the Force, Great Mystery, etc. are familiar labels; some are religious and some not. But we could also think of prayer as the conscious ten percent of the brain speaking to the 90 percent that is mysterious, or the self speaking to everything beyond the self. Prayer starts with what we know and where we are, but it stretches toward something beyond that. As such, prayer is an offering and impulse towards something greater, an impulse toward what's unknown and the illumination in its realization.

Night becomes day, and winter becomes spring. A seemingly new world emerges that's larger and richer. Everything seems different than it was before. Moments or experiences of illumination happen when that expansive unknown enters. Embedded in our forms, language, and customs, we view the world through our stories, concepts, and definitions — all the boxes, judgments, and limitations we put on experience. But we reach out *toward something greater* than what we've put in those boxes. Illumination happens when somehow "it" enters, and we have the experience of immensity, a moment of "aha!" The boxes may be shattered, they may dissolve, or we may transcend their walls and perceive outside their limits.

IMAGES OF THE FORMLESS

Albert Einstein, through his famous equation $E=mc^2$, stated that the fundamental stuff of the universe is not "stuff." Instead, our foundation is *Energy*, and energy is fluid, malleable, shape-shifting. It appears in many forms, such as heat, light, matter, gravity, chemical reaction, radiation, electrical charge, thought, you, me... All those forms can be sensed, measured, perceived, and described, once they arrive as in-form-ation, but energy itself is more primary. It may be called Spirit, Wakan Tanka, Nierika, the formless, the great bubbling forth, etc., but this source remains fundamentally unknowable. It is the source of, yet behind-beyond-outside of, all we can know.

The east is associated with sunrise and the element fire. Fire is neither solid nor static. Fire is energy that brings warmth and light, but what is it, really? (A verb? A noun?) We can add sticks, pour on gasoline, and pile on logs, but they are not the fire. These substances, all solid and concrete, are transformed before our eyes. The wood and fuel become coals, ash, and nothingness as we are illumined by the light, warmed and bathed by something shifting and formless.

The east is identified with spirit, inspiration, the in-breath. (*Spiritus* means breath.) Something invisible (called life) enters us, and we become animate. Inspiration is birth; it's generative, creative, associated with divinity. In ancient Greece, the Muses were goddesses who ruled creative forces that could become manifest in dance, music, poetry, and song. When poets create poems, they use the forms of the known — words, meter, and rhythm. But something larger enters a poem, something far greater than the prose meaning of the words. In music, the composer or musician also employs the known — notes, rhythm, harmonies, etc. — but something magical and new is birthed.

The path or journey toward illumination is always an act of faith. We are drawn beyond the known, loving or opening to something new, boundless, and greater, offering ourselves to transformation. Starting in the known, through intention, ritual, prayer, or practice, we reach out to that grander "something," offering it space within us. If grace, fortune, or "the gods" smile on us, we may be answered. Something enters, and we are different than before. A caterpillar spins the cocoon willing and ready to die. Its form and identity dissolve, and a different order of being emerges, one that's not a caterpillar any more.

GOING WILD: DANCERS, MYSTICS, AND CLOWNS

"To live outside the law, you must be honest."
— Bob Dylan

In Tibet, Dakinis, like woodland sprites, are female spirits associated with the wilderness. They often befriend, teach, and help those on spiritual pilgrimages. If one comes to you, you are blessed. *Dakini*, literally translated, means "wisdom gone wild," pointing to another image or metaphor of transformation.

Entering life, we take on various forms: the form of the body, the forms of our culture and language, the form of relationship, family, twenty-first century America, etc. As we mature, we learn and acquire *wisdom within these forms*. Hopefully, we learn to be adults, each of us capable of being good person in this time and place. But growth need not stop there. To complete the circle, our hard-won wisdom must go wild again; it must transcend the limits within which it grew. We become an artist, a mystic, a clown.

Picture a great dancer like Baryshnikov. As he dances, you marvel at his fluidity, spontaneity, and leaps that seem to defy gravity. But all that fluid grace and apparent spontaneity rests on a foundation of thousands of hours of ballet practice, perhaps the strictest, most disciplined form of dance ever developed. A master must first acquire and incorporate this form, becoming ever more adept and advanced in its "wisdom" and competence. Then, if he's fortunate or "accident prone," something totally new may burst into being. His craft blossoms and flowers, and he gives expression to something far beyond the forms of his training. Finely-honed technique becomes art; wisdom goes wild.

A true artist — teacher, painter, musician, poet, spiritual guide, etc. — can break all the rules. But the novice cannot. Beginners must enter the world, apprentice to its techniques, and learn its competencies, rules, and outlook before they can find wisdom beyond all they have learned. Knowledge is not bad. It is, in fact, completely necessary, but the wildness and lack of boundaries in a child or adolescent is not wisdom, mastery, or "spiritual." An adolescent substance abuser is not a shaman, even though he may use the same "medicine." Building a foundation of knowledge requires discipline, but its full flowering is not guaranteed. That flowering is beyond achievement and the ego. The wildness that leaps the fence of the corral and explores landscapes beyond any previously experienced cannot be planned.

Another image comes from the Plains Indians. The Heyoka clowns — a compelling example of the trickster archetype — could show up in any situation. They might interrupt the most serious rituals, mock everything, sow the seeds of chaos or humor. And they were considered sacred for they reminded the people of something very important: you must take your practices and rituals seriously. Whatever they are — the pipe, sweat lodge, poetry, music, yoga, or meditation practice — apply yourself to them fully! But do not become rigid or trapped by the forms.

If you begin to think that yours is the only right path; that you have the true teaching or exclusive ear of God; that Spirit only comes through the sweat lodge, Jesus, or this or that teacher... you have lost your way. You must take on the forms of your practice, whether taught to or developed by you, and learn their medicine. You meditate as you have learned to meditate; learn ceremony as you've been taught; pray as you have learned to pray. You do your best. But if you limit "God" or the appearance of Spirit to the forms of the path you have chosen, you are mistaking the light bulb for the light. And then the clowns and forces of *crazy wisdom* will be called to pop your balloon and shatter your self-righteousness.

In matters of the spirit, there's always a paradox. Spirit is formless, but we have to use form. We participate in the form of a vision quest, a form of meditation, the form of marriage, but Spirit can come in any form or its opposite. Spirit can make itself known to those who have never prayed in their lives. But if you are meditating, or praying, dancing, or marrying, you attempt to do it well. Illumination happens when that formless, unbound energy sets foot in your small doorway. The door jamb may break — one way or another, the boundaries of your perception and practice must expand as it enters. This is what we pray for, to be visited by a presence that may affirm or annihilate all we know so well.

In the Western world, we associate wisdom with knowing more. We seek more facts, more training, more degrees and education. We think knowledge is cumulative, akin to amassing poker chips in your circle of competence. But in other traditions, attachment to what we know can be an obstacle. In a well-known Buddhist story, the teacher keeps pouring tea in the student's cup as it overflows onto the floor. The message — "You are too full. You must empty yourself before you can learn anything" — is considered a very important lesson.

In the Toltec tradition of Mexico, the most important quality of a "man of knowledge" is his relationship with, and ability to enter, the unknown. The known is such a small part of life, while the unknown is vast.

It is there the seer looks for his personal power, true nature, and capacity to dream. The power of the east, of illumination, comes through the willingness and effort to open ourselves to something greater than what we know, to what's beyond reason or logic. We speak from what we know; we pray with words we know, and we practice what we know. But all "spiritual" practices reach toward what is unknown, what's mysterious and beyond form.

Our language fails us and reflects our confusion. We equate knowledge with in-form-ation; we want to be in-formed. But *reality*, as energy, is formless, fluid, able to appear in any form. It can be found in the pipe, sweat lodge, or church; in silence, singing, or sex. It may not follow our rules, and it's often found where it's not "supposed" to be. A Hindu story tells of a yogi who left his students to go into the mountains and join a band of thieves. He robbed many. After a few years, he returned illumined. Recognizing the lavish container he'd constructed for his spiritual journey, he had to step outside that box.

THE SELF OF THE SAGE OR SHAMAN

As we travel around the medicine wheel, we begin with a child, centered in itself. In adolescence, we develop the separate self, one that (hopefully) includes the other. The adult incorporates a new perspective and identity that includes the people, the circle, or the community. The self of the east we might call the higher self, a presence that can be sensed but is ultimately indefinable, outside of and beyond all the descriptions and roles our daily selves must act and manifest within.

There are a thousand different ways to describe what, ultimately, cannot be said. We think and live in a conceptual world of language with all its attendant polarities. If you have an *up* you must have a *down*. If you have a *left* you have to have a *right*; an *in*, an *out*. If you have a *self*, then you must also have a *world*. Having a self — any self — creates a membrane, a boundary, a definition. Inside is the self, and outside is the world. Thus, our daily self only exists in relation to what is not *self*. It exists in contrast to the world, to what's "not-I."

In one sense the work of the east is about knowing the reality that is not only "in here" but also "out there," beyond what we know or would normally define as ourselves. This could be called the higher self, the double, the "not-you." Some cultures assert that we are twinned — who we are is as much unknown as known, is as much *there* as it is *here* — and practices have been developed to meet, access, and embrace our double, our sacred twin — the self that is not us. The impulse of the east opens to the *out there* — beneath the surface, beyond the horizon, within the material. We seek that pregnant and fertile no-thing, which could appear as anything or all things. If the opposite, the *west*, involves an exploration deep within the self, the journey of the east moves outside or beyond it.

STUCK IN THE EAST: SPIRITUAL UNREALITY

A vision without a task is but a pipe dream.
A task without a vision is just drudgery.
But a vision with a task can move the world.

As in each of the directions discussed previously, our relationship to the energy represented by the east shield could be labeled too much or too little. If this leg of the stool is too short, our energy may be tied up in the details of daily life with little connection to the numinous and archetypal forces that have guided the human spiritual impulse through millennia. Life may be mostly a collection of tasks, duties, and roles — drudgery. They may be meaningful and even satisfying in many ways — spouse, parent, doctor, etc. — but the human psyche has developed over millions of years at the call of and in response to the living earth. Trying to live without connection to the great powers and grand forces at play in the world is to let something magnificent atrophy — our ability to perceive the face of God and the universe's story ignored as we play our parts in the cultural drama of today.

But this leg of the stool may also be too long, our allegiance to, or longing for, spiritual reality and the *other world* coming at the expense of this one. This can take many forms, some mildly amusing and others quite serious or even dangerous.

AVOIDANCE

A mild version of "stuck in the east" may appear in someone we label spacey or flaky — living a "pipe dream" as mentioned above. This person may spout new-age slogans — "Let go and let God... If it's meant to work out it will... This is a wonderful opportunity for growth... The universe is giving you a message... " — as rationalizations that justify not assuming responsibility, not applying yourself and doing your best to make a difference... as a way to avoid the suffering and pain of a real life, or justify not fully participating and possibly failing. These strategies all fit the description of a "spiritual bypass," the attempt to experience only the high moments or good feelings in life while avoiding our "shit" — all that's uncomfortable, disagreeable, or difficult.

When we remain stuck in the east in this way, everything is identified with God. There is a spiritual truth in this, but turning everything into an expression of the divine can be a refusal to enter life and deal with the limitations and suffering involved. I want to escape, be on top of the mountain, experience the highs and be happy, happy, happy. When you tell me about grief, pain, or suffering in your life, I say, "What a wonderful opportunity for growth!" These spiritual bypasses are rejections of real life with its attendant frustrations and sorrows.

SPIRITUAL REALIZATION

In the culture of traditional India, there was tremendous support for the journey toward spiritual realization, and people who realized their "god-essence" were revered and treated as saints. All day, their attention would be focused on and merged with the transcendent nature of the divine, and their devotees would care for them and take care of their needs — feeding, clothing, cleaning, and providing shelter for them. This exclusive focus on the divine (the east shield) made them incapable of attending to even the simplest tasks to care for themselves. This tradition, accepted and supported in traditional Hindu culture, makes little sense to those raised in other parts of the world. To someone from the West, a god-realized saint would appear filthy, helpless, and indistinguishable from a homeless man in a diaper — a generally unattractive proposition.

ADDICTION

While the use of plant medicines and teachers has a wide and well-respected history in the human experiment, their use in traditional cultures took place within a different context than is prevalent in modern life. These societies were intimately connected with the world around them — plants, animals, mountains, rivers, ancestors, spirit guides, the unborn (those to come), etc. The use of plant allies for healing, spiritual guidance, divination, and connection to the forces and powers of the nonhuman world was part of a rich toolkit helping the community live in harmony and balance with the world around them. When these substances, including those created in a lab, are used to avoid or ease the pain of certain aspects of life, we enter the landscape of addiction, where the plant or substance ceases to be an ally as it comes to dominate or diminish the capacities of those who use it.

SCHIZOPHRENIA OR OTHER MENTAL ILLNESS

The "other world" and the unknown are vast. This landscape is far-larger than the dream of daily life and the roles and tasks required for human society. Those who can contact this realm — artists, visionaries, shamans, ground-breaking scientists, spiritual teachers, etc. — and report back to their communities can be priceless resources in finding our place in the cosmos and living in balance with the rest of creation. But some enter this world and become lost, and they can't find their way back to their community. In that event, they can become insane and even dangerous.

Joseph Campbell once remarked, "A schizophrenic and a yogi live in the same ocean. One is swimming, while the other drowns." Some people who enter the other world lack the resources, human connection, sobriety, or whatever else it takes to return with vision, a gift, or a tale to tell. They become disoriented as the bridge between the other world and this one disappears. This can be sad and tragic. It can also be dangerous. If God instructs you to speak in tongues, that is one thing, but if voices tell you to kill your children or sister, and there's no "reality check," you may need to be locked up or restrained.

THE CIRCLE AND THE CROSS

Our medicine wheel is made up of two symbols. The circle represents wholeness and universality — "we are all one" — while the directions, or cross, evokes individuation, polarity, and separation. Unlike the Christian cross, which accents the vertical direction, in the sacred hoop, the arms or thrust of the directions are equal and contained within the wheel.

Each shield is an equal part of this circle we've divided into four directions. But there's also an affinity, balancing, and mirroring along the horizontal and vertical axes. North and south are about manifestation, how we show up in the world. The lessons of the south, trust and innocence, are learned by the child from the adults around him or her. If there are severe wounds in our south shield, we'll need to ground ourselves in the north in order to create a loving adult that can protect the child, tell the truth, and provide safety and belonging. This adult might reassure the wounded child that it is not responsible for someone else's anger and judgment. It would explain that everyone's responsibility in this world is to be as loving as they can, and if people have not been kind, they are simply not doing their job. This voice would say, "This issue is not about you. And I want you to know that I feel your hurt, love you, and am here beside you."

Most people have an inner critic, some version of a nasty adult telling us we've failed or messed up. Finding or creating an internal loving voice — a north shield task — can ultimately heal the child who feels worthless and not enough. That loving and strong adult presence is needed to fulfill the promise contained in the child. And the opposite is also true. In order to enact our *giveaway* as an adult, we must not only perceive reality and make choices. We must also have passion enough to follow through, and that passion comes from our child self.

East and west both ask the question "Who are you?" One looks deep within, the other far beyond, the self. If the north-south axis is about doing or manifesting, east and west focus more on being. Though the direction and focus of east and west might seem opposite, they are complementary. We live in a world that is whole, spherical; a circle is round. If you travel far enough west on the earth, you will eventually appear over the eastern horizon, and vice versa. There is an implication, or promise, that if you deeply explore who you are (the west) you will ultimately discover what's seemingly opposite: a place where you are one with everything, not separate at all.

These balances and alliances also imply that if you get stuck in one direction, the obvious medicine and antidote may be to invest more attention in its opposite. If vision is ultimately "seeing what is," ask if you are walking in balance; if your stool has four useful legs. Does your intention for your vision quest invite all your directions — your shields — to be activated and present? There may be moments when it feels right to fully express your south shield energy as you're moved to explore or experience the physical joy of hurling rocks and watching them fly. Another time you might be drawn to the west, opening your journal and examining what this experience is all about. "What did it mean when the hawk flew over me so low? What is the significance of my dreams?" At those times, we've moved to the west.

We enter the north (adult) shield whenever we attend to the practicalities of the experience — setting up the tarp or deciding whether to put the sleeping bag under that fractured rock shelf — as well as when making choices about what to do with our time, the rituals we'll undertake, and our priorities about what's important to engage with on our solos. This shield is also important in making plans and commitments about our return — what is possible, what's required, and what we're able and willing to do.

The vision quest should include all the directions. Some may "come to the mountain" seeking a visionary experience. For them, the word *vision* may be describe an illumining moment when something grand opens up and they are forever changed. Focused only on illumination, they imagine lightning bolts flashing and luminous eagles landing in their purpose circle to tell them they are ascended masters from lifetimes ago. I, in good humor, call this the "neon buffalo" experience. Sometimes it happens.

Time in the east shield may include much prayer and ritual, but another image sees *vision* as the flowering of a rose. Those stunning red blossoms are surely the reason anyone plants roses, but we cannot make it happen. We can't coax or drag the petals out of the limbs. But there are things we can do. We can weed, water, and prune, and if we do those things, the rose may become "accident prone" and flowers may emerge by themselves. The weeding, pruning, etc. represent the *work* — the effort of healing in the south, claiming the powers and wisdom of the north, and developing the unique individuality of the west. This is something we *can* do! And if we do it well, perhaps our roses will come. We can't pretend to control illumination or capture vision, but choosing to weed, prune, fertilize — doing the work — can make a difference. It may not result in a luminous eagle, but we may be rewarded with something totally unexpected.

A vision quest seeks a balance between the known and the unknown. In preparing, we write letters, read books, and sit in the circle to learn and sharpen our intention and direction. But intention and purpose eventually meet the unknown. As when shooting an arrow, before we enter the wilderness we draw the bow. We clarify intention — our aim — as we focus, examine, and plan, becoming as true as we can. And then we have to give ourselves over to the breeze, forces, and elements — we have to let go!. We open to the wind and make space for whatever is meant to happen.

NOTES ON MEDICINE ANIMALS

While working with medicine animals is not the focus of this manual, I mention them a) to complete the archetypal arrangement of the Four Shields teachings and b) to suggest the following possibilities.

1. If someone on a quest has a profound encounter or dream with a coyote or eagle, you might want to explore whether the message of that encounter applies to the themes of the relevant shield – in this case, the South or East
2. Conversely, if someone's quest highlights a need for serious work in a particular shield – take West for example – and he/she were open to shamanic practices, exploring a relationship with Bear may be a starting point.

BEAR, MEDICINE ANIMAL OF THE WEST

The lesson of the West – introspection – involves looking within. Bear is the master of this, leaving the outer world for months at a time before retuning in the spring. Our actions and behavior are visible. The inner life – created in adolescence – is not. Dancing and balancing between these worlds – while holding each as sacred – is the challenge and task of adolescence. In his descents into dreamworlds and darkness, Bear affirms, explores and reaps the harvest of worlds that are concealed.

EAGLE, MEDICINE ANIMAL OF THE EAST

The East, signifying sunrise, the urge to illumination, and the lure of the Unknown is represented by Eagle, who flies highest and approaches what's infinite and formless. He catches the first rays of sunlight, sees what's beyond the horizon, and -- like a sage or elder -- perceives the day-to-day scurrying below within a much-larger perspective. In his love for the formless, Eagle casts off gravity and any chains binding him to the confines of a limited life.

SECTION III:
PHYSICAL-PLANE CONCERNS

Back to the Source: An Overview **67**
Coming to Our Senses 68
Physical and Spiritual Reality 69

Outline of Basic Physical Plane Talk **71**
Notes on the Outline 72

Fasting **72**
Hunger 72
Low Energy 72
Dizziness 73
Headaches 73
Nausea 73
Water 73

Safety and Safety Systems **74**
The Stone Pile 74

Flora and Fauna **75**

Related Physical Plane Concerns **76**
Choosing Locations for a Quest 76
Thoughts on Equipment 77
Wilderness Ethics 78
Knowledge and Skills 78

SECTION III:

PHYSICAL-PLANE CONCERNS

BACK TO THE SOURCE:
AN OVERVIEW

(This overview — "Back to the Source" — need not be presented in detail during the preparation period.

It could be emailed to participants beforehand as part of an information packet, as could the entire section on physical-plane issues and concerns.)

Vision quests nearly always include a profound encounter with different spheres of "reality," as our inherited dreams and stories — often separating us from the earth, ourselves, and each other — encounter that primal reality out of which humans arose in the first place.

Human beings experience three kinds of reality. The first is *objective or primal reality*, which comprises what we call the physical universe: rocks, mountains, deer, cactus, sunlight, rain, heat, etc. This reality exists independently of anyone's beliefs or feelings about it. You can disbelieve in gravity, but if you fall out of a plane, you'll plummet to earth at the same speed as everyone else.

Subjective reality is an internal experience, manifesting within an individual's thoughts, feelings, and beliefs. Whether it be a powerful dream, a cluster of emotions, an acid trip, or a shamanic journey, it's unique to and localized in the person and perceived by no one else.

Humans also live within *intersubjective realities*. These initially have no objective existence, but when communicated among and agreed on by many people they acquire power enough to structure behavior and blind us to the fact they are totally imaginary. The idea of a "week," a repeating cycle of seven days, exists only in our imaginations, yet seven billion people organize their lives around it. Other intersubjective fictions — the set of rules defining money; stories and definitions of nationality, race, or what makes a "family"; beliefs about God; and legally created fictions like "Toyota" or "Google" — form the context or "reality" in which most people act, think, and live.

Intersubjective realities occupy an enormous slice of our conscious bandwidth, their unexamined assumptions crucial to some of the best and worst of human behavior. These shared fictions have led to unprecedented achievements like the creation of the corporation and nation-state, the Bill of Rights, putting people on the moon, the discovery of antibiotics, and the development of the internet. Intersubjective beliefs can organize and create common goals and commitments among millions of people who have never met each other. But believing in these imaginary "realities" has also led to religious wars, racial discrimination, the subjugation of women, living in our heads, and ecological disaster.

One current fiction/belief — humanism — states there's something special about our species because we alone have eternal souls, are self-conscious, have an inner life, or have developed our intellect beyond any other animal. Unfortunately, this belief about the sacredness of human life also implies that all those other, nonhuman, lives — from coyotes to coral reefs — are not so sacred. And today, primal, objective reality — plants, animals, and entire ecosystems — are at risk of being destroyed or irreparably damaged by the forces and assumptions of imaginary realities like nations and corporations that humans have created and live within.

Subjective realities, since they're neither objective nor measurable, are often dismissed as "unreal." But inner experiences can be extremely important to an individual. They can indicate truths yet to be articulated and brought to the outer world. Dreams, for example, do not fit the standard for reality held by our cultural consensus, but they can be invaluable in expressing feelings, longings, and desires the conscious mind is unaware of. Mystical experiences of rapture, spirit-filled journeys of shamans, and the enchanted worlds inhabited by primal peoples also fail our standards for reality: the intersubjective but arbitrary standard held by the mostly unhappy souls considered "normal" today.

When one's inner world is ill-matched with the outer (with society's rules and expectations, for example), it doesn't follow that a person is maladjusted. Feelings of depression related to going to work may be about work — the job, the people, or the mindless pursuit of conformity or money. It may well be that today's consensual reality is too small, too shallow, and too devoid of meaning to give allegiance to, and becoming well-adjusted may be like a death sentence — a feeling often expressed by those returning from a vision quest. If this is one's truth, it's good to know it. Trusting your inner voice — listening to your subjective reality — is not easy. Changing your commitment or direction will require allies, a community subscribing to a different set of values — a new reality — that can support and feed the seeds in you that want to grow.

People undertaking vision quests walk into the solitude of nature, consciously leaving the daily world, the intersubjective dream, behind. This allows the presence of outer primal reality and inner subjective reality to expand and come to the fore. Having an intimate encounter with a vibrant inner life and the living, sensuous Earth can be in stark contrast to programmed and inherited beliefs that disconnect us from the earth, ourselves, and each other. It creates an opportunity to sever some unconscious beliefs, downloaded since infancy, that define the world and limit the possibilities of who we can be today. And it offers a chance to commit to a different set of stories.

COMING TO OUR SENSES

The vision quest happens in nature. Being in the wilderness is far different than being in a house or an apartment in a city. In urban or suburban life, we see roads, electrical wires, and rectangular objects everywhere. Inhabiting a sensory world almost wholly constructed by technological or industrial processes limits our ability to know ourselves. How can we "meet our maker" if we live only within a world we (humans) have made? Experiencing primal reality requires stepping outside the world that we've created into a world that has created us.

Humans have grown and evolved out of the living earth. We were not dropped off by extraterrestrials or fashioned by some god outside time and space. The human body was molded through millennia to live in the natural world, our senses honed and developed to perceive patterns and adapt to the challenges of a living landscape. The organs we perceive through — skin, eyes, ears, smell, and taste — evolved within a feedback loop, a call-and-response relationship with the also-evolving environment. We go to the wilderness to reconnect with our roots, our source... to remember what we have forgotten.

Today, most people live in a human-fashioned world where little of the natural world remains. Each day our senses take in our own creations. Morning comes, and we find ourselves in a room with floors, walls, clocks, and mirrors. We look out the window and see buildings, telephone poles, and streets. Our day is extended by artificial lighting. Our eyes may be glued to a television or computer screen for hours. Those eyes may find nothing in the visual world that's natural other than the potted plant on the windowsill — and even that could be plastic. We take in a landscape that's artificial, molded, and managed. What we see is us.

We hear sounds coming from buses, traffic, airplanes, and radios. Houses hum with refrigerators, whirring fans, and air conditioners. Canned music plays in supermarkets, malls, and elevators. Cars honk; sirens wail. We listen to ourselves. We have become unfamiliar and uncomfortable with silence. Turn on the TV, plug in your iPod, and chill out.

Our remaining senses experience much the same. Physical contact is primarily with manufactured objects like silverware, dishes, steering wheels, polyester clothes, combs, sheetrock walls, mattresses, and toothbrushes. We breathe recycled and conditioned air; smell exhaust, air fresheners, and pine or lemon-scented cleaning supplies. Shampoos and deodorants are made to smell like flowers. We may still interact with the physical, sensuous world through eating food, but that becomes less and less true as we consume soda, beer, sugar, artificial flavoring, and fast or processed foods.

It's inaccurate to say we "have" technology. The situation is actually reversed — technology surrounds and envelops us. We live within it. The world we touch, hear, smell, and see is overwhelmingly human-created, and interacting and touching only ourselves and our creations is, ultimately, a form of incest.[5]

To leave behind that world, to come back and interact with nature, is healing in and of itself. In the natural world, we encounter something different, something larger, something we did not create. We meet that which created us. Other, older sensibilities reawaken when we are allowed to freely interact in natural environments. Pavlov's experiments with stimulus-response, in which dogs salivated upon hearing a bell associated with food, failed when the dogs were allowed to run free. Only after they were penned within cages and kennel was he able to create the programmed, artificial association between sound and food.

We are like Pavlov's dogs. We stay in lines, living within mostly unnatural environments: constrained by streets, locked doors, and parking spaces; hemmed in by appointments, schedules, and structures of time. The bell rings: we get up in the morning, change classes, or are let out of work. Healthcare waits on the doctor's appointment book; therapy takes place in a 50-minute hour. Recreation is put off until the weekend; rest and relaxation bide time till vacation. Living within social roles, schedules, regulations, habits, and consensus reality, cages have been fabricated in the physical world and in our minds. We're penned and shackled on every side. Mostly unseen, we live within boxes constructed by our language, thought forms, and ways of looking at reality.

Returning to the natural world, senses gone dormant begin to reawaken. The body starts to remember what has been dismembered. Responses and capacities developed over thousands of years stir and become alive again. Beyond the borders built by walls and words, in interaction with a real and living world, we engage with a landscape and process where our lives can, once again, start "making sense."

Lost

Stand still. The trees ahead and bushes beside you
Are not lost. Wherever you are is called Here,
And you must treat it as a powerful stranger,
Must ask permission to know it and be known.
The forest breathes. Listen. It answers,
I have made this place around you.
If you leave it, you may come back again, saying Here.
No two trees are the same to Raven.
No two branches are the same to Wren.
If what a tree or a bush does is lost on you,
You are surely lost. Stand still. The forest knows
Where you are. You must let it find you.[6]

PHYSICAL AND SPIRITUAL REALITY

Physical reality ranges from the mundane to the magnificent, and a vision fast is a complex blend of ecology, intention, sense, and perception that's woven into the way we relate to the world around us. It includes matters of the soul and spirit as well as simple survival. A participant's experience can range across a broad membrane, permeable and somewhat arbitrary, separating self from world, and this encounter may include overwhelming feelings of oneness with mountain, sky, forest, earth, or river, as well as the basic and practical concerns of how to stay warm, keep dry, or go to the bathroom.

Spiritual and practical concerns are not separate. Comfort is not the primary purpose of the vision quest, but some minimal or satisfactory amount of it is necessary if we're to give full attention to our purposes in being there. Some environments are generally mild and nurturing, and one's physical preparation can be relatively minimal. But to be prepared, you must have knowledge about situations that are possible, as well as what's likely to arise. If you are cold, wet, sick, and shivering, the energy available for song, ritual, prayer, and other actions in service of your intention will suffer. And there is a basic, bottom-line consideration: the vision and the gifts you want to bring back to your people require making it back in order to give them.

Vision fasts are both physical and spiritual experiences, and one must prepare for the physical event. Culture trains us to look at the world through the lens of its categories, and our conceptual system is arranged in pairs of opposites — spirit and flesh, heaven and earth — as if these "things" were separate. They are not. They may be intellectually distinct concepts, but the living world of nature is a woven-together fabric of multi-textured experience.

Walking into the wilderness with intention, prayer, and hope, we must attend to those things, pleasurable or challenging, that are usually labeled as "physical." Ultimately, "vision" involves seeing beyond our conditioned limits, acknowledging a larger framework, seeing all that is. Wholeness requires balance — the sensing, feeling, thinking, imaginative, and visionary realms all functioning together — and we will not have a more profound experience by dismissing half of them.

Certain practical concerns need to be addressed in any quest:

1. What to expect from fasting, the process of going without food and drinking only water for several days;
2. The basic logistics of the safety system and what's to be done in case of emergency;
3. Issues or factors relevant to the particular place and time in which you are questing (information about the landscape, weather, flora, and fauna, etc.); and
4. Simple and basic survival skills (orienting, how to stay warm and dry, necessary equipment, etc.). Having a basic knowledge about all of these helps create a sense of safety and confidence that will allow people to give more attention and energy to the deeper and ultimate purposes and intentions of their quests.

OUTLINE OF BASIC PHYSICAL-PLANE TALK

FASTING

SIDE EFFECT

- Slow energy
- Dizziness
- Headache
- Nausea (and antacids)

DRINKING WATER

- How much? (Check urine color)
- Logistics: Springs, filters, containers, etc.
- Miscellaneous: Bring toothbrush

STONE PILE

- How
- Two- and three-person
- Signs - obvious and permanent
- Minimalist vs. artistic
- Stone pile from base camp

EMERGENCY PROCEDURES

- Miscommunications
- Getting lost
- Injury
- Leaving time (afternoon shift)

FLORA AND FAUNA (RELATIVE TO QUEST SITES)

PLANTS

- Cacti
- Poison ivy/oak

ANIMALS

- Predator-prey relationships — never run!
- Snakes, scorpions, ants
- Coyote, bobcat, mountain lion
- Javelina
- Bear
- Moose
- Other people

STAYING WARM AND DRY

CLOTHES

- Synthetic vs. cotton or wool
- Layering
- Chimney effect (close openings)
- Hat (for cold and sun)

OTHER EQUIPMENT

- Seeping bag rating
- Round insulation (sleeping pad)
- Rain gear
- Ground cloth (or garbage bags)

TARP-TYING INSTRUCTIONS

- Equipment
  - Rope
  - Tarp - plastic or nylon
  - Tarp size
- Principles: Look up, look down
  - Drainage — ground and off tarp
- Practice:
  - Knots
  - Tie-downs — rocks; logs; trees, roots
  - Grommet reinforcement

MISCELLANEOUS

- Coming in early
  - Quest continues at camp
  - Stone pile responsibility
  - Conversation limited
- Bathroom etiquette
- Fires
- Leave no trace

HANDOUTS

- First aid/emergency procedures
- Maps (?)

NOTES ON THE OUTLINE

The outline above lists subjects to be addressed in presenting the physical-plane aspects of a quest. Different locations will greatly influence how simple or extensive the conversations on certain subjects are, specifically flora and fauna, water issues, and, to a lesser degree, tying a tarp.

- Fasting, its side-effects, and issues around drinking water are addressed below.
- The stone pile is also described below.
- Flora and fauna will differ by landscape. General notes are found below, and a sample description of flora and fauna is provided in Section VIII: Requirements and Resources.
- Equipment and clothes: see sample equipment list in Section VIII.
- Bathroom etiquette requires digging a poop hole. Feces should be disposed of in a hole, 6 to 8 inches deep, at least 200 feet away from any water source (rivers, streams, springs, etc.). Toilet tissue should be either packed out (a Ziploc bag works fine) or burned. Unburned toilet tissue should not be buried in the hole or left on the ground.
- Fires: Sometimes people make fires while out on their solos. Check and be aware if there are any fire restrictions and regulations in effect. Also, it's useful to talk about possible motivations for having a fire. Some motivations, such as a severance ritual that involves burning something, are well-aligned with the purposes and intentions of a quest. But building a fire at night "because I always have a fire when I'm camping" is not. A vision quest is not a camping trip. Having a fire can be a form of escape and diversion, a way of avoiding boredom or being alone in the dark. It becomes the substitute television, a form of entertainment or distraction, a way of not experiencing uncomfortable feelings.
- Leave-no-trace camping and wilderness practices are described in the Wilderness Ethics Statement included in the resources section. Further information on leave-no-trace practices can be found at https://www.rei.com/learn/expert-advice/leave-no-trace.html and several other sites.

FASTING

Fasting is one of the oldest forms of changing consciousness. Going without food and drinking only water expands our awareness. Perception widens and magnifies, becomes more all-encompassing, more dream-like and less narrowly focused. This change in the quality of our attention is desired and part of what we're seeking on a vision quest. But fasting also affects us physically, and it's important to know what these physical changes are so we can be prepared for them.

HUNGER

Most people anticipate they will be hungry. In fact, this is rarely the case. Feelings of hunger are usually fleeting, arising and passing within several minutes and returning in a few hours. These pangs are temporary, connected to the shrinking of the stomach, but after a day or so this shrinking is completed. At that point, hunger disappears and people can enter a zone that seems timeless and eternal, as if they are sustained by something else and will never need food again.

Though hunger may not be an issue, there are other side effects of fasting that can be challenging. They are, in order of frequency, low energy, dizziness, headache, and nausea.

LOW ENERGY

Usually, this begins on the second day. In normal life, our bodies contain reserves of carbohydrates, or "blood sugar." It takes about 24 hours to use these reserves up if they aren't being replenished. Once they run out, the body begins breaking down fat to burn for fuel. This period of transition from sugar to fat metabolism can be difficult, and feeling a lack of energy, tiredness, or a simple lessening of motivation is a common side effect of going without food.

The sense of low energy can range from mild — more like a slight drop in motivation rather than in actual strength — to quite strong, like the energy floor is dropping out from under us. We may need to sit and rest after walking 50 paces. But whatever the case, tiredness and low energy are not dangerous by themselves — one simply adjusts by slowing one's pace, decreasing activity, or doing things more deliberately. By the end of the second day or the beginning of the third, the intensity of this feeling usually passes.

While it's more common for tiredness (and other side effects of fasting) to arrive on the second day, every person is different. Some people will feel very little physical difference on a vision fast. Others can feel lighter and have even more energy than usual. A few have reported being tired all of the four days. General rules are based on statistical norms, and people are not statistics. These generalities may have little to do with any particular individual's experience.

DIZZINESS

A second (possible) side effect of fasting is dizziness. In general, the cessation of food intake produces a slight drop in blood pressure. For those with normal or high blood pressure, this is not a problem; it may even be beneficial. But those whose blood pressure is already low may feel dizzy when they stand up quickly because the flow of blood pumped up to the brain falls temporarily behind the head's quick increase in elevation. The visual field can swirl; you may see lights or "stars." This is a minor problem, not necessarily unpleasant, that's easily solved by getting up more slowly.

HEADACHES

A third potential discomfort is a headache. This should be expected if you're withdrawing from coffee or nicotine during the quest, but it's reasonably uncommon, happening to about one person in five, otherwise. In this case, a headache is likely due to temporary toxicity that results from the body breaking down fat for fuel. When one consumes toxins and unnatural substances in daily life — preservatives, additives, food colorings, etc. — the body removes them from the bloodstream and stores them away in fat cells. When, as happens in fasting, the body is denied carbohydrates and starts breaking down fats for energy, these toxins can be released back into the bloodstream. A headache can result. Drinking water usually relieves this within a few hours.

NAUSEA

The least common but most difficult potential side effect of fasting is nausea. This results from excess acid in the stomach. In normal life, people eat or snack every few hours, and their gastric juices have something to "grind their teeth on." When fasting, nothing arrives in the stomach, and some people continue to produce stomach acid. Indigestion or nausea can follow.

Participants can usually predict whether this condition is likely to happen. Some people can eat anything and describe themselves as having a "cast iron stomach." That person will likely not have a problem with nausea on a fast. But those who often have stomach upsets or have to be careful about what they eat and which foods they combine may find nausea a real concern.

Nausea can be difficult to deal with. It affects our physical core, is hard to ignore, and can dominate a person's experience. People may resist drinking water if their stomach's upset or vomit it up after swallowing. Either makes dehydration more likely.

There is a simple solution. Carrying some form of antacid (a roll of Tums or Rolaids) will usually take care of the problem. One can resolve to not use them unless absolutely necessary, but just having them there can help, since anxiety and worry contribute to indigestion. Having something nearby, just in case, should lessen any worry, and should nausea or indigestion arise, a remedy is at hand.

WATER

It is important to drink enough water during a fast. When hungry, drinking water fills the stomach and brings a sense of relief. Drinking water is useful when one has a headache because it helps flush out the system and hastens the elimination of toxins in the bloodstream. Good hydration helps increase blood pressure, reducing the potential for dizziness as well. In hot or dry environments, water can be critical to guard against dehydration. Dehydration can be life-threatening, and it makes many other potential problems, such as hypothermia, worse.

How do you know if you are drinking enough water? The amount of water people need can vary based on many factors: their size, physical build, and activity level; whether it is hot or cold, humid or dry. One rule of thumb is to drink a gallon per day — and this may be necessary in hot, desert environments — but there is no absolute formula that works for everyone. In cold or cloudy conditions where they not moving around a lot, people often return having consumed as little as a half-gallon per day.

The best indicator of whether you are drinking enough is the color of your urine. Waste products filtered from our blood by the kidneys give urine its color. If your urine is copious and light to clear, you're doing fine. If waste products are more concentrated because there's less water available to dilute them, urine becomes darker. If you notice that's the case, increase your intake of water.

One helpful hint when fasting: bring a toothbrush! During a fast, the systems related to absorption of nutrients become dormant while those focusing on elimination become more pronounced. The body's organs of elimination are the lungs, kidneys, skin, and tongue. One's tongue will likely become coated, producing a feeling of "cotton" or "crud" mouth. Rinsing out your mouth and brushing your teeth and tongue, though not a safety factor, can make for a more pleasant experience.

(Before moving on from this subject, it's good to ask participants about equipment — the number of containers they're bringing and what they have to filter or purify their water. Make sure everyone has adequate resources and plans.)

SAFETY AND SAFETY SYSTEMS

A vision quest is, ultimately, an encounter between the known and the unknown, and the unknown includes both the inner and outer world. Trying to cover all the bases so that "nothing bad will happen" is both impossible and a way of approaching the quest ruled by one's fears. In every myth of the heroic journey, and in the history of most people's lives, the discovery and development of new capacities come in times when we are forced to deal with issues outside our comfort zone. A vision quest is, by design, a journey outside the comfort zone of our current self, and physical-plane preparation is not an attempt to eliminate all risk but to make sure one has the knowledge about environment, equipment, and what to do so that effective action can be taken should certain issues arise.

Vision fasts and other rites of passage have varied widely throughout history and across cultures. Many involve stillness and immobility — solitude atop a lonely bluff, confinement within a small medicine circle, or endless dark hours within a cave or covered pit — while others, the Australian Aboriginal walkabout, for example, encourage a far-ranging encounter with the land. Most guided vision quests include certain safety precautions when someone is alone and fasting, and these precautions may be comforting even if the person wants his quest to be totally "off the grid." Whatever the plan or expectations about physical movement, there are ways to address safety concerns without peoples' solitude being interrupted or compromised.

In small-group quests led by professional guides, members are sometimes told to stay in specific areas where they're observed visually, or there can be a system of signals for participants to communicate they're okay. In quests where people are free to wander the landscape following the call of their hearts, there could be a buddy system, a series of signals, or a checkpoint such as a stone pile, where each day people leave some sign of their well-being. The possibilities are varied, and they may be relatively simple or complex, but people need to know what those procedures are, as well as what to expect and do if a problem arises.

THE STONE PILE

The stone pile is a system widely used among professional vision quest guides. Combining a few agreed-upon signals with the presence of a buddy, the stone pile allows the safety concerns of participants to be addressed without limiting either their freedom of movement or their sense of privacy. A basic outline of the stone pile follows:

Once the areas for the solo fasts have been chosen, buddies are determined by physical proximity — whoever's spot is physically closest to yours will likely be your buddy. Before the solo begins, usually the day before, the buddies show each other where their home base will be during their vision fast, "Person A" (Angie) knowing exactly where "Person B" (Bill) will be on his solo and vice versa. Once the buddies have seen and know the way to where each other will be, they choose a place approximately halfway between their respective areas to create a stone pile. This place needs to be somewhere that's clearly marked or easy to find.

The stone pile itself is something physical — a simple cairn or circle of small rocks will do the trick — that will be visited and modified daily by each buddy, one coming in the morning, the other in the afternoon. For example, Angie comes to the stone pile in the morning, and within the circle of small rocks, she places a large white stone she found on her way there. Later, in the afternoon, Bill arrives and sees the stone placed in the circle, which tells him, "Angie was here this morning. She's okay." Bill then removes the stone from the circle. The next morning, Angie returns and sees that the stone she left has been moved, which tells her "Bill is okay." She then places the white stone back in the circle, which Bill will see later in the day.

In this way, the stone pile system continues throughout the solo time of the vision quest. The system above — one putting the white stone within the circle, the other taking it out — is remarkably simple. Often people on a quest create something more elaborate: meaningful symbols, intricate mandalas that expand daily, found objects such as bones, feathers, driftwood, etc. But as far as safety goes, there are only two requirements: the changes made to the stone pile should be obvious enough that they can't be missed, and they should be solid or stable enough to remain clearly visible in case of rain or strong winds.

In this system, each buddy has a daily responsibility, one during the morning, one in the afternoon, to journey to the stone pile. If someone arrives at the stone pile to find their buddy has not been there, this initiates a series of actions that constitute the "emergency procedures." This series of actions is too long to elaborate here, and it can vary in different terrains and conditions. In quest programs led by professional guides, participants should receive clear instruction about what those procedures are. In the vast majority of cases, situations requiring emergency procedures never come to pass, but having a safety or backup system in place can be crucial if they do. (See "Emergency Procedures" in Section VIII: Requirements and Resources.)

Physical-plane preparations that require knowledge about location, skills, and equipment are also factors relevant to safety. These will be addressed in the sections to follow.

FLORA AND FAUNA

On most vision quests, concerns about flora are minor. The bulk of safety issues regarding plants revolve around what is dangerous to eat. For those not eating, the remaining factors are sometimes obvious (cacti and other spiny plants can puncture the skin) and usually limited — learning to identify species that produce allergic reactions, such as poison ivy, oak, and sumac.

The opportunity (or risk) of encountering animals that are often beautiful but also powerful and potentially dangerous varies from region to region. These might include bears, snakes, scorpions, mountain lions, coyotes, ticks, javelinas (wild pigs), moose, or smaller animals potentially carrying rabies or other viruses.

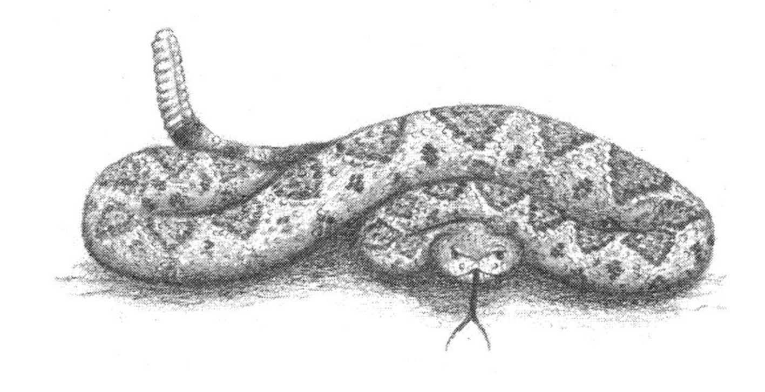

And, of course, we should include the most dangerous animal of all — other humans.

Many people unfamiliar with being in nature or wilderness focus on dramatic events or project unrealistic fears — attacked by a bear! bitten by a rattlesnake! — when speaking of safety on their solos. Those things are highly unlikely. Tripping on a rock and falling or slipping on a log when alone and without immediate help are very ordinary occurrences, and far more likely sources of injury.

Guides should be aware of the possible dangers in the particular area of the quest as well as what to do about them. Providing handouts with the relevant facts and recommended responses or requiring reading pertinent to the location in question may be helpful. Section VIII: Requirements and Resources contains a sample description of flora and fauna specific to the Gila Wilderness. Some general rules can be stated.

First, in most of North America at least, humans are the top of the food chain. Living in urban or other artificial environments, we rarely experience wind, rain, and weather, and it's easy for people to lose touch with their physical vitality, strength, and resources. Many, even most, forget their competence and become fearful. Caricatures of a person screaming at the sight of a mouse or spider or running away from a wasp that flies through a window are exaggerated examples of something fairly common: a disconnection and lack of knowledge about basic physical reality as well as our own power.

We forget the obvious fact: most large and "dangerous" animals — be they bear, mountain lion, wolf, or buffalo — are being killed and driven to extinction by *us*. It is human beings, not bears or coyotes, who are dominating and overrunning the planet. It's important to realize and remember who is dangerous to whom. Most creatures see humans as threatening and avoid them if they possibly can. Mountain lions, bears, moose, or rattlesnakes, if aware of our presence, usually disappear. They want nothing to do with us.

Second, humans are not prey; they are predators. Predators have eyes in the front of their heads to better focus on, track, and stalk whatever they are seeking. Prey have their eyes on the sides to see what is behind or coming down upon them. Look in the mirror. Where are your eyes? Take a moment to acknowledge who you are, even if these feelings seem far away from you. When entering the wilderness, you are a predator; you are dangerous. And most animals know it.

Relationships between predator and prey exist all throughout nature. Some animals, like mountain lions, are pure predators. Others, like rabbits and mice, are always prey. But many animals can be a predator to some animals and prey to others. Predator-prey relations can be complex and dynamic. The definitions are not always fixed.

When encountering a large predator, one rule nearly always holds true: *do not run away*! There are two good reasons for this. First, and most obvious, whatever you encounter can likely run much faster than you. The second reason is even more important. Since the lines between predator and prey are not always fixed, those relationships sometimes get determined situation by situation, encounter by encounter. A 40-pound wolverine has been known to drive a 600-pound bear from a kill. If there is any doubt or confusion in the mind of an animal you meet, fleeing will erase it. Running away waves a large sign announcing, "I am prey." Demonstrating obvious prey behavior — running away — can bring the predator out, luring it into giving chase even if its first impulse was to flee.

When confronting a large animal, it may be hard to claim your position at the top of the heap. But stop, take a deep breath, and remember. Don't run away, either from the animal or from who you really are.

RELATED PHYSICAL-PLANE CONCERNS

CHOOSING LOCATIONS FOR A QUEST

Vision quests take place in natural settings, often places of beauty and power — places different from where we spend most of our lives. People often ask, "Would it be better to fast in a place familiar or unusual to me?

Should I quest in the forest or in the desert? Does it make a difference?"

The answer is yes and no. A simple framework for answering this question involves the concepts *set* and *setting*. Set refers to one's motivations and purposes, the collection of attitudes, intentions, and reasons for undertaking a quest. Set could include concerns and issues just now being faced in someone's life due to circumstances such as divorce, aging, or the death of a child. Or it could involve burdens carried for decades, such as guilt, addiction, low self-esteem, and self-sabotaging frames of reference from a dysfunctional childhood. It contains what people hope for or fear; what calls to them, and what they are ready to leave behind. The deep, core motivations urging a person to quest are not likely to change based on location. They remain the same in deserts, mountains, forests, or canyon. The set stays constant, no matter the setting.

But a vision quest is a meeting of set and setting, and settings vary. The lush, deciduous forests of the Northeast are rich in earth and water. The red-rock canyons or the stark, harsh deserts of the Southwest abound in fire and air. Each ecology and landscape will carry different energies and powers. For one person, it is important to fast in an area that is familiar and become closer to and more intimate with the forces and forms of the environment he lives in. For others, facing what's unknown and unfamiliar is a higher priority, and they leave behind the ecologies they know to enter landscapes that are unusual, novel, or exciting to them.

Whatever reasons draw a person toward one area or another, in some sense the setting — weather fluctuations, animal encounters, etc. — always represents or embodies something unknown or mysterious. The landscape, or Mother Earth, is the visible face of this mystery, and our interactions with her bring us into an encounter with a story and source larger than the self and its ideas about the world. Most preparation for a quest focuses on the set — on peoples' intentions, attitudes, and rituals and processes to facilitate a useful and coherent encounter between the known self and what is beyond it (the unknown or mystery). A person's set is (somewhat) accessible to her conscious influence and control.

The setting is not. Limiting our scope to the physical plane, even if one consciously chooses the time and place of a vision quest (spring in the desert or fall when the colors turn), most of what is met in nature is outside our control, preconceptions, and expectations. Weather, cloud patterns, dragonflies mating, shooting stars, and animal encounters cannot be predicted, and their power and relevance to the set people bring with them constitute the miracle and mystery of this process.

THOUGHTS ON EQUIPMENT

When undertaking any out-of-doors adventure, someone's equipment, knowledge, and procedures must be relevant to the environment he's in. These will vary according to different locations and times of year for the quest. The relevant safety issues are not the same for summertime in the desert, early spring in the northeast woods, or fall in the Pacific Northwest. In different environments, the major concerns could be cold, heat, rain, sunstroke, animals, or lightning.

Equipment should consist of those things needed — kept to a minimum — to keep a person warm, dry, and safe in the wilderness. Packing can be a revealing exercise. People find themselves bringing items that have less to do with safety or necessity and more to do with comfort and convenience. This may be a mirror or allegory of their lives, an expression of karma: "How much baggage do I carry? What am I afraid to do without? How weighted down am I by my needs for comfort and security?" Exploring these questions in a group can be valuable entry points to explore the deeper waters along that shifting shore where our physical and psychic selves meet.

Different landscapes, climates, and times of year require slightly modified equipment lists. People should bring items appropriate to the time and place where they are going, but weather can vary greatly even in those places whose climates seem consistent and stable. Over the years, I've guided quests that included unexpected snow in the desert, floods, gale-force remnants of a hurricane, freak late-winter storms, and, of course, just knock-your-socks-off beautiful days. The equipment brought to a vision quest needs to reflect the reasonable and possible weather conditions for that area, and program leaders should provide participants with a list of equipment specific to that particular time of year and location.

Some things are virtually universal: a sleeping bag rated appropriately to the temperatures you would expect to face on the coldest night, hiking boots, sleeping pad, and a tarp or a tent to provide a dry place should significant rain occur. Other items, like water pumps and filters, may or may not be required. For an example, refer to the "Sample Equipment List" in Section VIII: Resources.

On Circles of Air and Stone quests, we recommend using a tarp for shelter. The quest involves being in and connecting with nature. Sleeping in a tent is like being inside a room. A tarp has almost all of the advantages of a tent (the exception being protection in mosquito or insect-infested environments) while being more open and spacious. One has the sense of living in nature rather than in a walled environment. An 8' x 10' tarp is adequate, though a larger one will give more room. Learning to string a tarp is not difficult, and it can be done in almost any landscape. A guide's role should include instruction for those who do not know how.

WILDERNESS ETHICS

Our own safety and health are not all that must be considered on a vision quest. We can feel warm and protected by building a large bonfire and keeping it burning day and night, but the land and environment will suffer.

Knowledge of how to leave no trace, when to use or not use fire, and what to do with waste all help ensure the safety and continued vitality of natural systems. Vision quests involve breaking down our habitual separation between self and world, and that includes recognizing the sacredness of the living earth that created us. Rediscovering our own true nature *in nature* requires we treat the earth as well as we treat ourselves as we enter a sacred space where the flowering and enlivening is both internal and external. We should walk out having done no harm, leaving nothing behind but our love, prayers, and footprints.

A simple statement of "Wilderness Ethics" can be found in Section VIII: Requirements and Resources.

KNOWLEDGE AND SKILLS

Guides need to have basic knowledge about the area being entered — plants, animals, landscape features, and likely weather patterns — as well as familiarity with safety and emergency procedures and how to put them into effect. Other relevant expertise includes familiarity with equipment, how to tie a tarp, possible environmental dangers, and competence in basic first aid — what to do if people cut themselves, are stung by an insect, sprain an ankle, or become seriously disabled.

Summer or desert quests have a higher risk of sunburn, heat stroke, and heat exhaustion. Guides should have basic knowledge about these. On organized quests, leaders should instruct participants on how to prevent, recognize, and treat them should they occur. Wet or cold conditions are common outside the Southwest, and the dangers of hypothermia may need to be addressed. Warmth is related to staying dry, and keeping oneself and one's clothing dry depends on rain gear and having a tarp and knowing how to string it.

For all this to work, people need to follow through on their knowledge and use their equipment in the proper way. No matter how well you know how to put up a tarp, it won't keep your sleeping bag dry if the bag is not under it. No matter how good your equipment is, you must know how and when to use it in order for it to be effective. This seems simple and obvious, but most problems, dangers, injuries, environmental damage, and loss of life result from poor judgment or simply not following through on what people should know about. In the vast majority of instances, people's fears and concerns about safety prove to be unwarranted. But in rare events and under severe conditions, having basic knowledge, the right equipment, and following established procedures can be critical and even lifesaving.

Developing a deep knowledge base and a full set of skills is beyond the scope of this manual. Most guides have taken some form of wilderness first aid or wilderness first responder courses. These are offered in various locations around the country. The resources section, under the heading "Knowledge and Skills," lists a selection of companies and organizations offering equipment, first aid training, and other useful knowledge.

SECTION IV:
RITUAL AND CEREMONY

The Language of the Old Brain 81
Marking vs. Making Changes 82
Making Good Ritual 82

Ritual Aspects of Practical Tasks 83
Finding Your Spot 83
Fasting 84
The Stone Pile (Safety System) 84

Where Custom Meets Choice 85
Threshold Gates 85
Death Lodge 86
The Purpose Circle 88
Summoning the Darkness 89
Medicine Songs, Names, and Animals 91

Self-Created Rituals and Ceremonies 94
Rituals of Severance 94
Rituals of Incorporation 99
Rituals of Attunement 103

SECTION IV: RITUAL AND CEREMONY

THE LANGUAGE OF THE OLD BRAIN

(Note: For simplicity's sake, I've chosen to address most of this chapter to the second person — "You." Though a manual for vision quest guides, much of the text includes instruction on how to perform various ritual acts. It seemed cumbersome to switch between the first or second person — "we" or "you," referring to quest guides — and the third person — "he," "she," or "they," referring to participants.)

The vision quest is a ritual that's both powerful and profound, but other rituals and ceremonies performed within it may make up core elements of the quest. Creating and participating in ritual acts aligned with one's purpose and intention can bring deeper engagement, power, and magic to the process.

Brain physiologists have long asserted we have three distinct brain structures, each one wrapped around the one beneath. The oldest and deepest is called the reptile brain. Concerned with issues of safety and biological survival, it sits atop the spinal column, controlling instincts and our automatic and autonomous functions — those things (like temperature regulation, metabolism, and breathing) that we rarely need to think about.

Surrounding the reptile brain is the limbic system, or mammalian brain, associated with deep, primal emotions. It's activated when an infant looks into its mother's eyes, and significant neural development and patterning is lost if this connection is lacking. Our mammal brain seeks connection or communion, and it responds to the presence or interruption of this necessary human element. Its activities are responsible for gut feelings, hunches, and all those ways of perceiving and knowing below our conscious awareness.

Lastly, the neocortex, or new brain, is the thinking, calculating, planning, speaking brain, the one humans consider themselves so special to have. Concepts and spoken language are the media of choice for this new, outer brain, and it responds to our conscious conversations.

The words of daily life rarely penetrate our deeper structures, but ritual and ceremony appear to be languages that the older brain structures understand. We gather stones, cast circles, offer cornmeal, sing or speak to the various directions, and a part of ourselves — ancient and primal — that doesn't listen when we just talk, is stimulated. It recognizes, reacts, and responds to these physical, emotional, and metaphysical alignments. And if you're curious about where the power in your life lies, each moment our subconscious mind is processing a million times more

information than the languaged landlord in the house of reason. The power of rational choice and will to make real change has limits, and if change is what we seek, we'll need to use languages — ritual and ceremony — that the depths below the surface understand.

MAKING VERSUS MARKING CHANGES

Rituals are transformative; they make a change. Ceremonies are confirmatory; they mark, celebrate, or ratify a change that has already happened.

Many cultures have puberty rituals for boys. In those instances, it is the ritual itself, which could involve isolation, ordeals, tests, and teachings, that makes them men. It transforms them. Another culture may have a puberty ceremony for girls. The ceremony is important, and it may be long, arduous, and elaborate, full of dances, tests, and presentations. But the change — girl to woman — has already happened. Nature and the Spirit have transformed the girl, and the ceremony announces, celebrates, and confirms it for everyone to see.

These categories and definitions — transforming and confirming, making versus marking a change — are logical distinctions. They exist in the abstract and make sense in our minds. But in real life, many acts wander over the lines, acts that have both ritual and ceremonial aspects.

MAKING GOOD RITUAL

It's important to find forms of ritual that work for you. This is *your* vision quest and, as with boots or a backpack, a good fit is important. Try to free yourself of any preconceived notions about "doing it right" or comparisons to others. There may be a right way to do a Catholic mass and a right way to lead a Lakota sweat lodge, but this is *your* quest. You are the authority here, and your relationship to Spirit, like your relationship with a partner, does not have to look just like everyone else's. *You do not have to be good.*

Many have gone before you and found their unique way. Black Elk discovered a visionary universe through sickness and descending into a coma. Christ wandered for forty days and battled temptation in a desert. Moses climbed to the top of Mt. Sinai; Mohammed retired to a cave, and Buddha entered the forest to face and dissolve illusion under the Bodhi tree. A Plains Indian may sit inside a small circle and not eat, drink, or leave for days, while an aboriginal youth in Australia wanders on walkabout for months.

All the above were vision quests or rites of passage. Each took place within the context of a particular time, place, culture, and person. Considering the many possibilities, it's absolutely appropriate to create the form of vision quest that's right for you. Like plants and animals that adapt to different environments, all throughout history the forms of religious and spiritual seeking have had to adapt to the landscape and soil they took root in. When Buddhism left India for Tibet, it met a shamanistic mountain people, and the meeting and mingling of these strands wove into the rich and colorful cloth of Tibetan Buddhism. Traveling east, it encountered Japanese culture and produced a much different result, the sparse simplicity of Zen. You have your own psychic soil, and the forms of rituals and practices that will grow there are for you to learn and decide.

Your choices around rituals and ceremonies involve not only *what* you decide to do, but *how* you choose to do it. Ritual forms may be simple or elaborate. What's important is to bring your full being — all your attention and energy — to the moment, to make an act of power. For one person, keeping it simple is better; all the elaborations or trappings feeling like distractions and tangents subtracting from the essential core act. For another, the reverse may be true. Burning incense, collecting stones to make a circle, speaking to the mountain, calling in the directions, and evoking the spirits of the ancestors all build energy and power, moving him from the ordinary to the extraordinary. The choice is up to you.

RITUALS ASPECTS OF PRACTICAL TASKS

There are practical tasks in every quest that also have ritual aspects. Some choose to celebrate and honor these tasks as ritual and symbolic, and for them these activities may be some of the most important experiences of the whole process. For others, they are background, necessary things to do and be done with, for their focus is elsewhere. A few are listed below.

FINDING YOUR SPOT

In choosing the place for one's fast, there are rational and practical elements that are important to consider: "Is there shelter from the wind? Would the area flood if it rained? Can I hang a tarp there?" But choosing a spot is not like buying a car; it's more than a checklist. You are looking for a sacred connection, a place outside that resonates with the depths of what is inside you. This resonance can include senses, feelings, and images. You're seeking a place where the inner and outer landscapes say "Yes!" to each other. This match, and its confirmation, may best be found or facilitated through ritual. Just as in rituals of courtship surrounding a relationship we're searching for, it's important to invite and welcome the other — nature and the spirit — into the decision-making process.

There are many ways to include the natural world in this search, ways both profound and practical. You could speak your intentions as you walk into the wilderness, letting the land hear and respond to you. You might let yourself be led, turning this search over to some force other than the rational, planning mind. You could follow gusts of wind or the flights of birds or butterflies or wander until hawk calls from the sky.

When you find a place you like, speak to the spirits who live there. Tell them why you've come and ask permission to visit there. Speak from your heart, asking to be welcomed and wait until you hear a "yes." These are ritual actions that can move us out of the closed, static, and separate self (and out of our heads) into a present, open, and evolving relationship with the living landscape.

Finding your spot may also be a metaphor for your life. The search process and actions may be a mirror that reflects your values, modus operandi, fears, and hopes. One person looks for a place that feels protective, while another seeks the highest ridge, its exposed discomfort secondary to the search for grander views. One person marches out and soon stops, saying, "This is good enough." The attitude is indiscriminate or flexible. Almost any place will do. Another spends the whole afternoon roaming the canyons, frustrated and anxious, discarding spot after spot, dominated by indecision or standards set so high that nothing is ever good enough.

Our experience is a metaphor as much as a fact. The world is created from possibilities, and there is no hard, absolute, and objective reality. Nothing is just as it is. The practical and necessary hunt for your place contains other dimensions and resonances; larger themes are playing out. In seeking the place we belong, the quality of our searching evokes differing responses from the world. Embracing the larger dimensions of this act can move us beyond ourselves. It can transform this practical task into a ritual engagement with forces far greater than the familiar *me*. The story we play out in seeking our spot is sometimes among the most interactive and compelling of the entire quest.

FASTING

Fasting has undeniable physical effects. It also is a ritual, one of the oldest ways humans have found to change their consciousness. During a fast, awareness gradually expands. It becomes less focused, more open and peripheral. It produces a dream-like and fluid energy, a palpable change from our everyday altered state. Images bubble to the surface; people we've not thought of in decades come to visit.

Fasting is also a statement of intention. It says, "Spirit, Great Mystery, I come to you asking for help. But I do not take this lightly. I am not a child wanting to take and only receive. I do not ask for something for nothing. I have given up conversation, company, comfort, food. Look kindly on me and find me worthy. I put myself in your hands. I surrender my habits, routines, and protections. I go without food in hope that you might feed me in different ways. Feed my senses, my heart, soul, and imagination. Sustain me with insight and beauty, fill me with your presence, and show me my place and your will for me."

Fasting is a sacrifice. The Latin origins of this word are *"sacer"* (sacred) and *"facie"* (to make). You "make sacred" this time by your sacrifice. You give up food, companionship, comfort — the pillars of daily and domestic life. In forsaking these you are making an offering, sacrificing something valuable at the altar of your longing. You offer up the social and survival instincts — the lower three chakras — so the spiritual body (the upper chakras) may awaken. You empty, open, and humble yourself.

Many choose to mark and affirm this ritual of fasting. It can be done simply. Each time you drink, offer some water to a nearby plant and acknowledge what is already happening. You *are* making a sacrifice. Why not do it consciously? By recognizing this sacrifice (and participating joyfully and willingly) in your choice to fast, it becomes an act of power and not merely something that happens to you.

THE STONE PILE (SAFETY SYSTEM)

While various quests may have different safety systems, the issues of safety and security, as well as being watched over and responsible to others, are metaphors and fertile ground for self-observation and insight. The following description uses the stone pile — a safety system requiring you to show up at a certain place and leave a sign of your well-being — as an example.

Visiting the stone pile is a practical task; you have to go once a day at a certain time. Its primary purpose is safety, but it can also have symbolic or ritual aspects as well. It's a metaphor representing your connection to your people, your human family. The stone pile is a responsibility to care for another — your buddy — who also cares for you. It could be your lifeline to help if you need it.

Once you begin your solo, your time is almost totally yours. You can do or not do rituals, stay up all night, or sleep and dream most of the day. There is only one thing you must do — go to the stone pile. Because it's required, it can symbolize authority or duty, representing the negative side of your connection to people — the obligations, responsibilities, and "shoulds" of social life. But it could also evoke the opposite — your lifeline of friendship, help, support, care, and compassion.

Since you're required to do it, you will, but there's the option to make it a ritual. You can journey to the stone pile as a victim, dragging your feet as you go. You could go as a warrior, lover, or religious pilgrim, turning it into an act you are not resisting or subject to. You can literally walk your talk. It can be an offering that represents your gift to your people. What you leave is an offering to your buddy. Turn it into something rich.

This required task contains lessons. If you are called to fast miles up a canyon so you will never be bothered or interrupted, going that far commits you to retrace those miles every day to leave your mark. The stone pile represents your minimum, but necessary responsibility to your community. You can make it difficult and long. You can waste the afternoon avoiding it and drag your feet all the way. It's your choice. But if you wish to be alone and uninterrupted, you have to fulfill your duties to your community well. Because if you don't, people will be roaming all over the hills wondering what's wrong and calling your name. The stone pile teaches that, like figure and ground, self and others are not separate, and freedom involves accepting our minimum responsibilities, great or small, and doing them well. It offers a metaphor that weaves together the perceived polarity and tension between individual liberty and community needs.

WHERE CUSTOM MEETS CHOICE

Time-Honored Traditions in New Forms

The rituals and ceremonies described below have long histories. Often done within vision fasts, their lengthy tenure is due to their power and efficacy. They offer profound encounters with inner and outer landscapes and create structures that can bring insights and catalyze commitments. Your quest will be unique to you in marvelous and myriad ways, and it could involve the choice to do none, some, or all of the following.

THRESHOLD GATES

The word threshold comes from harvest times. As farmers threshed their grain, a board or barrier was placed across the threshing floor to hold the germ — the valuable and useful part of the seed — while the chaff was blown away. It marked a transition point, an important and necessary separation. When you enter or exit a room, you step over a threshold that marks the boundary between different spaces. Crossing signifies a passage from one state or place to another.

If you are part of a vision quest group, there may be some sort of threshold ritual before you leave camp to begin your solo. As you walk away, for a short period you might still be able to see or hear other people. But a time will soon come when you are beyond sight and sound of everyone. You realize, "I'm really alone now." At that point, many choose to do a threshold ritual to formally mark their entry into their solo and the sacred world.

This threshold could be simple. You could draw a line in the sand, collect stones to mark a border, or find a stick and create a gate. There may be a stream to ford, a fallen log across the path, or a passage beneath limbs that create an arch. You could state simply, "When I step over that line, I will enter the sacred world and begin my vision quest." Then you stand, waiting until you feel fully present and filled with energy to cross.

You could be drawn to do something more elaborate. Some choose to smudge, sing, pray, rattle, and announce their intentions to the mountains. Some state a desire to step away from something as they cross over, while others focus on entering the new. Each additional act or prayer feels like gathering energy until there's a readiness to move forward. Whatever is your way, it's important that it feel right to you. Crossing the threshold will happen, one way or another. You will walk out of camp and journey into solitude, leave everything behind. Why not create a ritual that makes it an act of power? Rather than just feel the wind blow, why not spread your wings and fly?

Speaking your intentions to the mountains, the landscape, or the mystery in all things is helpful, but people's clarity varies. Some know they seek specific guidance to end a part of their lives. Others come to find direction or renewal. A few leave for their fast not fully clear about what their intent is. A threshold ritual can challenge us to create or claim a purpose. One man, fresh from a breakup with a woman he expected to marry, had difficulty focusing on his fast because he was in so much turmoil. He walked out of camp, stopped, and drew a line across the trail, declaring, "I'm not stepping across until I know why." He stood there feeling how hurt and wounded he was, how disappointed and let down. He began to soothe himself by rubbing his belly (home to his inner child). Eventually, he stated his intention — a commitment to be fully present with that child who felt so much pain. Four days later, he returned with one of the most tender and uplifting quests stories I've ever heard.

At the threshold, you winnow the grain. You marshal your intent and gather your purpose; the chaff blows away as you step across. Speak your intention out loud. Like taking aim with a bow and arrow, you focus on your purpose and direction. You are aware of the tension as you pull the string. When you step across, you let go.

Those who choose to do this ritual usually do another on their way back. This time the direction is reversed. You consider everything you leave behind as you walk out of the wilderness and everything you walk toward as you return to people, conversation, life, job, responsibilities. This is also a major step and a powerful moment.

DEATH LODGE

Long ago, people lived simpler lives. More intimate with their bodies and natural cycles of life, they knew when their dying time was at hand. Entering the death lodge marked this important transition. Word would quickly spread throughout the village, everyone realizing they had limited time to visit with the departing person.

The death lodge offered a last chance to complete relationships with the dying. Some visitors would come to thank the dying for gifts given and received, to acknowledge their importance to their lives. Others might come burdened with a lingering conflict, for this represented the last chance to talk and resolve issues between them. They arrived prepared to speak their truth, their intention to make things good (or as good as they could be made), to let the pain and problems go while there was still a chance. In these cases, anger might need to be voiced, but it was expressed to get to what lay beneath. Its objective was release and resolution, so the relationship and the future journey of the departing would be free from attachment or resentment.

The death lodge was closed when the allotted time was up. The dying person was then free to "take his last walk to the mountains." If someone didn't visit during the set-aside time, he had no right to intrude upon the final preparations of the one leaving. The time had passed; the window was shut. The ritual of the death lodge gave closure to the community as well as to those departing. The person heading toward the afterlife would have completed earthly business. There would be nothing undone, no karma tying him to the daily world of form and manifestation. He could enter the spirit world freely. And the people, to the extent they completed what was unresolved, could say goodbye without regret.

Many people choose to do some form of death lodge on a vision quest. The basic procedure is simple, with some variations. First, one chooses a place. It could be naturally occurring (a hollow or a clearing among the trees) or a circle could be created with rocks gathered and placed to mark its boundary. Whether found or created, begin by announcing your intention, asking this place to support you in your death preparation. If moved you could include offerings of tobacco, cornmeal, smudge, or prayer. Then, step into the circle, walk to the center, and in your own words declare, "I have entered my death lodge. Death approaches, and I want to walk freely to the spirit world. All who would speak with me are welcome." Sit down and wait.

Let it happen. Clear your mind; try to be present. Feel the sun, watch the wind moving the plants, hear the sounds of the forest. Wait and witness. Soon a thought enters the mind: "I wonder how my daughter (friend, partner, father, etc.) is doing at home." When you notice your attention going to your daughter, this signals that she has entered your death lodge. Imagine her approaching and sitting down before you. Speak to her aloud, as if this is your last conversation and you will never have the chance to speak to her again. Say everything you would want to say. It may be extremely difficult, very emotional, but do it.

At some point, you will know that you've finished; you've said it all. Imagine her acknowledging that she's heard all you've said. Wait a moment. Watch her walk out of the lodge and disappear.[7]

Sit. Watch the mountains. Feel the breeze. Your mind wanders again, remembering a time you went camping with your brother. This signifies he has arrived at your death lodge. Watch him approach, enter, and sit before you. As with your daughter, have your final conversation.

People's death lodges can take their own, unique form. As illustrated above, you can let your mind wander and allow whoever "shows up" to enter your death lodge. But you might know you want to speak with specific people and call them in, one by one. When this list has been completed, an open lodge could follow.

Visitors to the death lodge can include people no longer living. Grandparents or friends lost to tragedies decades ago may appear, and it's important to say goodbye. There's no need to question why. Every visitor does not have to be human. A beloved pet may come, and your grief may be stronger than with any person. The most unexpected people can arrive, and sometimes those you think "should" visit, don't. A death lodge visit could be with a former version of yourself: "the man I was while drinking" or "the frightened girl after the divorce." One person may have a few major visitations while another has many, as if a line were forming outside the door.

Time in the death lodge can be very emotional. There may come a point where you are just not able to do more. Releases of long-held feelings are both liberating and exhausting. Pace yourself. If you become tired, yet want to continue, acknowledge there is more to do. Take a break and return later. Give it the time it needs. Everybody will eventually come.

Commonly, death lodges are done early in the quest. The intention is to complete business, finish our affairs with daily and ordinary reality so that our remaining energy is unencumbered and available to Spirit. But people sometimes choose to speak with these significant others whenever moved, or in the darkness, or on the last day. The choice is up to you.

During the death lodge, we ritually visit our last moments. Death is ever stalking us. Eventually, though we don't know when, there will come a time when we will say goodbye to everything. It is good to practice beforehand and face the bittersweet truths of our lives, for denial limits and diminishes us. As we learn to face what's temporary and accept the inevitable, our attention is freed to attend to something larger and eternal. Acknowledging our impermanence as physical beings, and conscious of the journey to the spirit world awaiting us, our time becomes precious. Our perspective on what is important in life begins to change. We begin the process of working things out.

This ritual can initiate a shift in our lives and relationships, even if we are not soon leaving for the spirit world. In the death lodge, we give our very best to resolve issues, to release resentments and blocked energy. The next time we experience a particular relationship with all its old triggers we may discover we have a new power to stop the usual reactions. We remember that we have done our best to say it all and be done with it. This may result in a new freedom to not play the game, to say "No, I do not have to put my energy there." The triggers themselves may still arise, but you have cleared your energy field; given the old relationship and dance its time. Your "appointment book" is now oriented to new business, and you have an inner receptionist to screen your calls. Having choice over whether we repeat and replay situations that hurt us or violate our boundaries is a wonderful power. It has happened for many.

THE PURPOSE CIRCLE

The purpose circle is a space one enters on the last night of the quest. This space incorporates your purpose — your intentions and gifts — and is "peopled" with your allies — those who support you in living from this center. Within it, you will pass the whole night, holding to this resolve and commitment.

The physical part is straightforward. You choose a place that feels appropriate, possibly different than where you have spent your previous days, and construct a circle of stones. You could start by placing stones for the cardinal directions, speaking aloud about what they mean to you and asking that those qualities, energies, and powers be present within your circle. Rocks are then added, representing the elements of your life — practices, relationships, etc. — that support you in living this purpose, including them until the circle feels complete.

For example, a stone could symbolize a group that encourages you to pursue your dreams. You would speak to this group about their support — how they listen to, assist, or inspire you; how they affirm your best — as you set the stone in the circle. Rocks can be added for all those who bolster you on your path — groups or individuals whom you can count on to be there — speaking to each in turn. You can add symbols of activities that connect you to your soul or path — writing, dance, tai chi, prayer, meditation, etc. — affirming their importance, meaning, and benefit as you invite them into your circle. All the situations, relationships, and practices that support your purpose can be included.

(Elements of severance are occasionally included in this ritual. You can speak to a stone and place it outside the circle, to affirm a practice or relationship that no longer serves you.)

When done, you have created a ring of power, a circle of allies alive with intention and purpose. As the sun settles beneath the horizon, you step inside, intending to stay awake through the long dark night.

The purpose circle can evoke the energies of death and rebirth, the enclosure both tomb and womb. Those who've been pronounced dead and then return consistently report a journey through a long dark tunnel that emerges into the light. We enter this circle of darkness as the sun goes down, trusting we too will pass through to a realm of light (morning). Staying all night, we consciously enact our dying, intending to remain awake through it all.

In the *Tibetan Book of the Dead*, a departed soul encounters various Bardo states after death. These are energy or dream states in which the soul faces — is confronted or enticed by — the karma and issues of his life. The seductions of the living world, as well as the opposite — anything inducing fear, loathing, or repulsion — must be faced. The one who has died strives to remain in equanimity, neither craving the enticements nor turning away in aversion. Lured or repulsed, all of them are confronted, the departing souls challenged to stay centered in their true nature or essential being.

Entering the purpose circle engages the process of death and its Bardo states. Demons appear, each pulling you off-center, telling you to act unconsciously, to pack it in. One voice whispers how cold it is and how nice it would be to lie down. Another tells you the circle doesn't mean anything; you'll be tired in the morning, and you might as well sleep. It whispers there could be something far better, an important dream you will miss by staying awake. The purpose circle can be practice for life, for the tasks of life and death are often the same: to remain conscious and not become slaves to gods spawned from our fears or desires.

We enter this purpose circle as a warrior, magician, or servant of the source, determined to stay awake for one night of our lives, persisting through everything that tries to dissuade us. It may be an ordeal — uncomfortable, difficult, and long. We have entered the dark night, been interred in our tomb. Our will may wane, our soul be tested. But we have placed allies in a circle around us, and we are not alone. In olden times, the bodies of the dead were placed in a sacred place along with special objects — knife, bowl, staff, or lance — that were needed to make the journey into the spirit world. We too have our aids. The allies in our journey, all that support our spiritual life, have been placed around us, waiting to be called on, to help us get through the night. How we do that will be part of our emerging story.

What is your purpose? What does that mean? Our purpose could refer to our gifts, intention, path, or work. Some people come to the last night knowing their purpose in concrete and practical terms. It could involve a specific decision: to leave their job, go home, and start an alternative school. It may be a commitment — new or renewed — to truly being a father, or a pledge to invest in a dream locked inside you for decades. Your purpose may be the same as or different from your original thoughts when you began the fast — much can happen in these four days.

But you may also arrive on the threshold of the last night and still be unsure what your purpose is. If so, you can enter the circle and pray, asking to be told who you are and what your vision is. Your purpose circle may be what the Sioux used to call *hanbechyapi*, or beseeching for a vision. In undertaking a vision quest, we put ourselves in the hands of the Mystery. Whenever we are in the presence of greater powers the outcome is not in our hands. What we can control is our attention, intention, and effort. We can pray; we can hope; we can ask and affirm our longing. In doing so, we can stay in our center, whether we've been shown the form or process of our purpose or not.

How you "stay in the center" of your purpose can vary greatly. Some sit all night as if meditating, while others walk the perimeter and talk to the stars, directions, and spirits. Many dance, sing, rattle, drum, or hold conversations with stones, ancestors, guides, and themselves. There is no right way, only *your* right way, and for some, this realization can be the greatest gift of the night.

This night may be long and arduous, but there is light at the end of the tunnel. As dawn approaches, the horizon changes from cobalt through gray to red. Finally, the sun rises. Choose how to close your circle consciously and purposefully, then prepare to begin your journey back to the human world.

Though the purpose circle is a ritual enactment of dying, it is also a metaphor for birth. The emergence out of the womb can also be a difficult journey, traversing a dark tunnel — the birth canal, to enter a world of light. If you entered this circle as a tomb, greet the morning as someone who has died to this form. Walk back into daily life as a spirit, free from fear, survival concerns, and material things. Others, having undergone a gestation from which they emerge newborn, can walk back toward the world with childlike wonder, eyes open and sparkling, free from preconceptions and judgments.

When finished, take your circle apart. Leave no trace. The experience may be dear to you, but the circle only needs to exist within you, as an energy field within your special place. Reborn into the life of the spirit, undo your material attachments and assemblages. In doing so, you bless those who will follow in the coming years, saving them the experience of coming upon your creations and feeling like the spot has been used. Walking lightly and leaving the earth unblemished is one gift we can all give to our people.

SUMMONING THE DARKNESS

Entering nature, with its harsh and exciting landscapes and forces, moves us beyond the polarities of good and evil, the polarities of daily life. Heavens, whether they be on puffy clouds with everyone dressed in white or filled with 200 virgins, and hells, below the earth and fiery, are irrelevant. Everything is right here, and the urge to make some parts of it good — babies and bunny rabbits, for example — and other parts evil — crocodiles, spiders, and ticks — is artificial and a distinctly human overlay.

Humans — one species among 10 million — are also neither good nor evil. Human history is filled with extraordinary achievements, from the pyramids of Egypt to the Sistine Chapel, as well as cannibalism and mass sacrifice. The species that produced Buddha and St. Francis also created Hitler and Vlad the Impaler. The forces that can produce saints and monsters, crusades and jihads, totalitarianism, slavery, and the Bill of Rights are swirling within every human psyche, and every culture and era has labeled some of these expressions "good" or "normal" and others "dark" or "deviant."

In modern life, we're all taught to be a "good boy" or "good girl," and in this process, we deny or repress parts of ourselves that don't fit the preferred self-image. We may grow up to be quiet approval seekers or people-pleasers and repress certain unattractive emotions, like fear, anger, or sadness, or downplay a core part of our identity, like sexuality. Whatever the specifics, dismissed or suppressed impulses become part of our shadow, all the pieces of ourselves that fade from view and become lost in darkness as we "turn toward the light."

But the shadow never goes away. It doesn't disappear because we refuse to look at or acknowledge it. The limbic system and reptile brain do not need the conscious brain's approval to function. Their relegation to the land of darkness merely means they function out of sight, their expressions now unconscious, surprising, and irrational. Self-sabotaging behaviors, depression, psychosomatic illnesses, eating disorders, addictions, explosive emotions, the "nice kid" who guns down his classmates at school... if we refuse to acknowledge and invite this unruly guest to dinner, he may come anyway, and we'll be sipping tea while he burns down the house.

Summoning the dark is a ritual for calling forth the shadow. Our intention is to have a conversation, to see and integrate what has been exiled and denied. This ritual must, of course, take place in the dark, after the glow of twilight has faded. Its beginning, the creation of a circle of allies, mimics the purpose circle, only this time your allies are there to give support and courage as you make ready to face what you least want to look at, what you've invested much of your life avoiding. When this circle of support has been created and all ambient light is gone, open the circle, simply or with smudging, prayer, etc., and step into the center. Face the dark and announce, "I'm ready, come show yourself." Then wait.

Wait until you sense something. Some people are visual, and they may see shapes or apparitions in the darkness. Others, noticing a particularly black area, perhaps under a tree, may have the feeling there's something there. Those less visually oriented might perceive a chill moving up the spine, sense a shifting wind has entered the area, become aware of a sudden silence, or notice the air feels clammy and oppressive. When you sense this presence — in whatever way — speak out loud, "Who are you? And what do you want from me?" You've now invited the darkness to speak.

What you "hear" may appear to be outside or seem like an inner knowing or words forming themselves in your head. Perhaps the voice answers, "I am your depression. I want you to die!" If so, you would answer, "I'm sorry, I won't give you that. What else would you like from me?" You have denied its request. The price is too high, but you are still open to negotiating. Perhaps this energy responds, "Then I want you to live your life in fear." The price is still too high, and again, you deny its request. "What else do you want from me?" This process may go on for a bit. "I want you to avoid risks; to play it safe; to always focus on security... " But eventually, the darkness — your depression — may ask for something you are willing to give: "I want you to acknowledge all the power I have held in your life."

Can you do that, comply with this request? If so, you must agree and make a commitment, letting this darkness know what you will do to fulfill your end of the bargain. You might say, out loud, "I will acknowledge you and honor your power. During the coming year, once a month at the full moon, I will light a candle in your honor and recite a litany. I will make a list and speak of all the ways you have affected my life, from when you first appeared to this moment. I will give you your due."

Something has changed. You are speaking to and negotiating with this entity that has been outside of your control, that has operated independently and sabotaged your plans. You have listened and agreed to its request. (Be sure to follow through!) Now it's your turn. Having granted its wish, it must grant you yours. Again, speaking aloud, articulate your desire. "Having agreed to address you and honor your power one night a month for the coming year, I want you to keep that appointment and stay away from me for the rest of the month." When you have struck your bargain, say "good night" and close the circle.

MEDICINE SONGS, NAMES, AND ANIMALS

Our word *health* derives from the old English word *hale*, which means to be whole. So, in the larger, traditional sense, medicine is anything that helps you to become more whole. Our contemporary view of medicine is very limited; it usually refers to a surgical procedure or drug. But wholeness can mean (or be brought to you by) many things. Ultimately, medicine is anything that helps you on that journey.

In the final analysis, becoming whole involves realizing your connection and relationship with your larger self. This includes many dimensions of reality: physical, emotional, and spiritual. In this broader definition, medicine could be a substance, whether comfrey, Tylenol, psilocybin mushrooms, or holy water, if those elements help bring you into balance or usher in a larger awareness or expression of being. But medicine could just as well be a story if it teaches you something that supports your growth and makes you more well-rounded or complete. It could be a parable, a meeting, a name, or a song. Any of these could contain medicine.

SONGS

Music can be medicine. Most of the time we realize that, but our knowledge is unconscious. If we're tired and need to clean the house, we put on rock and roll, something energetic enough to get us through the chores. When we want to relax, we play something quiet and melodic, perhaps classical. Some tunes celebrate marching off to war, while others convey the message that all's right with the world. Lovers often refer to "our song," and, when it is played, they're transported back to the moment they met or remember something that unites them. Songs carry energy and associations. They have medicine.

I know several people who lead sweat lodges. One, before beginning, enters the lodge to pray and center himself. His preparation includes a medicine song that helps ready him to lead the ceremony. On vision quests, songs often come to people. They can arrive in the moment, with words and melody that have never been uttered before. They might be songs learned in church as a child or something remembered from pop radio.

These songs can appear at the most profound or profane moments. The spirit moves in mysterious ways. They can come in a dream, be coaxed out of memory, erupt full-blown, or emerge slowly and develop. They could bring insight or energy, make us laugh, respond to a need, or arrive seemingly out of the blue.

Perhaps you find yourself resisting something, like going to the stone pile. You drag your feet because it feels like a chore, but you go. Your movement sets your arms swinging, and you feel the breeze, observe the dance of flowers, listen to the buzz of insects. Soon you start to hum, slowly settling into a melody. Words start to collect chorus and cadence. Before long, you are singing, boots moving with rhythm and purpose through the landscape. Notice this. There is a medicine — medicine of a particular kind — in this song. Its arrival changed your mood; raised your spirits and energy.

There is nothing unnatural in this, but don't ignore it. You've received a gift of medicine. Just like pills or prescriptions in a pharmacy, songs can assist us in different ways. They can bring comfort or courage, give hope, or summon an animal guide. They can help you forget your troubles; remember your purpose; relax; or evoke determination, devotion, or dispassionate distance. Like penicillin, Prozac, and Viagra, they are not interchangeable. They are gifts. They've been presented to you, and they're meant to be used. Honor them; carry them with you. Sometimes we forget and throw away a gift from lack of attention. Don't leave them on the shelf, passively consigned to the category of "coincidence."

NAMES

There is power in naming. Something formless is brought into form through the use of words. In many cultures, it has been customary to receive a second, or sacred, name at some point in life. In the West, our last name locates us within the lineage of males, our father and the fathers before, while our first and middle names result from our parents' preference. But there is a much older tradition of receiving a name that describes our journey, declares our gifts, or defines our relationship to the spirit.

Many Native Americans have come back from a vision quest with a holy name. You may know of people who studied with a guru in India and returned with a Sanskrit name — Ram Dass, for example — the new name crystallizing something important about who they are. Cassius Clay became Muhammad Ali. In doing so, he made a powerful political statement, a declaration announcing, "I reject your slave owner's name and do not hold dear being white or Christian."

Contemporary culture does not have a tradition, in adolescence or adulthood, of taking a name that defines a larger framework of who we are. Some people come to a vision quest wanting a name. Others aren't looking, but a name arrives. Seeking a spirit name through a vision quest is both common and appropriate, but remember the old saying: "The desire for enlightenment is the last impediment to enlightenment." Looking too hard can get in the way. Sometimes there's an essential paradox: a new name symbolizes a new status, a new orientation and being, but the old self — willful, craving, and perhaps dysfunctional — who wants the name badly must move out of the way. Take the point of view the name will find you. Speak, affirm, and announce your desire for a name to the mountain. Then let it go and put it in the hands of Spirit.

If a name does find you, there are choices about how to receive it. A name can be between you and the spirit; it does not need to be shared with anyone else. Honor what feels right in your heart. Some people have medicine names they use only in ritual contexts. They are addressed by that name in a sweat lodge or sacred circle but they do not take the sacred to the supermarket. Some use their new name only among friends, while others go all the way, changing their passport, social security card, and driver's license. The choice is not all or nothing. There are many places to draw a line between private and public, sacred and profane. You can decide which most respects, affirms, and sustains the name's medicine and power.

ANIMALS

Encounters with animals can contain medicine if they teach or guide you to a greater sense of all you are. Many people receive medicine from these encounters. Suppose you are tired, your mind wandering into swamps of self-pity, thinking, "Oh god, I'm exhausted; I have no energy. Why did I decide to do this?" A swallow-tailed butterfly appears and lands on your boot. It rests there for a minute, wings opening and closing. Your internal chatter stops, fascinated by its colors, beauty, delicacy, and strength. Eventually, it takes flight again, dancing across the meadow. You watch until it disappears, shaking your head in surprise and delight. You have received medicine, an infusion of light, joyfulness, and wonder that washed away the doldrums of the one feeling depressed and sorry for himself.

People on vision quests often have significant encounters with animals, and medicine may come in many forms. It can arrive as an emotional lift, as in the butterfly example above. It can appear as insight, arising out of an observational process as hundreds of ants teach you about your connection to community. Or a hawk may provide guidance, its call showing you the path at each junction where you wonder where to turn.

Sometimes encounters with an animal are oft-repeated, or the meeting may be so striking you cannot ignore it. This can lead to the question, "Is this my spirit guide or power animal?" At various times, I have been charged by bears, had birds land on my chest, and stared into the face of a raccoon, our noses two inches apart. Once, on top of a high flat-topped butte in New Mexico, I smudged and entered my purpose circle. As soon as

I placed myself in the center, a ringtail — a weasel-like creature with a long, striped tail — summited the butte, came to my circle, and watched me for several minutes, walking the perimeter four times without entering. Something like that you cannot ignore.

I welcome all medicine encounters, but I make a distinction between receiving medicine from an animal and encountering a "medicine animal." Think of the difference between having a great connection with someone you met at a party and making a commitment to a relationship with a partner. We may have numerous highly positive interactions with people, but committed relationships are far fewer. Repetitive or particularly intense encounters with animals on a vision quest invite you to question if these could be allies or guides. If so, there are ways to follow it further, investing attention and energy in developing real relationships with the spirits of the animal in question.

Developing Relationships with the Earth

Reciprocity is a fundamental requirement of a healthy relationship, yet western culture trains us to approach nature with the idea that we are dominant and more important. We see the natural world as secondary, a background to our story, a place we can enjoy ourselves. We use it for our purposes; our national forests carry the title "Land of Many Uses." We ask, "What can I take?" and we take timber, minerals, grazing rights, etc., rarely thinking about what we can give.

Even on vision quests, we are trained to focus on what we can get out of it. We're conditioned to think this way. It's like a virus in our consciousness and language. Our ideas, images, and expressions predispose us to take. We take a pill, take a photo, take a break, take a vacation. We take a hike, a piss, a trip; we get stoned, get laid; get away... We take everything, but what do we give other than a damn or a shit? We have poverty of phrases for giving.

We were born from and evolved out of the living earth, and we must have a healthy relationship with the earth if we're to know ourselves and be whole. No relationship lasts long or is healthy without considering both parties' needs. Harmony, balance, and power require reciprocity. We and the beings of this earth have evolved together. We are equal and related, with different gifts and medicine. If we're to develop a relationship to a medicine animal, we have to give to it as well. What can you give back? How can you do this?

After a profound encounter with a red-tailed hawk, I might begin by reading. I learn how it mates, hunts, and lives, seeing if there's a lesson about how to live or relate to my family. Perhaps I go back into nature to befriend, observe, and speak with Hawk. I can begin to take shamanic journeys to meet and communicate with the spirit of this ally. I assume I have things to learn, "homework" to do, requirements to fulfill, and commitments to keep if I'm to receive its friendship or gifts. I must learn to show up in this relationship, and I ask what it might want or require of me.

There are many possibilities for developing a relationship with a medicine animal. In shamanic dancing, you loan your body to the animal spirit that it might enter and experience this world. Let deer dance through you. Offer gifts to this friend and ally. Raymond Stone, a well-known Paiute sweat lodge leader, counted Bear as an ally. As the fire roared in preparation for the lodge, he'd come to its edge to pray. Holding a jar of honey over the blaze, he spoke to the spirit of Bear as he poured the sweet nectar into the flames.

Whether small or large, encounters with animals can help on your journey to wholeness. A wide and deep path is available to be pursued beyond the formal time of your quest. Bring these animals into your modern life, so cut off from the natural world. Remember to give back. If you want this spirit to guide or teach you, ask what it needs in return. Why did it come to you, and what can you do for it? It may want you to speak a certain truth, articulate a position, advocate for the environment in your community. It may ask you to grow a garden, perform a ritual, or help heal a logging site. Acts of reciprocity are important. Nature is alive, sentient, aware, and the plants and animals are waiting for us to wake up, to listen and come home — to act like one of the family.

There are no hierarchies whereby one animal is better than another. Alienated from our own imagination, power, and creativity, we live in a culture of celebrity, and we often bring it, like a virus, into our spirituality. Everyone has a past life where they were a witch, a high priest, or gladiator, but no one was ever an accountant, waiter, or janitor. This need for self-importance leads to a fascination with eagles, elks, dolphins, or cougars, for these big animals are considered powerful and we want to feed our hungry egos by associating with them.

Mouse and dragonfly are wonderful medicine animals, and they are neither lower nor less powerful than rattlesnake or hawk. Dragonfly eyes have thousands of lenses through which they observe the world. Through their medicine, aspects of the universe beyond our wildest imaginings come into view. Ants have a selfless, relentless focus, a trans-personal group mind as they work together with and for their community. Forget any ideas of higher or lower. Instead, think, "God comes to me in a dragonfly mask. Here is god as a raven, frog, or porcupine."

These meetings are rich and mysterious. No one knows why some animals come to us and others do not. In human relations, we hold to the principle that all people are created equal and everyone partakes of the divine. Yet some we relate to much better than others. Similarly, who can say why a particular animal has chosen us to establish a relationship? Just say "Yes" to the gift and follow it up.

SELF-CREATED RITUALS AND CEREMONIES

People choose to do a vision quest for many reasons. Some seek a non-ordinary experience that's different from and beyond daily life. Others want a rite of passage that ends one phase of life or way of being and initiates, claims, or welcomes another. Some come for renewal, to rekindle their spirit during their time on the land, while others seek purpose, direction, or answers to important questions. What follows is a compendium of rituals, ceremonies, and practices for letting go, ending, and saying goodbye to the old; for discovering, embracing, or integrating the new; and for attuning, deepening, and being present with what already, or eternally is.

RITUALS OF SEVERANCE

Severance means cutting off. You can sever a limb or sever a relationship. You can cut off contact or ties with someone. Rituals of severance are about ending things: ending attachments, obligations, situations, circumstances, behaviors, or roles. These may refer to what is external — relationships, careers, material objects, where one lives — or qualities we define as internal — addiction, self-pity, people-pleasing, or playing victim. Severance is analogous to extractions in the world of shamanism — the removal of what's toxic or doesn't belong. The following are commonly practiced and powerful forms for making these changes and ending some aspect of one's current reality.

VOMITING/EXPELLING

The ritual of vomiting (or expelling) can be undertaken as a general cleansing — all the toxins you've swallowed in life — or focused on freeing oneself of a specific poisonous residue; for example, emotional remnants from the relationship with your father, mother, abuser, etc. Vomiting is primal and graphic. It represents severance in its most literal form, and, used in ritual fashion, it's a method for release and rejection. When you vomit, something inside is cast out, and it no longer resides within you.

Begin by finding a spot where you can dig a hole in the ground. Make a prayer to Mother Earth that whatever "poisons" you carry might be released and transformed into something useful. Our request is directed there because the earth has an immense ability to break down and transform what's waste or toxic to one form of life and turn it into something beneficial, nurturing, and useful to the next.

In this ritual, we "vomit" the inherited or swallowed "poison" into the hole. In practice, this may involve speaking into the hole about the pains, hurts, attitudes, or disappointments in your life. You could spit, cry, scream, or wail out the hurt, suffering, or burden of self-hatred carried as a result of some part of your past. You might mimic the sounds and motions of vomiting as you expel the dis-ease from your being. Some have come close to vomiting or actually vomited.

When finished, rake the dirt and leaves back into the hole. Pat it down. Pray that you remain free of this poison and that it be converted into medicine: something useful, helpful, and nontoxic. Imagine that cleansing yourself of this creates space for something new to grow. Thank Mother Earth for listening, for accepting the poison, and for being your witness and friend as you free yourself to live a new and more fitting dream.

Expelling or excreting could also include defecating, spitting, pouring out, bleeding (for example, menstrual rituals), or sweating, part of the purification process in a prayer lodge. As you pray and sweat, you are also cleansed and purified, physical, mental, and spiritual toxins released as perspiration drips down into the earth. In expelling rituals, your physical body is both ground and metaphor for the severance taking place.

BURIAL

In the West, we bury the dead, and our language has phrases and metaphors of endings related to burial — "bury the hatchet," "bury the past," etc. The above-mentioned vomiting ritual also included burial once we released toxins into the hole. Burial includes the acts of covering, concealing, and reabsorbing as an expression of ending. But we also plant. We prepare for new growth through a very similar act, putting seeds in the earth. Both death and rebirth have the potential to be ritually enacted through this process of laying to rest.

Circles of air, circles of stone...
Earth circles, and night follows day.
We bury our seeds, we bury our bones,
While sacred birds circle and prey.

Some people on vision quests have brought ritual objects for this purpose, and they enact an ending through burial. One man, approaching retirement and seeking a positive vision of his new status, had worked as a high school principal for "way too long." Bringing the nameplate from his desk, he ritually laid to rest that symbol of his past life within the humus and roots in the woods of Vermont. Many objects might signify parts of your life that you wish to sever from. People have brought wedding rings, dolls, appointment books, jewelry, diaries, and mementos from childhood for use in these ritual endings.

If you don't have or don't wish to carry symbolic objects, they can be created by whittling, weaving, or writing. What no longer serves you may be instilled in a rock or twig. Symbols or statements can be written on birch bark, and thus invested with the essence of something you want to terminate. What you wish to say goodbye to may seem external — roles, positions, relationships, jobs, or things — or you may want to sever from qualities within yourself like self-pity or obsessiveness. By speaking to, breathing into, pressing, or writing on the object, you can imbue it with whatever qualities you want to leave behind. You might find things that embody some of the qualities you wish to be free of. A piece of obsidian — volcanic glass — may represent an attitude or belief that's hard, dark, cutting, or brittle. Burying it can help free us from its effect on our lives.

Doug, a man from the Pacific Northwest, "buried" himself. Finding a thick branch about 8 feet long, he placed one end on a low stump and the other on the ground. Using this as a ridgepole, he collected smaller branches, leaned them against this pole, and then covered the whole structure with leaves and pine needles to create a debris shelter. When evening arrived, he spoke to the setting sun about aspects of his life he was determined would not live to see the light of day. When darkness fell, he crawled into his cocoon, pulling sticks and leaves behind him to seal the opening. Like the caterpillar, he waited and endured the dissolution of his "old body." When the sun crested the hillside the next morning, he broke his way out of his sarcophagus to emerge newborn.

SMASHING

Smashing can be a powerful act of severance. Things broken are no longer whole; they have dis-integrated. A couple no longer together have "broken up," and people talk about their "split." To breach a contract, promise, or agreement means it no longer exists. At the end of your quest, you will "break" your fast.

Bob, separated and then divorced from his former wife, had two small girls from the marriage. Though the divorce was a year past, he had yet to finish. He ruminated, regretted, and wondered, "What if?" He felt emotionally stuck, mired in endless remorse and repetition. He wasn't moving on, and he wanted to be done.

On his quest, he found a large white stone that represented his marriage, hopes, and dreams. He placed the stone before him and proceeded to hold a death lodge. He spoke to the rock/marriage for one last time, articulating each of his regrets and ruminations, expressing all the failed hopes and griefs of the marriage. He talked, shouted, and cried, voicing every thought and feeling until he was finished. Finally, he stood, lifted the stone up over his head, and hurled it down, shattering it into pieces.

The largest piece represented his relationship to his former wife. He buried that stone to be free of it. Two of the smaller stones symbolized his daughters. These he put in his daypack, carrying them with him wherever he went to represent his commitment to their ongoing relationship. Through smashing and burying he ritually completed his marriage. Then he moved on, carrying his children forward in a tender and touching act of incorporation.

Sally's life was ruled by fear. Her parents had left her unprotected from her mentally unbalanced older brother, and her childhood was filled with torment. In her teens, she had been raped by her first boyfriend and later given a sexually transmitted disease by her cheating fiancé. She felt limited by ever-present and sometimes paralyzing anxiety.

During her solo, she created a "house of terror." Whenever she came across a solid branch in the woods, she'd drag it back to her spot. When her pile was large enough, she laid them up, tipi-style, naming each pole of the tipi to represent the various forms — abuse, betrayal, abandonment — of her uneasiness, foreboding, and panic. When finished, she crawled inside to feel and express her lifelong feelings of imprisonment. She screamed in anger and sobbed with grief. But eventually, she stood and, pressing against the bars of her "cage," felt the full force of her fury at what her life had become. Breaking out of her enclosure, she hoisted a hefty log she'd left outside and, wielding this staff of power and possibility, smashed that stockade to the ground.

In similar instances, people have built up walls with rocks or branches. These walls represent the walls they've fashioned in their lives, and they're later broken down. Others have shattered wristwatches, created and crushed clay figurines, or demolished other symbols of what imprisons them. If smashing seems appropriate to a ritual you want to perform, stay aware and respectful of the ecosystem around you. We do not want to enter the sacred world and leave a trail of rubble behind us.

BURNING

In much of the world, the dead are cremated. When something burns, what was formerly solid and substantial disintegrates and is reduced to ash and smoke. Little or nothing is left.

In the political arena, flags, draft cards, brassieres, and effigies have all been set afire as statements of severance. They signify that adherence to and participation in certain ideologies or ways of thinking are over, that some fidelity or allegiance no longer applies. Love letters are often burned to "clean house" and signal the end of relationship, and metaphorically, bridges are burned in situations where we never want to go back.

Many symbolic objects have been brought from home to be burned on quests. One man burned his wedding jacket to make closure on his failed marriage, while another burned his bar card and never practiced law again. Diplomas, photos, letters, a Ph.D. thesis, clothes, and citizenship papers have been taken to the mountain to be consumed by fire.

One can sever from qualities, habits, roles, situations, or relationships in the outer world, or from patterns in the mind, body, or psyche. If you are without symbolic objects, severance ceremonies can still be done with fire. Build a small blaze and gather a pile of sticks. Pick up the sticks as the flame is burning, and one by one, invest each with something you wish to let go of.

If this happens to be an internal quality or habit of thought, you might hold a piece of wood and state, "This is my self-pity" or "This is my sense of myself as a victim." Speak aloud. Describe your relationship to it, how long you've known it, and where it came from. Express gratitude for this quality and what it has given you. Perhaps at one point it helped you cope, comforted you, or gave you hope when you were blamed unjustly for things. Thank it for that help, tell it you no longer need it, and say goodbye. Wish it well and place the stick in the fire. Watch it burn and shrivel, giving you the last warmth and light before it leaves.

Pick up the next stick. Sense its qualities and energy — perhaps the conviction that you are responsible for how everyone is feeling. Speak to it. Appreciate how it once served you. If you were physically punished, it may have given you hope, the idea you could change your behavior to control the situation and avoid being hit. Thank it for once helping you to manage your distress.

People are endlessly creative. A woman collected dried grasses and fashioned them into dolls to be burned. Another wove cattails and reeds to make shields of her defenses. Wood has been carved into figurines; birch bark, written on or painted, goes up like a torch. Imagination can run wild in the wilderness. Materials and possibilities offer themselves to you.

If you are planning a ceremony involving burning, use fallen wood or plants that are already dead. Take care not to scar the earth. Collect a small number of sticks, branches, or roots, keeping it minimal if you are fasting in the desert or an area with limited resources. Make your fire in gravel or on rocks to avoid burning grass, humus, or organic matter. Erase any traces afterward. Make sure your fire is safe. Rake away dead grasses or leaves and protect it from winds that could send off sparks that would endanger the environment.

Many people's experience in nature has included time around a fire at night, but a burning ritual is not a campfire. You are not camping; you are on a vision quest. Fire is comforting and hypnotic, but on a vision quest, it's usually a form of avoidance. Fire becomes a substitute television, an escape from boredom, a retreat from the fear of being alone in the dark. On a vision quest, a ritual fire takes us deeper into our relationship with ourselves and the world. It's not intended to take us away.

WASHING OFF

Washing off includes removal, cleansing, and severance. Lady Macbeth cries, "Out, damn'd spot," as if removing the blood from her hands would cleanse the stain on her soul. Pontius Pilate washes his hands of "this affair" to deny participation in the condemnation of Christ.

In landscapes with lakes, rivers, and streams, the elements of washing rituals are readily available. Mud or clay can usually be found on the banks. Coat yourself with this muck to represent the poisons of your life, the pollution of your thoughts, the layers of falsehood or conditioning that mask your true nature or soul. Then let it dry. As it dries, it will shrink and feel confining. Sense how these habitual responses limit you. Speak of this constriction and your need to be free of it. Then enter the water and wash it off.

If there are no lakes or streams nearby, you can cleanse yourself with a jug or bottle of water. Many have used soil, clay, or ash to make marks or motifs on their face, legs, or chest, these designs representing whatever they wished to be free of. Someone may have written the word *shame* or *fear* on his chest, later ritually washing it off. Perhaps, after a few days, you just feel dirty, and rather than washing out of fastidiousness, you instill and infuse the dust and dirt with some quality of your life. As children, we come into this world receptive and innocent, like a fresh, clean towel. But after years of use or abuse, that towel becomes soiled and encrusted. Washing can be a way to return to one's state of innocence. Pour water over your head or dance in the rain.

CASTING AWAY

If you observe our highways, streets, and parks, you might conclude that throwing away is a national ritual. But, unfortunately, this is not done with connection or consciousness. Casting away can be a powerful ritual of release. Name and invest any object or substance — sticks, stones, sand, soil — with energy or impulses you are ready to part with — fears, obsessions, addictions — and let it go. One can cast sticks into a stream, rocks into a pond, logs into a swamp. Watch them disappear or be carried away. If you come to a high place, you can hurl objects over the edge. On a windy, gusty day, leaves, pine needles, small sticks — the chaff of our lives — can be cast out and taken by the wind.

CUTTING

To sever is to cut off. *Severing ties and cutting off contact* are expressions describing the end of a relationship. The act of cutting splits, divides, separates, divorces. In marriage, the wedding ring represents the circle of oneness and union. Upon separation or divorce, this ring is removed. Cutting hair can mark a change. In the biblical story of Samson, cutting his hair removed his power, his untrimmed locks a connection to his earthy wildness and strength. When entering the military, a person's hair is shorn, the old identity removed, and a uniform provided to signify the new. Many people have returned from vision fasts with alterations to hair, mustaches, or beards. They sever from an old look, an old face, and in the process incorporate a new one.

Cutting has similarities to breaking. We cut ties, cut classes, and cut corners to express our unwillingness to participate in some situation. One young mother, feeling her life was comprised of pleasing her two small children, husband, parents, and in-laws, brought several skeins of yarn to her fast. In a thicket of saplings growing closely together, she stood in the center, stringing the yarn between the shoots to signify all the ties, obligations, and responsibilities to her family and relatives. Finally, she was hemmed in, the expectations of mother, father, aunt, sister, children, husband, and in-laws trapping her in their midst. She shouted, screamed, cried, and prayed, fully feeling her frustration and victimization. Taking out her knife and hacking her way out, she severed the bonds limiting her freedom.

Tearing is a slight variation on cutting. Many have torn up letters, photos, or documents; ripped off clothing; and shredded uniforms or other items representing unwanted qualities. Untying is another version of severance. When we marry, we tie the knot. Dissolution would be the opposite, untying or unraveling. Rituals can be performed with string, rope, or cloth, the knots representing ties to people and situations or the twisted or constricted condition of our emotions or psyche.

Powerful rites of cutting, scarring, circumcision, or sub-incision exist in other cultures. In some native tribes, parents cut off a knuckle or piece of flesh to grieve when a child was killed in battle. These practices expressed both loss and transfiguration since they resulted in a changed body. Among the Maori of New Zealand, their elaborate scarring and tattoos announce to the world that the initiate is a different person. These changes cannot be overlooked. The upsurge of interest in tattooing may partly represent a deeper, mostly unarticulated desire for rites of passage and initiatory experiences.

If you're considering scarring or piercing as an act of initiation, I suggest caution. Some people can be drawn to it out of unconscious and unexamined self-hatred. Scarring skirts the edge of self-mutilation. It can express psychic states on the unhealthy side of the spectrum, a desire to hurt rather than know or claim one's self. I know some who have done it well. A man in his forties, finishing a divorce and entering a new relationship, received a medicine name, Two Crows, on his fast. He returned with the profile of two crows on his shoulder. He'd built a small fire, heated the blade of his knife, and blistered the shapes into his skin. It was a powerful ritual, an incorporation of a new identity and a new name, and he took it on with a new body.

LEAVING BEHIND

The form here is simple, concrete, and obvious. Walking away from and leaving something behind is a literal and metaphorical way of saying goodbye. A partner walks out on a relationship; someone abandons his commitments; we exit a bad situation.

People sometimes come upon parts of the landscape that can represent qualities of their life or psyche that feel negative, limiting, or dysfunctional. These places can then become part of ritual processes. A swampy wetland — a place that's hard to move through, clingy, and sucking you in — could symbolize depression, apathy, or hopelessness. Moving through thickets of spruce or hemlock, dark and crowded with dead branches, could remind someone of endless obstacles or incessant difficulties, whether that be paying the bills, other peoples' wants and needs, or critical voices that never stop. A washed-out arroyo could symbolize an internal barrenness or devastation; a cave evokes a sense of isolation or living in darkness; debris piles left by a flood signify the residue and damage of some traumatic event.

Finding (or creating) spaces that evoke negative associations gives an opportunity to enact rituals of severance. In simple terms, the person questing enters and spends some significant time in the negatively charged area, expressing, much like in the death lodge ritual, everything that needs to be said (or done). This could include someone's personal history of how this condition came to be, the power it has held over her, the limitations, cost, and feelings of being in it, throwing stones, etc. At the end of this time, the person leaves the space behind, announcing that she has finished and will not be coming back. And this promise is kept for the rest of the time out on the land.

RITUALS OF INCORPORATION

Incorporation is the opposite of severance. Severance is a removal. Incorporation — literally, "in corpus" — means into the body. This could include the physical, etheric, emotional, or energy body. To incorporate is to add, grow, include, or integrate something into one's life and existence. Rituals of incorporation can be considered analogous to techniques of soul retrieval in shamanic practice.

INGESTION

The most basic expression of incorporation is to swallow or eat something. Cultures familiar with the sacrament of medicinal plants like mushrooms or ayahuasca believe consuming the vine or mushroom invites the god or entity that lives in the plant to speak, teach, and heal them from inside. By ingestion, they welcome in a deity, doctor, or guide.

Incorporation-by-ingestion rituals have persisted in religious life. In communion, one takes in the wine, bread, or wafer to represent the flesh and blood of Christ. This hearkens back to primal rituals from more ancient times. In these older traditions, when a king or great warrior (many of whom were considered representatives of God) died, his followers would literally consume the body to take in his power. The spirit that enlivened him would thus be absorbed by his people.

On a vision fast you're only consuming water, but that does not preclude ingestion rituals. In full moon ceremonies, groups often gather and pass around a crystal or sacred object. Each member speaks or breathes his or her intentions for the current lunar cycle into the crystal, which is then dropped into a bowl of water to sit under the moonlight. The water, imbued with the moon's energy and group's intention, is then taken in, drunk in the morning.

On a vision quest, you can choose a small stone to invest with your intention and drop it into a water bottle. If you want to take in the energy of Father Sun, you can place your water out in the daylight. There are many possibilities for putting your hopes, intentions, or goals into your water. You could add stones, acorns, or other objects to drink in the energy of the earth, mountain, or your own unacknowledged anger or grief. Your voice, tears, or breath... a drop of blood, a wedding ring, or pendant from a lost friend can be dropped in. Drinking and taking in the power invested into these objects is a direct and visceral incorporation into your body.

ENTERING OR IMMERSION

You enter something — a college, relationship, temple, contractual obligation, stage of life — as a manifestation of beginning anew. The threshold ritual at the start of a vision quest includes the act of entering. During your solo time, you may discover and enter canyons, caves, groves, ponds, or rivers. Sacred or symbolic space can be either created or happened upon. As mentioned in the description of the severance ritual, many participants find elements of the landscape that speak to them of certain energies. These circles of power, swamps of despair, charred forests of burnout, lakes of fear, etc. can be occupied, inhabited, or left. Entering is a spatial movement from one area into another. The regions may be distinct or loosely defined. You might enter your inner darkness by crawling into a cave and staying there, but a more open area with sunshine and shade may serve for a ritual about encountering your shadow.

Immersions (or baptisms) are also acts of entering. If there are no streams or ponds where you quest, the earth in her various guises — sand dunes, mud banks, craters from fallen trees, masses of leaves — can function as places to be absorbed in. Burial can be symbolic of severance, but it can also evoke renewal and nurturance. In the spring, new life is conceived and gestated by being planted — embedded in the earth. You can ritually immerse yourself in the ground and "drink" of its energy, absorb the rich, sustaining power of mother Gaia.

But quest sites with water are common. In those, baptism can be a sacrament of initiation and purification whereby we are washed, cleansed of an old state, and anointed or consecrated to a new. In religious baptisms, one is immersed in a particular form of spiritual life, but other ritual acts of baptism may evoke or mark an entry into anything physical, social, or psychological.

BEARING AND WEARING

Across the broad range of human culture, incorporation has often been expressed by symbolic objects being linked to the body. What you wear and how you decorate or display your physical form sends a message for all eyes to see. In primal societies, images of masked, painted, or tattooed torsos spin tales of elemental energies and relationships to a more-than-rational universe. On a New York subway, Catholic nuns, Hare Krishnas, Hassidic Jews, Buddhist monks, and white-turbaned Sikhs are easy to tell apart, their religious commitments and outer loyalties made manifest by what they wear.

Our complex, modern life would be difficult to manage without the information communicated by dress. Knowledge and expectations about roles, authority, competence, class, and social norms are quickly conveyed by the "uniforms" of doctors, nurses, police, waitresses, priests, soldiers, TV repairmen, and judges, to name just a few. Even when our outfit doesn't serve any practical or necessary purpose in terms of social organization, it may well tell the world about our intentions and allegiances. Important messages are broadcast by what we wear to parties, work, church, or when we get into bed with another. Something as simple as the donning of a hat may announce something about the occasion we are going to, or our tribal bond with those who ritually chant and howl for the same football team.

Dressing in certain attire or decorating ourselves to incorporate desired commitments or energies is a ritual as old as humanity. In the past, going into battle could involve putting on war paint, particular colors and designs evoking courage, protection, strength, or the gods needed for victory. The chief dons his headdress of eagle feathers, hoping to see today's decision in the context of the big picture, while the jester puts on his outfit and clown face, giving him permission to do what otherwise might land him in a psych ward.

On vision quests, many people have clothed (or unclothed) themselves in ritual fashion, their change of status marked or announced by their changes in physical appearance. Leather has been sewn into medicine pouches; ferns, vines, and birch bark woven into wreaths; feathers braided into hair. Roots or branches have been twisted into and worn as bracelets, cattails made into shields, shirts painted or decorated with signs of a new dream. In one simple but meaningful ritual a man painted words, images, and symbols of all he wanted to leave behind on the back of his shirt, while the front displayed all he wished to move into. Whenever he walked, he moved away from his old life and toward the new. Others have painted themselves with ash, mud, or berries; put their hair into dreadlocks; and wandered through woodlands or across mountains surveying their realm in order to experience and claim their warrior, wild-man or magical energy,

Bearing or carrying expresses the same energy as wearing, and in many cases, the line between them is blurred. Police wear uniforms; they carry guns or badges. Kings put on crowns, carry scepters, and wear robes. Warriors shoulder their spears and don their armor. A cowboy might wear spurs and a Stetson while carrying a lariat. Earth-based people once wore medicine pouches with something sacred — cornmeal, a crystal, or bone — inside. Carrying these things was a reminder to bring into life a certain energy, relationship, or commitment.

In almost any gathering of people today, the majority will be carrying or wearing medicine objects. Wedding and engagement rings are commonplace, but many others sport necklaces, pendants, earrings, bracelets, or tattoos — objects or images that, consciously or unconsciously, have symbolic or ritual significance. The use of Christian crosses, Celtic knots, rose-quartz hearts, or Sanskrit letters adorning the body to embody certain energies or announce social commitments is widespread, and the popularity of silver, gold, turquoise, crystal, and gemstone jewelry comes from its symbolic associations, not its material or practical qualities.

It's common for people to bring medicine objects back from a vision quest. A rock in the shape of a heart, a riverbed stone evenly divided into dark and light, a stick whose knots and whorls create the face of an owl... the earth can speak to us through her physical forms in innumerable ways, and carrying those forms is one way to remember and bring the message back.

The aforementioned man who created a smashing and burial ritual around his marriage also carried forward two stones for his daughters. This ritual was simple, powerful, and beautiful. Simple is oftentimes the best approach, but peoples' creativity during their vision quests can be astounding. Many "spiritual warriors" have returned from their fasts with shields, staffs, or scepters, or with their faces, arms, or chest marked with patterns or paint. One fellow who embodied "wild man" by running through the woods covered with mud and ash was later determined to get in touch with his "king energy," his sense of generosity, strength, and connectedness. Gathering willow branches, twigs, ferns, crimson berries, and yellow flowers, he returned to camp with an enormous crown, this headdress trimmed with scarlet and gold.

Many a person has returned from his solo carrying a staff. Practically, staffs can serve as walking sticks, but they are also medicine objects signifying the vertical dimension — the connection from earth to sky, the joining of above and below. Staffs have their own natural and unique energy, but they can be modified and invested with meaning through carving — spirals, geometrical designs, the head of a snake, hawk, or raven — or tying on feathers, colored ribbons, or yarn.

PRAYER TIES AND PRAYER ARROWS

On the plains of North America, a vision quest site might be marked and surrounded by "prayer ties." Prayer ties were created as tobacco was placed in the center of small squares of colored cloth while prayers were made. The cloth was then tied into small pouches or bundles, hundreds of these embodied prayers enclosing and encompassing the area where the supplicant would cry for a vision.

The tradition of prayer arrows originated with the Huichol people of central Mexico. A prayer arrow is a medicine object that embodies and incorporates one's intentions, hopes, and vision into a form that is visible and concrete.

One begins by choosing a small branch or, better said, letting the branch call to you. After the stick is selected, people slowly and deliberately wrap it with colored yarns. Praying as they go, each turn of the thread represents a prayer. Eventually, they hold a staff, beautifully decorated with bands of different hue, which carries all their hopes or visions and incorporates their prayers. Other meaningful pieces — ribbons, feathers, etc. — may be added to the "arrow."

The stick is an arrow because, through the conscious and deliberate wrapping, one's intentions are focused; one's aim is made pure. The arrow is then presented to Mother Earth — given away to a tree, stream, or the ocean. Through this offering or giveaway, the arrow is let go. Or, if it feels right and important, it may, as a sacred or medicine object, be placed on an altar or incorporated into one's living space and life.

A brief note about prayer for those raised in the Western world: In the worldview of shamanic cultures, we pray for something that exists right now. Prayer is not about the future. Prayer is about present reality. Prayer is not, "I hope to win the lottery." If I were praying to be a better father, I would engage myself fully in the act, seeing, feeling, sensing, and imagining myself being a better father with my daughter. By itself, the sentence, "I want to be a better father," could be a string of words about a wish for tomorrow. It could stay on the surface.

In shamanic traditions, this better father already exists. It is a promise and a possibility, already a reality in another world that is not too far away. In active prayer, I invest energy in that potential — existing already — and through this investment, I make the likelihood of that potential blooming into this reality greater. In wrapping the prayer arrow, I see, sense, feed, and come to know the better father that exists already, and as I do, it blossoms, manifests, and grows within me.

WEAVING

Weaving incorporates. It gathers things together; it mingles, merges, and makes connections. Among the Navajo, weaving is a sacred art that combines and blends the separate threads of existence into the cloth of reality. Spider Woman, a major figure in southwestern mythology, represents the universal feminine principle of joining and interconnectedness, and the woven blankets, braided baskets, and beadwork, as well as the interlaced lines of dream-catchers, are expressions of this rich tradition among native peoples.

Many on vision quests have used grasses, reeds, twigs, string, hair, rope, and even dental floss to wrap and incorporate the various energies of life into a single, often artistic, entity. The father thread, lover thread, career and calling thread... weaving combines strands that may have formerly felt separate.

DANCE AND MOVEMENT

Embodying — whether images, energies, or commitments — is the bottom line, the core definition of incorporation. We've all seen people walking along the street that have taken on the posture and bearing of resignation and defeat. They shuffle along, bent over as if the whole weight of the world is on their shoulders. A warrior, lover, or child would never walk that way.

In yoga, as well as in Qigong and the martial arts, different poses or asanas (for example, the child, warrior, crane, or corpse pose) are associated with particular powers and attitudes, and one practices these poses to stretch the mind and energy body as much as the muscles. Ritual can directly engage the body, and you can examine, explore, and practice your "walk" as you go to the stone pile or wander the landscape. Notice how you sit — like a queen or like a monk? "Sculpt" your body to express something you want to incorporate; invite in the power of a particular pose or posture. Can you walk your talk?

Many have used movement or dance to articulate purposes, intent, or themes of their vision quests. Step into a circle to embody everything you want to leave behind. Perhaps you curl, tense, or shrivel up. Would you cower and hide, freeze into immobility, or adopt a defensive posture? Step out of that circle. Move into an area dedicated to all you wish to be, the new expression on your face and form announcing and celebrating your new "stance." Move back and forth between these areas. Find (or formulate) a fluid movement that connects the two — what you are leaving behind and what you are heading toward — in so doing create your incorporation dance, the embodied movement you intend to make in your life.

Though other humans are far away, one can still dance with a partner... or many. Grasses sway; leaves flutter; branches undulate in the wind. Butterflies bounce across the meadow; bats plummet past; stars spin and sparkle in the heavens. Join in! Don't be a wallflower; mirror and move with all that is in motion. Everything is swaying and shifting! Let whatever moves you come out into the world.

RITUALS OF ATTUNEMENT

To engage with the unknown, the vibrant present, we have to move beyond our everyday self. The "I" is not the center of the universe, and when this self is shrunk or removed from the center, the world around it expands correspondingly. The techniques and methods of all spiritual traditions involve forms and practices to break the obsession and constant self-referencing of the "I" and open to the other, that vaster, unexplored realm beyond its confines.

The traditional avenues beyond the self are many and varied. Some involve expressions of surrender, praise, gratitude, or prayer — energetic offerings in which we act and *speak from* the self (the known), but what we intend to *speak to* is beyond that (the unknown). Others use disciplines of the physical, sensory world that include ordeals, fasting, breath, yoga, or sound; evoke the emotions through fear, love, compassion, devotion, or ecstatic dance; focus on the mind, usually in the form of quieting it, as in meditation; or nurture the imaginative/visionary realms through dreams, art, poetry, shamanic trance, or the use of plant allies.

These practices can range from austere to elaborate, easy to difficult, from the vision quest and other initiatory rites to the simple expression of gratitude, but at their core they all seek to remove attention and energy from the self in its ordinary, consensual reality, and to emphasize and focus on everything beyond that... the changing, fluid, magical, and mysterious world of the unknown and the profusion of possibilities for perceiving and engaging with it.

The following rituals of the threshold focus on attuning to the present. They intend to neither leave behind nor welcome in. Instead, they aim toward deepening our attentiveness or access to inner or outer realities in their various forms, removing blocks and barriers we normally put between ourselves and the rich, vibrant existence we are embedded in. These practices, within the larger ritual of the vision quest, seek to alter, change, or shake up the ordinary self and its collection of habits and routines that keep us separate and disconnected from the world.

OFFERINGS OF ATTENTION – SPEAKING AND LISTENING

Making offerings is a means to connect with larger, unseen forces. The word "sacrifice" comes from the Latin, meaning "to make sacred," and human history is replete with stories of sacrifice to deities. These giveaways are based on a belief in reciprocity: that we and the universe (or gods) are in communion or dialogue, and by giving back we keep our relationship with the universe in balance. While some expressions of these sacrificial offerings — animals, blood, humans — seem distasteful in our current cultural milieu, we routinely bury thousands of blown-apart young men or women while praising the sacrifice they've made for their country. One could certainly question this form of worship and wonder why our gods are so ravenous.

Gestures of gratitude need not be dramatic or bloody, but they do need to be heartfelt. Gratitude is often part of smudging (see "Smudging" in Section VI), its expression carried by the smoke to the four corners of the earth. The act of giving, in this instance praise or thanks, is a way of connecting, acknowledging, and returning something to the spirit of the earth. It is the attitude and intention of giving, not necessarily what you give, that makes a difference.

Prayer is one example of an offering many people make daily. Anne Lamott (in *Traveling Mercies: Some Thoughts on Faith*) said there are only two prayers, the first being "help me, help me, help me," and the second being "thank you, thank you, thank you." The former is a request, but the latter is a gift of praise or gratitude. In many traditions, the first is done rarely and the second often.

Many native peoples offered tobacco, cornmeal, or herbs to the spirits when they hunted or gathered plants for food or medicine. Sun Bear, one of my early teachers, would search his pockets for coins if he didn't have tobacco with him. Gifting, or giving back, brings us to the world. The act of giving communicates with the spirits of place, acknowledging the life and presence about us. Giving up food as a sacrifice is part of every vision quest, and one can expand on this by consciously offering commitments, water, or other meaningful items to the mystery. And traditionally, the sacrifice of the ego or self — "thy will, not mine, be done" — was required at the doorway to illumination.

In modern, consensual reality, our attention is usually fixated on our internal dialogue, and we move through life preoccupied, somewhere else — at best, partially engaged in what we are doing. Speaking aloud — bringing our thoughts, words, and voice into, rather than away from, the world — can help us connect and weave ourselves back into the web of life. One may speak (or sing) to the Spirit, plants, mountains, wind, or sun. In the act of speaking, we come into the moment. Speaking out loud moves us to the here and now, and acknowledging what else is here — rock, canyon, cloud, raven, plant — brings us into a relationship with something outside ourselves. Addressing the world creates an "I-thou," rather than an "I-it" relationship. Speaking to "things" as the living presences they are brings them alive and makes them real to us.

When I Was the Forest

When I was the stream, when I was the
forest, when I was still the field,
when I was every hoof, foot,
fin and wing, when I
was the sky
itself,

no one ever asked me did I have a purpose, no one ever
wondered was there anything I might need,
for there was nothing
I could not
love.

It was when I left all we once were that
the agony began, the fear and questions came;
and I wept; I wept. And tears
I had never known
before.

So I returned to the river, I returned to
the mountains. I asked for their hand in marriage again,
I begged — I begged to wed every object
and creature.
And when they accepted,
God was ever present in my arms.
And He did not say,
"Where have you
been?"

For then I knew my soul — every soul —
had always held
Him.

— Meister Eckhart

The "dream" we believe is the reality we live. If our dream — our cultural story and presuppositions — says nature is dead, dumb, or without a soul, our "reality" will reflect its philosophy and emotional tone. If our dream recognizes the universe as a living, sentient entity, even in the middle of the desert with no human around, we are not alone. Something is listening and capable of responding.

We have to invest that dream with attention and energy in order for it to come alive. The literal meaning of recognize is to "know again." Recognizing and addressing this "Other," giving energy to this "parallel world" through speaking, calling, and singing to the river, mountain, or creosote bush, creates rapport and alliance with this living presence.

Prayer is one form of deepening and attuning through speaking. In its most basic or generic form, prayer is an offering from the known to the great and fundamental unknown. In prayer, we speak from the self, the personality, the identity we know, but we address something larger and outside of that. Prayer, no matter what name we choose to speak to, engages us with what we don't or cannot know, what we somehow sense and can only imagine. It attunes and moves us closer to The Mystery, toward something greater.

Prayer and various forms of focused attentiveness are large components of most vision quests. The word "quest" implies reaching for something outside the sphere of the self we currently know. To pray, speak to, and reach toward that something — whether we call it Great Spirit, higher power, Mother Earth, mystery, God, or "the Force" — is an almost natural expression of the urge underlying a vision fast itself.

Meditation is sometimes conceived of as a complement to prayer. If prayer is speaking to, meditation can be thought of as the practice of listening to the unknown or mystery. Traditional forms of meditation practice are varied and diverse. They may be religious or secular, gentle or rigorous, but there is a fundamental constant: the investing of one's attention in particular ways — breath, physical sensations, silence, mantas, an image of a deity — and its corresponding removal from the torrent of thoughts and dialogue. As the languaged, word-driven reality of the self or ego slows down or atrophies from lack of attention, space develops for other sensibilities and possibilities of perception to emerge.

The unknown is vast; its forms of expression are infinite. Listening to the unknown may involve receptivity to dreams or the recognition of signs or omens in sunsets, light reflecting off water, or the shapes of clouds. It can include engagements and encounters with dragonflies, rocks, gusts of wind, or callings that motivate us to follow butterflies, animal tracks, or the songs of birds, to name just a few. Conversation is a two-way street, and like the tree whose roots support the crown, the depth and sincerity of our prayers and spoken words open us to what could be, and surely is, speaking back.

OPENING OTHER WINDOWS OF PERCEPTION

Carl Jung said humans have four capacities, four "windows" through which they can know the world. These are named Sensing, Feeling, Thinking, and Intuition/imagination. As modern people who've inherited the worldview of Newtonian science and the Age of Reason — people who have been trained through a decade or more of public education — we have overdeveloped our rational minds, learning to view the world through the window of thinking, thinking, thinking, and more thinking. Rational analysis requires we distance ourselves from what we observe and think about. It values being detached — neutral, uninvolved, and unemotional. As a rule of thumb, any practice that leads us toward the other windows — our sensing, emotional, or imaginative selves — will bring us more into the present and engage us more intimately with the reality within and about us.

SENSING

Any of the common five senses can crack open a doorway to different realities, and many forms of changing perception can engage us in the moment in new ways. These practices can be entertaining or instructive, but they can also help us "stop the world," as Carlos Castaneda says. Much of our perceiving is driven (and limited) by the structure and syntax of our thought process and language. As a result, some aspects of the world we neither pay attention to nor perceive because they are outside our conceptual framework. Looking at the world in unusual ways helps us disassemble the consensual and socially constructed reality we inherit, and it may crack open the door for other possibilities to emerge.

Sight has been used as a vehicle to alter reality in multitudes of spiritual practices. Focusing one's attention on a single point, a candle, or sacred paintings or geometric designs (mandalas and yantras in the Hindu and Buddhist traditions) are methods that have been employed over centuries. In the world of nature, people can also practice using their eyes differently to see the world in new ways. A few of these practices are described below.

One can choose to "take on the eyes" of something else. Lie down and observe the world like snake or mouse, from ground level. Stay for 20 or 30 minutes, and you'll perceive many things you've never noticed before. Or, as children do, bend over and look back through your legs to see the world upside down. It is still a world, yet a different one. Stay until that sky becomes "real" for you, the blue sky becoming bright mountains and the mountains the darker sky.

Reversing foreground and back is another way to open perceptual doors. Lie down; gaze up at the sky through the branches of trees. Make the dark pattern (the branches) the background and bring the sky (the light pattern) to the fore. Create a "tree made of sky." Or, looking at the natural world, observe all the shadows. Bring them into focus until you have a "landscape of shadows."

We can change our focus through different forms of "gazing." Our habitual attention is similar to taking a series of snapshots. These "snapshots" may last a few seconds at most. We walk through the world paying attention to what is in front of us. Our eyes move, our heads turn, and we refocus on what now enters our line of sight. Gazing is a practice where one does not focus on anything. In it, you allow your eyes to go soft, to not "grab" anything. Sit and gaze at lichen on a fissured rock, or the textured, layered bark of a ponderosa pine. In a short while, shapes begin to change, images emerge, and new worlds open up in what was once just "rock" or "bark."

Or, walk slowly while allowing the whole visual field to be like a river flowing by. Let it move past or wash over you like a steady visual stream, your eyes relaxed and grasping at nothing. Soon your feet, belly, and fingertips become more alive and sentient as you move through a landscape different than before: separation diminished, vision peacefully resting within rather than "looking at" things.

One can practice this form of gazing along with non-rational wandering to evoke a nonlinear, dreamlike state. In normal walking, we head out with a plan for where we want to go. Instead, walk with no plan at all. Meander. Let yourself be led by whatever calls you; go wherever "something else" wishes to lead you. When the ego — the control-seeking I — is surrendered, other voices have a chance to be heard.

With practice, **hearing** can also "bring us to our senses" and closer to the presence in all things. The spiritual traditions of the world have long used sound to change people's consciousness. Rattles, drums, and musical bows have been employed by shamans on every continent to journey or heal. Incan flutes, the overtone droning of Tibetan monks, and the intense staccatos of the Balinese monkey chant bring listeners and practitioners to altered states. Specific rhythmic beats are known to alter brain waves, entrain the mind, and promote trance states and highly receptive forms of awareness. Newer technologies have developed ways to embed subliminal rhythms into music to promote concentration, meditation, or sleep.

Chanting, rattling, drumming, and singing have been important parts of innumerable vision quests, the vehicle of rhythm and sound ridden into visionary and other landscapes. Spirits have been called and prayers sung through the long nights of purpose circles. Many have brought rattles, drums, or flutes to the mountain. Others have fashioned instruments while there. A tin can, duct tape, and a handful of stones can create a perfect-sounding rattle. A plastic water jug can make a drum; a bottle with a neck, a flute. Every stick, stone, or branch has its particular resonance. How many of the world's instruments have evolved from finding the right things to hit together?

For the ancient Hebrews, the vowels — A-E-I-O-U — were sounds that expressed and shaped the breath, while consonants represented the breaking and cutting of this breath. Early written text included only consonants because breath was considered spirit, and spirit was not to be made concrete or fashioned into "graven images." In India, every sound in the Sanskrit language represented a spiritual energy or principle, and to chant or sing the names of the gods, as practiced in Kirtan, was to evoke their presence. The primal word/sound of A-U-M (or OM) combined *A*, the beginning of the breath; *U*, its shaping; and *M*, its closing or ending, and finished with the silence underlying all. And, in Castaneda's books, Don Juan has Carlos "listen to the silence" underneath or between all the sounds.

On a vision quest, we both literally and metaphorically leave the daily, familiar world behind. This provides an opportunity to explore and experiment with these worlds of perception. We can listen in different ways, sing or drum to the mountains, hear the voice under all the other voices, sense the sound of hearing itself. Many have reported hearing their own heartbeat or a swish as blood moves through their inner ear. Sensitive instruments report the planet itself has a regular rhythmic wave, and many have returned from their solos having heard melodies, rocks singing, or ancient voices carried on the wind.

We can also come closer and more attuned to the earth through the vehicle of **touch**. The skin is our largest organ, but the vocabulary of touch has become an atrophied language in Puritan-influenced cultures. We can become more intimate with the earth when we remove our defenses. Taking off our clothes, stripping away the buffers between ourselves and the world, will do that quickly. Many on quest explore being naked.

The smell and texture of moss on the skin, the cold, silky shock of one's body entering water, and the rough abrasiveness as rock meets foot stop all thinking and bring us to the moment.

Some choose to close their eyes or blindfold themselves and explore an area tactilely for a period. These experiments can seem initially uncomfortable and unfamiliar to an "I" identified with a visual reality within a stream of thoughts. But a quiet joy slowly grows as we become closer to the earth, sun, wind, and water, rediscovering our sensuous bodies with all their strengths and vulnerabilities. Our minds abhor the unknown. But our bodies love it.

FEELING

Feeling is very different from thinking. Thoughts have distance. They are "about" things, separate from their objects. Enshrined in the Western world as the basis of real knowledge, true "objectivity" is defined as unaffected by emotion, not influenced by anything below the neck. Highly educated or intellectual people have decades of training in this activity, having been taught that emotions and feelings are unreliable and not to be trusted.

Feeling is the purview of the mid- or mammalian brain. It is home to our longing for connection, love, and resonance... and the distress when all that is missing. When we feel something, we become very present. Distance shrinks, perhaps to nothing. Feelings can wash over and overwhelm us, and it could be they have us as much as we have them. In a flood of feelings, the separate self, or "I," may disappear.

Since feelings are hard to control — in fact, may require a loss or lack of control — it is difficult to make them happen. If they offer an avenue or pathway to a different engagement with the world, how do we walk down that road to get there? Feeling is unlike sensation. Our musculature and motor skills respond to will, and we can change or manipulate our physical circumstances to alter our sensory experience.

One ritual for accessing feeling is called the "Truth Mandala."[8] A large circle is created — a border of stones, a line in the sand — and divided into four quadrants that represent difficult emotions. There is a quadrant for fear, another for anger, and one for grief, sorrow, or loss. The final quadrant is called emptiness, and this represents an absence of feeling, which could be experienced as numbness, apathy, or confusion. A smaller circle or stone is located in the center as a place of hope. Each quadrant is then marked with a staff, bone, or another symbol to remind us of the emotion being represented.

When you are ready, step in. If you enter the quadrant of anger, speak or express — out loud — all you are angry about. This can be past or present, personal or political, small or large. When finished or moved, step into another quadrant to express your fear, grief, or loss. Move around the circle as you are drawn. Return to quadrants you have previously stepped out of as memories or new feelings surface. Just begin. Speak your truth about love, dashed dreams, rivers and rainforests, your friends, your father, or your future. Oftentimes speaking the words will stimulate the feelings. Feel free to cry, scream, pound, or wail.

When you're done, having fully expressed your truth, step into the center and feel the power of your emotional life. Give thanks to the earth for having listened, for giving you the eyes, ears, senses, and heart to feel all this. Acknowledge the hope inherent in our capacity for feeling, recognizing that this pain alerts you when something is toxic or out of balance. Realize that your anger, fear, and sorrow are like your immune system, marshaling and mobilizing the possibility, energy, and opportunity for change. Say "Yes!" to your longing to live — truly live — even amidst all the suffering and injustice.

Another practice for moving past our habitual selves, "presenting your ego to a tree," can also be found in Section VI, More Rituals and Exercises.

IMAGINATION AND INTUITION

Mapping the Landscape of "Reality"

Our last nonthinking window through which we know the world is the realm of intuition and imagination. The myths defining modern life tell us that what's imaginary is unreal, train us to ignore the world of dreams, and demand we pay attention and focus on "reality." In so doing, they ignore, and we become blind to, the true power of imagination: the ability to draw otherwise separate phenomena into a single entity, into an image.

We live in three realities:

1. Primal or objective reality: the world of trees, rocks, stars, atoms, molecules, heat, light, gravity, etc. This world is unaffected by what we think of it.
2. Subjective reality: people's "inner world," with all its beliefs, stories, prejudices, joys, sorrows, dreams, and exceptional or dysfunctional ways of engaging life. This world is experienced and perceived by no one outside the subject.
3. Inter-subjective reality: the collection of "imaginary entities" like money, religions, corporations, nations, and "families," which — when masses of people agree on and believe in them — form the rules, structures, and codes that, mostly unexamined, define and give form to peoples' lives and experience.

Imagination's power is immense. Imagination strings the gossamer lines that join seven separate stars into the Big Dipper. Stars exist in primal, or objective, reality, but a sky populated by Orion, Leo, and Cygnus... by heroes, gods, bulls, and flying steeds who tell their stories across the heavens... testifies to the power of imagination. Rivers are a facet of primal reality, but the assertion that one wet, clay bank is in Ohio while its opposite resides in Kentucky is a totally imaginary distinction.

Financial institutions, savings accounts, towns, licenses, legal rights, and citizenship — most of what we experience as the reality of modern life — depend on agreed-upon imaginary concepts. Some consequences of these agreed-upon imaginary realities of the present and past — nations, kings, gods in heaven, Pharaohs, divine rights, and master races — have resulted in genocides, slavery, oppression, and the miseries of millions. Today, wars, economic injustice, and the epidemics of anxiety and depression are direct results of the unexamined belief systems (imaginary realities) that structure and set the rules for the world we inhabit. In fact, it is often the pain, emptiness, and dysfunctions resulting from that world that inspire or compel people to seek something else by undertaking vision quests.

On vision quests, people enter into a changed relationship with the various "realities" they are conditioned to inhabit. Embracing solitude and gaining distance from consensus reality allows the intersubjective dreams of the culture to dwindle and recede. Through fasting and living on the land, a person enters a much deeper encounter with primal reality and all the forces and beings that comprise it. Ans, as people remove themselves from culture (intersubjective reality), their inner subjective reality emerges and comes to the fore. As primal and subjective reality become more prominent, the contradictions and disconnections between them and intersubjective reality may become highlighted, and all those previously unexamined social agreements become more available for renegotiation.

Exploring Imaginary Landscapes

Vision quests are times when imagination — mostly ignored or dismissed in daily life — reemerges and flowers. There are some straightforward reasons for this:

- The lack of competing images (from computers, televisions, billboards, radios, etc.) leaves us to our own devices. Our inherent imaginative abilities no longer get lost in the noise and static.
- The effects of fasting — a decline of focused, hyperactive, "type-A" awareness and activity — ushers in a more dreamy, associative state.
- A radical increase in free time comes about as the list of tasks and "things to do" shrinks to almost nothing. "Nature abhors a vacuum," and this time that's newly empty is a fertile field waiting to be seeded by our imagination. Much of the preparation process supports a greater imaginary component. Many exercises or ritual processes require or assume imagination. For example:
    - The people spoken to in a death lodge are called forth and visualized. They're not in one's physical, objective reality.
    - When we call in the dark, our mind's eye sees into the shadows.
    - In prayer, we address forces and entities in other worlds.

This time of heightened imagination also results in an increased awareness and remembrance of dreams, which are often significant in the vision quest process. Dreams bring perspectives the rational mind hasn't thought of and certainly didn't create. They carry messages that can be arresting and emotionally charged. Freud labeled dreams the "royal road to the unconscious," and much of Jung's work was rooted in explorations of the dream world. And, if part of our intention on a quest is to free ourselves from the habitual, repetitive, squirrel cage of our internal dialogues and thinking mind, most anything arriving from the dream world is a valuable gift.

(For a further elaboration of this, see "Dreams and Dreaming" in Section V: Themes Within a Vision Quest)

Simple tools for dreamwork

As mentioned, being on a quest often results in an increase in the frequency, power, and remembrance of dreams. "Energy flows where attention goes," and in daily life, our attention is scattered and focused on a thousand other things. Walking into the wilderness takes us away from all that distraction, and attention and energy are freed up and more available for those things that are usually ignored, dreams being one. By using a few simple tools and techniques, we can augment and help ourselves access this rich and vibrant world within. Since energy flows where attention goes, just giving greater attention to the dream world will increase the likelihood of dreams responding and coming to visit. Here are a few simple ways of doing this:

- Have pen, paper, and flashlight nearby when lying down to sleep.
- Ask for a dream before settling in. (One can ask the night, stars, God, the mystery, Gaia, or the "other world.")
- Ask for a dream about a specific subject, problem, or issue. (If you then remember a dream, assume that it was in response to, and therefore about, what you requested.)
- Make your requests imagery-rich. Saying "please send me a dream tonight" takes six words. But a picture is worth a thousand words. For example, imagine picking up a heavy stone and carrying it to a well. Feeling its weight, you bring it close to your mouth and whisper, "Help me bring back a dream tonight." Then, placing the stone in the bucket and turning the crank, you lower it into the well. (Or just drop it!) Hear the splash, and you'll know your intention has entered deep waters.

When a dream arrives, thank the Mystery (or whomever you asked) and write it down. Once the dream has been recorded, there are several possible ways to listen to what it has to say.

- The most common method, used in most analysis, is just to write it down and ask what it means. This may lead to useful insights but analyzing a dream for its meaning takes it right to the head, back to the squirrel cage of rational thought. Something evocative and visceral can become intellectual.
- Let the other characters speak. It's useful to believe that every part and character in a dream scenario is a part of ourselves, a part we don't recognize (and hence is appearing as something else.) Normally, when recording a dream, we take the point of view of the "I-character": "I was walking down a path... I saw a cabin with a light... I was scared... etc." The I-character is our habitual self or ego, something we're all too familiar with. Letting the other characters speak allows different, hidden parts of our psyche to have a voice.
  - For example, imagine we dream of a fruit tree in a field, and, when we get to it, we became frightened upon finding a large bear eating apples on the far side of the trunk. We could record the dream again, this time speaking from bear's perspective. Or the tree — the voice of fertility or the knowledge of good and evil at the center of the garden — might tell its story, watching the human approach as the bear gobbles and snorts at its base. The apples themselves, or a hawk circling overhead, might have their own, different, stories to tell, stories the rational mind — the I-character — would never consider.
- Invite the dream characters into the daily world. The morning grows late, but you're still immersed in the richness of this dream. You remember you have to go to the stone pile. You put down the journal, get to your feet, grab water and daypack, and start to make your way down the hill. But something nags at you, and you stop, turn around, and say, "Hey Bear, want to come with me to the stone pile?"
  - Inviting dream characters to join us in daily life can teach us about their power, message, or energy. Imagine that dream bear walking beside you, or out front, or behind. Speak out loud; converse. Listen to what wants to be said. Imagine bear behind you, walking into and merging with you. Feel what it's like to move through the world as bear. Spend the day together. Discover who he is, and who you are when he's there and present.

- Reentering the dream: We've been taught that it's this reality (the daily world) that counts, and that dreams have value insofar as they contribute — insights, solutions, etc. — to our everyday life. Our relationship with our dreams, as with the natural world, tends to be exploitive — "What can I get from them?" But the ultimate authority on the dream is the dream world itself. Rather than "what can my dreams add to daily life?" I could ask a different question, "How can I change my routines or my daily life to improve my access to the dream world?"

After awakening, we assume the dream is over. Why assume that? If we were listening to a sporting event on the radio and then changed stations, we'd take for granted that the game continues. We might decide to tune back in later. Morning comes; our eyes open; the station changes to "awake!" But perhaps the game continues on, and we can return to its enchanted world. Going back to a dream — lying down, closing our eyes, and relaxing — we can pick up where we left off and through activating our imagination reengage and learn directly from the source.

(If you wish to "work" a dream in a group, simple instruction on running a dream council can be found under "Dream Work" in Section VI: Other Rituals and Exercises.)

SECTION V:
THEMES WITHIN A VISION QUEST

The Hero's Journey **113**
The Call to Adventure 113
The Realm of Primal Forces 115
The Return 117
More about Monsters and Allies 119
The Unknown 120

Dreams and Dreaming **123**

Myth: The Power of Stories **125**

Ritual and Ceremony **127**

Additional Themes **128**
Archetypes 128
Council 131
Death as an Ally 132
The Other Story 133
Paradise Lost 134
Prayer 134
Sacred Space 135
Wounding and Shamanic Initiations 135

SECTION V:
THEMES WITHIN A VISION QUEST

THE HERO'S JOURNEY

Many people have read the book *The Trail to the Sacred Mountain* as preparation for a vision quest. In it, a quest is described as a rite of passage that consists of three parts: severance, the threshold, and incorporation. But the quest also follows an archetypal mythic progression of three parts. Understanding this guiding myth clarifies the function and structure underlying a vision quest and helps people see their personal journey in a larger context

In the seminal work *The Hero with a Thousand Faces*, Joseph Campbell asserts that the multitudes of myths, legends, and fables throughout the world are variations on a single essential story, the heroic journey. He labeled it a "mono-myth," its universality derived from the fact that it mirrored a process of growth and change that is unvarying and hard-wired into human beings. The particular characters, faces, forms, landscapes, and locations may seem dissimilar on the surface because peoples with different cultures and beliefs work with different "software," but the basic configuration of the story remains constant.

THE CALL TO ADVENTURE

The three-part structure of this guiding myth begins with a Call to Adventure, in which the hero or heroine is compelled to undertake a journey. This journey takes the protagonist beyond familiar territory to a realm where he has never been before. He goes on this quest to seek, resolve, explore, or find something. The goal can be represented as a magic potion, the Golden Fleece, buried treasure, release from a curse or obligation, advice from an oracle, or a hundred other things, but the essential feature is the lead figure being summoned out of ordinary life to have an encounter with the extraordinary.

Sometimes this happens spontaneously as the hero follows some natural inclination. A hunter wounds a deer. Tracking it for what seems like an eternity, he finds himself in an unknown landscape where the forest is strange, foreboding, or magical, where his usual responses and old orientations don't work anymore. In a different story, Alice thinks it peculiar as a rabbit hurries by holding a watch. Curious, she follows it. As she tumbles down the passageway into Wonderland, the world around her changes dramatically!

In a second version, the adventure begins with the hero or heroine being swept up by outside events. The captain and crew are blown off course by a great storm and find themselves stranded in an alien land. Jonah is swallowed by a whale and descends into an abyss. Dorothy's life moves through a flat, featureless landscape until a swirling wind catches her up and takes her to Oz. This new land is colorful, wild, magical, and scary, with enigmatic wizards, frightening witches, and strange companions.

Finally, our hero may undertake the adventure willingly because something is unsustainable, threatening, or out of balance at home, and a solution beckons from some realm outside the everyday. Civil war rages in the kingdom, and the hero seeks the oracle to find who is the rightful ruler. The king is dying, and someone must search for the Water of Life to heal the ailing monarch. There are battles to be fought, dragons to be confronted or slain, treasures to be found, curses and enchantments to be lifted, gods to be propitiated. And each of these quests involves going forth into the dangerous unknown.

These myths and stories are still relevant because they are symbolic — outer representations of our inner psychic lives. The choice to participate in a vision quest may represent following some call. People may have desired to do something like this for years, and, whether they can articulate it or not, a deep longing or attraction draws them away from ordinary life to explore the landscape of the soul. Or, like sailors blown off course, some may come to this threshold having been swept up by life's events, their direction altered as divorce, a visit to the doctor, a work crisis, or a loved-one's death causes their world to become unsettled and radically different. Now, having been thrust into this new and unfamiliar landscape, they must walk down a path they've not traveled before.

Is there trouble in the kingdom? Does civil war lay waste the landscape in the form of a relentless self-critic that destroys the heroine's enthusiasm and vitality? Are there dragons demanding sacrifices — addictions and obsessions that consume her life energy; that prey upon her childlike, innocent impulses and rip them to shreds? Is our protagonist angry, sad, frightened, or depressed? Does she quest because there's an inner or outer demon that must finally be confronted and faced?

Some come to this journey to lift curses and enchantments. Enchantments represent a condition in which people are living lives that are not their own. In a myth or fairy tale, you might be a prince, but someone has condemned you to be a frog, so you live in the mud and croak. Or the princess lies asleep, dormant, unable to be awakened. Her unconsciousness is deep; her aliveness and vitality far away and inaccessible. In daily life, if we still struggle with our parents' expectations, the values of success our culture teaches us, or the presumptions of what a man, woman, or spouse is supposed to be, we are under a spell and playing out a life that's not truly ours. Some spend their lives struggling to make their way to the top of the ladder without realizing they've placed it against the wrong wall. To lift a curse or enchantment is to claim your own authority and values, write your own story, and live your own life.

The wind, one brilliant day,
Called to my soul with an aroma of jasmine.
The wind said, "In return for the odor of my jasmine
I'd like all the color of your roses."

I said, "I have no roses. All the flowers.
In my garden all are dead."

And the wind said,
"Well, then I'll take the withered petals,
And the yellow leaves, and the waters of the fountain,"

The wind left, and I wept.
And I said to my soul,
"What have you done with the garden entrusted to you?"

— *Antonio Machado*[9]

The mythic condition could be one of famine or drought. Like Machado says, the land may have become barren — the springs dried up, the crops withering, the cattle gaunt and infertile. Demeter grieves for her daughter, Persephone, and the earth turns brown and wasted. Myths of famine and drought represent a condition where spontaneity and creativity — the joy of life — have disappeared. We're tired, burned out, going through the motions. Life seems empty and meaningless. The vitality and happiness we knew as children are gone; the mythical garden appears as a bunch of dead stalks. What happened? How did we get here, and what must we find or do to make it live again?

Campbell reminds us these great myths and stories are about us, today, not superstitious tales from a faraway past. And the many individual ways through which someone may be called, compelled, or driven to face his or her unique monsters and challenges through a vision quest represent a healing process that is ancient, archetypal, and prototypically human.

THE REALM OF PRIMAL FORCES

Whether lured by a calling, swept up in a tempest, or driven to seek help by a crisis, our hero or heroine is brought to the second stage of the journey: entering The Realm of Primal Forces. Alice tumbles down into Wonderland. Dorothy is transported to Oz. Orpheus descends to the underworld. The three brothers embark on their adventure to seek the Water of Life. The sacred twins of the Navajo traverse swamps that suck and reeds that cut in search of their father. Strange, dangerous, and frightening, magical powers and possibilities abound as we cross the threshold into the second stage of our journey.

In every myth, the central figure must leave home to enter this numinous realm. The answers we seek are somewhere else. They are never in the tribe, castle, or village. They are not in Athens, New York, Kansas, or Sedona. The magic potion is not to be found at the pharmacy; the Golden Fleece does not lie on a shelf in "Home Furnishings." One must set sail across dark seas, climb mountains, enter the dark forest, or journey to the underworld. Unfamiliar landscapes harboring great forces await us.

Simply put, "leaving home" means you are not going to find what you're looking for by doing what you always do. The really deep questions, the conditions that trouble the heart and the soul, will not be answered by doing the usual things faster, more efficiently, or with better management. Change must take place at a deeper level. Magic, truth, passion, purpose, or power won't be found by playing the same old tapes and programs. We must step outside our habits, routines, beliefs, judgments, our opinions about the world and ourselves. The journey begins by leaving something — culture, comfort, convenience; our normal, habitual, socially constructed reality; our home and village... the old story — behind.

Leaving home always appears dangerous and frightening. There are monsters in the sea. A vicious, three-headed dog (Cerberus) guards the road to the underworld. Returning with the Golden Fleece requires sailing through a channel where rocks smash together and crush every ship. Dorothy must kill the Wicked Witch of the West, Perseus behead Medusa, and Alice face the Queen of Hearts without losing her own. In every instance, difficulties and dilemmas appear. Demons, dangers, and darkness inevitably lurk in the new territory.

The stories, with their terrors and wonders, delights and danger, reflect a fundamental truth. When we enter unknown landscapes — inner and outer — and engage with new energies and possibilities, the ego feels threatened. It is not at home. The self and its stories are all about the known; conventional life seeks security. The ego would say, "I'm interested in the unknown; tell me what it's like." The familiar self wants to turn the unknown into the known before it will consider it. But our strategies, stories, and attempts to get attention — to keep the self important and at the center of the universe — are useless in these new circumstances. The unknown lies outside the comfort zone, and it challenges the known and all its assumptions, rules, and definitions.

In the realm of primal forces, the ordinary concerns of daily life are far away. Security and the attempt to control the world to avoid discomfort and change dissolves as the world we know starts changing. Now, something in us must change and respond to meet it. The old self and all its strategies no longer serve us. What we've formerly clung to like a rock will sink us like a stone. We are confused, anxious, and uncertain; our defenses are down. Our fears appear as monsters, dangers, obstacles. The situation seems perilous. We feel unprotected, afraid, open, and at risk. We become vulnerable.

There are always dangers in the realm of primal forces, but the stories contain a saving grace. When the challenge is accepted and the commitment to the journey is made, allies appear. There are friends, healing forces, and guiding spirits in the primal realm as well. A dwarf by the side of the road tells the youngest brother the way to the Water of Life. Spider Woman reveals secrets that allow the sacred twins to pass through the swamps that suck and reeds that cut. A stranger offers a song to lull the dragon to sleep. A message arrives in a dream or a bottle; a goddess appears. A dove flies through the channel that crushes ships, and, as the rocks rebound and separate, your boat passes through. David Whyte, in *The Well of Grief*, says:

Those who will not slip beneath
the still surface on the well of grief,

turning down through its black water
to the place we cannot breathe,

will never know the source from which we drink
the secret water cold and clear

nor find, in the darkness glimmering,
the small round coins
thrown by those who wished for something else.[10]

The Well of Grief tells us to take the plunge: "turning down through the black waters to the place we cannot breathe." Our fear urges us to hold back, but if we do we'll find nothing, becoming like those who remain at the edge of the well, throwing in the "small round coins" with a wish their lives will change.

In these myths of heroic adventure, allies, spirit guides, and healing forces are there to aid us. But they do not appear until the commitment to the adventure has been made. Standing on the dock before departure, you worry about the monsters in the sea. You feel and sense them, wonder, "Is the craft sturdy enough?" Are your maps any good; is the crew trustworthy? You've heard tales of what lurks in the forest, seen strange shadows and shapes beyond the boundaries of the known world. Fear is your constant companion as you step across the line. Yet you set sail into the storm and resist the urge to turn away.

On a vision quest, we stand at the threshold, about to enter the primal realm. We enter nature, wilderness, the territory of the unknown. How could we possibly have an encounter with the unknown while staying in our own houses? How could we meet our maker by staying within a world that we (humans) have made? We must step beyond the worlds we have created and enter that larger world that fashioned us if we are to encounter anything worthy of the terms "god" or "spirit."

Campbell assures us that helpers and allies await us. But they won't be found if we refuse to take the journey. We are first called, challenged to make a commitment, to face our monsters in the unknown. Once we take that step, a beacon appears before us, and allies, friends, and guides arrive by our side. Those of good heart always succeed. The dragon is slain, the Water of Life found, the enchantments lifted. Golden apples and magic potions are carried back. The Lion acquires courage; the Tin Man gains a heart, and Dorothy finds her way home.

Participants in vision quests enter the realm of primal forces both literally and symbolically. They have left an actual and familiar home — house, family, work, community, conveniences — to journey to the quest site. When the solo begins they will leave behind even more of what's routine and familiar — phones, books, human conversation, and companionship — to enter a (more or less) unfamiliar landscape. Some may have never camped before.

The monsters that appear at this time may appear to be internal or external. Common external monsters are fears of animals (bears, rattlesnakes, etc.); concerns about being cold, hungry, or uncomfortable; and fears of getting lost, feeling bored, or being alone in the dark. Those fears can sometimes be great, but anxieties around external monsters are usually distractions from, or peripheral to, the core purposes of the quest.

Internal monsters are generally different. Fears and feelings of shame, worthlessness, depression, failure, hopelessness, or not being "enough" are old, and they have a life and field of action outside the wilderness setting of any particular quest. Consciously or unconsciously, they are closely related to issues of purpose, and often what the hero needs to face and confront to live a free and authentic life.

THE RETURN

The third and final stage of the heroic journey is The Return. The protagonist has heard the call and set off into a realm of great and primal forces. He vanquishes demons, slays or subdues enemies, and overcomes obstacles seeking a treasure, gift, or relief from some difficulty. The completion of the adventure entails coming back from that magical realm to reenter the life that was left behind.

Coming back, the hero must bring a gift. He may carry wisdom, the blessing of the gods, or a story that needs to be told. This gift can be simple or complicated, abstract or concrete. It's been portrayed as chests of treasure, sovereignty, healing herbs, love potions, magical wands, or cloaks of invisibility. As a metaphor, this gift represents new vision or commitment — a connection to truth, passion, power, or soul. The hero's final task involves becoming an agent of change, making a difference and manifesting a transformation of himself or his surroundings that bring benefit to the community. The cycle is complete when this fresh energy helps to heal and renew the world.

DANGERS

Sometimes, the journey home is the most dangerous part of the adventure. After the Trojan War, it takes Odysseus ten years to make his way back to Ithaca. On the way, he and his crew are battered by storms, tempted by sirens, captured by Cyclops, bewitched and turned into swine by an enchantress. By the time he spies his homeland, all his men and ships have been lost. And even then, he is not safe. His court is overrun by scoundrels, as dukes and lords scheme to marry his wife, dispatch his son, and steal his kingdom. Forces are at play that would be threatened by his return. Many do not want him back.

In Grimm's fairy tale, "The Water of Life," the youngest son secures the life-giving liquid to heal his father, the dying king. But his older brothers deceive and betray him. They steal the magical fluid in hope of winning favor and ultimately inheriting the throne. They take what is wondrous, precious, and sacred, hoping to turn it into what is social and profane — wealth and power.

After any profound encounter with something extraordinary — with Spirit, the rawness of your real experience, a sacred dream... finding your authentic voice, power, purpose, or direction — bringing it back into daily life is daunting. The tugs of comfort and inertia are strong. There can be forces at home threatened by, or hostile to, the new energy. Something important can be lost if we succumb to those interests. We must face the challenge of returning to our communities and the dangers lurking there.

In myth and story, this conflict between the old order and the new, between the sacred and the profane, can appear as danger in the return. Whether personal (habits, routines, attachments of the ego) or political, the old ways of being do not give up easily. Individuals and institutions are fond of their power and position. People have a stake in things remaining as they are. If the new energy cannot be co-opted, it may face outright assault. Wealth and privilege do not easily hand over the keys to the vault.

There is no guarantee that change, personal or political, will be welcome, no matter how brilliant the idea or needed the message. In the outer world, justice, peace, equality, ecological balance, available health care, access to goods and services — all fine goals and noble aims — will always be seen as a loss of power and profit to some. On a personal level, change is inconvenient and requires effort, and it can be seen as threatening by those who want to avoid their own call to adventure. "Security" is often a catchword for an unwillingness to face and confront one's fears, though it leads to a life forever ruled by them. Forces of inertia or injustice may need to be confronted. The castle may be full of scoundrels, and, like Odysseus, you may have to fight to claim your throne.

Danger in its various disguises — resistance, co-opting, and betrayal — can play out in an individual's psyche and in family systems, work environments, and the great stage of history. Gurus and spiritual teachers cash in on their popularity and fame; the Utopian vision of Marx is crushed by the iron fist of Stalin, and the teachings of Christ are overwhelmed by the church's obsession with opulence and authority. The great new hopes of JFK, Obama, health care reform, etc., are sucked down by the swamp of moneyed interests.

BALANCING THE SACRED AND PROFANE

The challenges of the return alert us to the difficulty in bringing a new vision or dream into being. As the hero arrives home and attempts to integrate into her community, an understanding or accord must be struck between the sacred and profane, the magical and the mundane. A successful return requires having our feet in both worlds. We must remember our journey, our time in the realm of primal forces. The connection to the numinous world of spirit — to an order of values outside social rewards — needs to remain strong. If we become distracted, and our attention captured by the common concerns of social reality, the gift will be co-opted, the new wine repackaged in old bottles, and our creative vision slapped on a billboard to sell insurance or real estate.

But there's an equal danger if our allegiance abides wholly with the sacred at the expense of the practical. Then, our ideas and intentions may go nowhere, our hazy hodgepodge of poorly articulated visions and airy-fairy dreams lacking incentive or grounds to galvanize or motivate anyone. The world is a play of light and shadow, terror and wonder. Cooperation and symbiotic relationships characterize every natural system, but so do predator and prey. Childlike innocence may be charming; vulnerability, openness, and surrender necessary to grow and embrace a larger dream. But naiveté and an otherworldly aura are sorry strategies for engaging our daily world. Monsters, obstacles, and challenges of another sort lie there as well.

If we do not address these important issues, something crucial can be lost. A negotiation, a reconciliation and agreement — between doing and being, between vision and current definitions of reality — is vital if the return is to be meaningful. Forgetting either of our sacred responsibilities — our connection to something greater or to the requirements of daily life — makes us one-dimensional and devoid of depth. Abandoning our footing and ground in either world is like losing a leg. Vision becomes crippled, and meaningful movement ceases as we're unable to walk our talk.

FINDING FERTILE SOIL

The return is the final stage of a great death and rebirth cycle. The hero leaves the old story behind and traverses territory outside the lines and limitations of the cultural consensus. Her encounter and engagement with what's both perennial and extraordinary lifts the veil, and it leaves her with new perceptions, powers, and allegiances. These new seeds must then be brought home and planted in the ground of community and daily life.

Growing this garden can be a delicate matter. The creative and renewing vision (the kernel to be germinated), needs fertile soil — allies and situations that will welcome the new way of being. It will require sure and steady work — weeding, watering, fertilizing, and pruning — to usher fresh ideas into reality. Whether we plant roses or apples, marigolds or marijuana — however we intend to bear beauty, happiness, peace, or nourishment to the world — husbanding those seeds through to harvest requires effort and consistency, for there is no lack of forces — weeds, scab, scale, and beetles in the natural world; hostility, indifference, laziness, or attachment to comfort in the human — that can reduce our dreams to rubble.

The challenges are not finished when the hero returns home. Like her, we must face all the voices, in the world and in ourselves, that drain our energy, deplete our resources, and hinder us from bringing the new dream to fruition.

MORE ABOUT MONSTERS AND ALLIES

DANGERS AND OBSTACLES

Myths tell of monsters in the depths of the sea, of forests with dense and tangled thickets. Sirens seduce the traveler and lure him to his death; the passage to the underworld is guarded by a ravenous, three-headed dog. Dangers abound on the journey: things that devour or maim; spells, riddles, and labyrinths that confuse; false treasures, rumors, and intoxicants that distract.

These dangers tell us the soul's "dis-ease" is not easily cured. The journey is difficult and hazardous; the Golden Fleece is not down at the local 7-Eleven. Simple solutions – eating blue-green algae, reciting affirmations, accepting Christ, or listening to the latest news channeled from the Pleiades – will not get us to our destination. We cannot skip over the dark and frightening sea. The road to life traverses the valley of death; the gate of heaven is accessed through a long dark tunnel. Spring's flowers follow autumn's dying and the numbing cold of winter.

This does not sit well with many. Modern perception is linear. We look for progress and see growth as a matter of more: more money, happiness or leisure time; more sex, knowledge, time with the kids; building a new addition on the house. Spiritually, we want to reach higher planes. We seek enlightenment (more light) and run from darkness and death. Our new-age metaphors celebrate transformation – a caterpillar becoming a butterfly. But a caterpillar does not become a butterfly by going on a SlimFast diet, repeating affirmations, and sprouting paisley-colored wings. In fact, a caterpillar does not become a butterfly at all – it spins a cocoon around itself and disintegrates.

Monsters, dangers, tests, and ordeals tell us something: that our healing process requires facing our demons, and that we must revisit and open, not cover, our wounds. We need to confront, know, accept, and befriend our rage, grief, unworthiness, bigotry, arrogance, numbness, cowardice, terror, losses, and judgments. We must enter and face the darkness, endure the long dark night of the soul, conduct what Alcoholics Anonymous calls a "searching and fearless moral inventory."

This healing process is shamanic, not additive or linear. The shaman drinks the poison and transmutes it to nectar. Christ turns water into wine. We recapitulate our lives, claim what we've lost, and give back what's not ours. The archetypal and mythic journey guides us from the personal to the universal. Engaging our personal demons ushers us into a universal story, and through this process, these personal wounds become sacred.

ALLIES AND GUIDES

We do not have to take this journey alone, although we must be ready and willing to do so. In the archetypal stories, assistance is usually available. Magical aid comes to those who are worthy and of good heart. Ariadne provides Theseus with a ball of string to find his way back from the labyrinth; Athena gives Perseus sword and shield to defeat Medusa; Dorothy finds companions and is assisted by the good witch.

Help is available, but it may not be apparent at the beginning. Magical forces and friends appear, but only after committing to the journey. Early on, the dangers seem obvious or overwhelming. The path looks dark, the sea stormy, the swamplands impassable. The heroic journey is not a Club Med vacation, and perhaps it's not surprising so few take it. Experiencing the grief and terror of an alcoholic childhood, exploring the landscape of physical or sexual abuse, plumbing the depths of one's loneliness, entering the darkness of repressed desires or self-hatred – these are difficult journeys all.

But when the die is finally cast, and the commitment made, allies, friends, guides, fellow travelers, and magical help does appear. When we follow the call, Campbell says, doors open where none appeared before. The alcoholic facing her disease finds the fellowship of AA and the guidance of the twelve steps. A chance conversation at the coffee shop leads to someone revealing her story; a friend or stranger guides you to a support group, workshop, or therapist. An advertisement for a retreat grabs your attention; books seem to leap off the shelf. Other travelers who share insight, courage, and hope walk beside us. Visible or invisible forces appear and convince us we're not alone.

THE UNKNOWN

The unknown is an unexpressed but major theme in the heroic journey. The hero is called to leave home and all that's familiar to enter the realm of primal forces. This realm, where the landscape, characters, forces, rules, and course of action are all strange, challenging, and mysterious, is synonymous with the unknown.

Since the unknown is fundamentally "unknown," it's hard to speak directly about it. Our whole world — our "reality" — makes up the known. This includes science and the laws of physics; our definition of self and who we think we are; our assumptions about the cosmos (such as that the world is made up of objects like atoms, rocks, and stars); and all our notions of God, source, time, etc. So how *do* we speak about it?

We come close to the unknown through symbols, images, and metaphor. "A picture is worth a thousand words" reminds us that images and metaphor can convey things our logical and linear minds have difficulty grasping. Where (and what) is the unknown?

When we perceive an iceberg, we know 90 percent of it lies unseen below the water. Science tells us that 90 percent of the universe is made up of some mysterious dark matter that we can't perceive. Neuroscience reports that our limbic system, or subconscious, processes information a million times faster than our conscious mind. And yet, the statement "we use ten percent of our brains" implies, among other things, that most of the brain seems to be attending to something we're unaware of. Psychology has coined the term "unconscious" to represent all aspects of psyche above, below, beyond, beside, or outside of consciousness.

We can think of the known as the conscious mind. Other images — dark matter, the limbic system, the unconscious, the iceberg, the soul or spirit realm, the dreamtime — can all be useful metaphors in our attempts to grasp the unknown. At the very least, bringing attention and energy to the unknown can enrich the landscape of daily life, and, moreover, provide insight or experience that's quite extraordinary.

Reaching toward the unknown involves moving beyond the self. Carlos Castaneda's teacher, Don Juan, constantly exhorts him to "shrink his self-importance," reminding him again and again that the "I" is not the center of the world. When the self shrinks and is removed from the center, when the self-referencing internal dialogue stops, the world around it expands correspondingly. The methods of all spiritual traditions involve forms and techniques to break the obsession and constant self-referencing of the "I" and open one to other (and vaster) realms beyond its confines.

In quantum physics, the known is dissolving. Reality looks relative and relational. The universe is probabilistic — a seething field of possibilities — and the old rock of reason has broken down into shifting sands. Primal cultures referred to the living presence of this Unknown as the Great Mystery. It was the source and origin of all facts, shapes, forms, and expressions of existence; the wellspring from which emerged all things of the world which could be experienced and known. It was a focus of reverence, symbolized the matrix and mother of our being-ness, and was background and field from which all our perceptions emerged.

The phrase "primal forces" conjures up images of power. The unknown implies mystery. This realm of power and mystery must be faced and encountered to find our strength, gifts, and magic. To experience the Great Mystery is to know God, the Source, the Creator. To experience does not mean to think about or understand. To experience means to be intimate with. Developing a loving relationship with this unknown, a relationship of appreciation, gratitude, and respect, is to find one's place in the universe, to belong and have a home. Creating and sustaining this relationship is the primary task of life, and it results in feelings of peace and a sense of wonder, purpose, and connectedness with all parts of creation.

FACES OF THE UNKNOWN

The realm of primal forces is the unknown. After the heroes leave home, they enter a realm that is strange, frightening, enchanting, and mysterious. The landscape is different — volcanoes, underground passages, seas with strange currents. Gnomes, dragons, dwarfs, fairies, witches, elves — unusual and sometimes magical, characters appear. It is a dangerous place, yet captivating and exciting as well.

Monsters and allies, both present in the realm of primal forces, are the twin faces of God, those powers and energies beyond the self we know. In heroic journeys, they arrive together, like sacred twins. In the landscape of the soul and the shadowy areas of the psyche, they are, ultimately, one and the same, monsters being the rejected or dark aspects of divinity. As Joseph Campbell says, "Every demon is just a god we haven't recognized yet."

Power and divinity appearing in both the light and shadowy ends of the spectrum tell us the unknown can manifest in many different guises. Expressed as an outer world in myth, the new landscape could be wet, swamp-like, and uncrossable except by boats. Or, it could be accessed by falling down a rabbit hole or being swept up in a tornado. It might be high in the mountains, a temple in the sky, a castle shrouded in fog, or a cave deep underground. Monsters and dangers manifest as wicked witches, dragons, or vile creatures with snakes writhing out of their scalps. They show up in impossible tasks that need to be accomplished, mist-filled bogs filled with quicksand, or seductive temptresses offering tasty herbs that take away your memory.

Viewing myth as metaphor, the realm of primal forces and the unknown are symbolic of the psyche and its inner landscapes, landscapes that appear differently to different people. And this is true, for the unknown is always relative to what one knows, to what is habitual, comfortable, and familiar. The word "shadow," in its broadest sense, refers not just to those things that are dark and socially unacceptable. All aspects of yourself that are invisible, that you can't see, can be considered to be "in shadow."

If you live in a psychological landscape where you are always, polite, helpful, and smiling, the unknown may fit the classical example of "shadow" — all those repressed impulses of the psyche that are angry, resentful, self-centered, and aggressive. You might kick the dog when no one else is around. If, however, what you are familiar with is shame — if your life has been saddled with low self-esteem and the acceptance of criticism or abuse — it may be your "gold" — the divine child, the heroic leader — that is invisible and unknown to you. In the realm of the unknown, elves, fairies, and grand soaring creatures are just as likely as things that slither in the dark.

Culture has a strong effect on what takes residence in any person's psyche. In a society disconnected from nature — or if one's personal history includes learning to fear the natural world — wildness, sensuality, and the body will represent the unknown and will tend to be located and expressed as part of one's shadow. In Western culture, indigenous people have traditionally been seen as barbarians, savages, or, at best, underdeveloped, as opposed to connected to their natural harmony and integrity. Similar forces may play out in anyone's psyche, where, in addition to repressing and judging the wild parts of oneself, nature itself may be demonized or projected onto others. Consider the emotional tone of "he's an animal."

In highly rational people and a society focused on being practical or reasonable, expressions of irrationality may be disturbing or threatening, and thus appear in the realm of primal forces — Alice in Wonderland, for example. In some systems (the Fool card is the first major arcana of the Tarot) there is a tradition of crazy wisdom, where the clown or fool has a perspective that's "out of the box." In the rational West, tricksters, clowns, cats who speak in riddles, and things that make no sense are generally, like the Joker in Batman, seen as dangerous or untrustworthy rather than a potential source of poetry or creative knowledge. For some, loosening up is dangerous, and having fun just isn't funny.

In patriarchal cultures, the feminine or "anima" may be exiled into shadow. Although changing rapidly over the last 50 years, this has been a powerful shaping force in Western Christianity. For two millennia we've had a heaven and vision of divinity with no female characters; blamed Eve for all our problems; and seen the feminine — Mother Earth — as something to be used, exploited, and dominated. Many men have been raised within this good ol' boy culture, and for them, the feminine qualities within them may be caricatured, demonized, denied, and/or projected. The demeaning words "sissy," "fag," "wimp," "cocksucker," etc. barely scratch the surface of some men's fear of the feminine. These forces and tendencies — like Medusa, the Queen of Hearts, or the Wicked Witch — may appear quite threatening.

In the heroic journey, everyone must enter this unknown, this primal realm, and encounter the divine and threatening forces there. What's threatening and unknown for one may be the polar opposite of what's uncomfortable to another. The shadow, the lost self, and what's unexplored, rejected, and exiled can differ for everyone, but it lives in the primal realm. These can include the feminine; our sensual, instinctual drives; the spontaneous, innocent self; our fierce protectiveness (warrior or mother bear); our passion, rage, or wisdom, etc. — any or all may be waiting to be discovered, experienced, and integrated.

Whatever is there must be faced, defeated, or befriended. The co-existence of monsters and allies tells us there's gold to be found in the darkness. There's a richness to be gained in facing what's been rejected or forgotten. Growth comes from accepting, even welcoming, the psychic forces that have been cast out and exiled from the Garden, however they appear, whatever they are. Whenever we encounter dragons or dark passageways, there's probably a chest of treasure nearby, waiting to be discovered.

But those trunks of diamonds do not come easily. The heroes must do their underground work. They must earn their gold. As mentioned, what's unknown and frightening exists in relation to what's known and comforting. If wholeness is our goal, we must travel in the direction we've avoided and invite to the banquet all those we've banished from the kingdom.

In the cycle of the seasons, the darkness and death of winter lead to light and rebirth at the spring equinox. In a world that's round, traveling westward ultimately brings us back to the east. The inner journey has the potential to bring us outside ourselves to the universal, and vice versa. In the story of The Devil's Sooty Brother, soot and ashes turn to gold. In the dark underworld beneath the earth's surface lives Hades (Pluto), the god of riches. The realm of primal forces invites us to accept, surrender to, or integrate the frightening or rejected forces within us. As Rilke says in "The Man Watching,"

Winning does not tempt that man.
This is how he grows:
By being defeated, decisively,
By constantly greater beings.

DREAMS AND DREAMING

On vision quests, the theme of dreams and dreaming can weave in and out of the presentation and the solo experience. First, participants often see an increase in their dream life — or remembered dream life — on their solos, and sometimes before. Leaving home and traveling to a new place where they meet new people — people also committed to working on their inner lives and matters of the soul — creates fertile ground for seeding the garden of dreams. This intentionality (of the group and themselves), along with fears and other emotional forces bubbling to the surface, makes the emergence of major dreams, sometimes even before arriving, more common. Since the frequency and power of dreaming appear so closely connected to the quest, the subject should be addressed in some way. Tools for working with dreams can and perhaps should be offered. They fit well within the subject of imagination or practices of attunement.

Although the theme of *dreaming* does not occupy a central place in the description of the heroic journey archetype, the realm of primal forces — those frightening, fluid, and magical fields of possibility outside the familiar, seemingly solid world of reason and fact — is in many ways synonymous with the world of dreams and dreaming.

When introducing the quest employing the metaphor of the heroic journey, issues and questions about "leaving home" — what it means — can be used to help the participants think more broadly or deeply about their intentions as well as think outside the box. Home (the box) is a frame of reference that can include desires for material comfort and security and outer attachments to energy-draining relationships, jobs, etc. It includes inner attachments to people-pleasing, low self-esteem, fear, judging others, etc., as well as cultural assumptions and attachments: to success, god-in-heaven, being reasonable, etc.

The reality of our daytime world — the box — is

a. "Objective," materialistic, and populated by objects that are separate from each other;

b. Disinclined to give credence to emotions or any non-physical realities that might affect that static and solid physical realm; and

c. Wedded to reason and thinking as the tools and processes for determining what's true and real.

In contrast, in the world of dreams, outer and inner realities are fluid and constantly influence each other. And it's this world, or an awareness like it, that has to be accessed on a vision quest. Because if our inner and outer worlds aren't connected in a fluid call-and-response with each other, there's no point in praying, no point in speaking about our intentions, no point to ritual, and no reason to go on a vision quest as opposed to a meditation retreat.

The following short exploration of the world of dreaming has proved useful to share in many groups, whether formally in circle or informally around a campfire.

....

In our current mythology, dreams are considered illusory and don't satisfy our requirements for "reality." Nonsensical and irrational, they're regarded as irrelevant to our daily lives But, in the view of many peoples throughout history, we dream all the time. Unaware that we might be dreaming, we call our dream "reality." In so doing, we consign other states of awareness — the "realities" of primal peoples; the ecstatic journeys of shamans; the consciousness of the night — into the trash heap of the "unreal." Those rich storehouses of other perceptual possibilities appear as threatening or unimportant, leaving our vision circumscribed and making us destructive and dangerous to all those whose consciousness roams outside our fenced-in yard of respectability.

In our daily dream, the elements of the world (the tangible nouns of existence) are separate. I am myself, a tree is a tree, a stone is a stone. This separation is relatively permanent — it will be there tomorrow and the next day and the next — unless physical interactions intervene to change it. A stone can be broken, crushed into gravel, ground into sand. A tree can be cut into lumber, chipped into mulch, burned to ash. I can die, be eaten by worms, decompose into soil.

For us, dreaming awareness differs radically from waking awareness. In the dreamscape, things change constantly. We can transform shape or appearance and perceive from different vantage points. Our perception can be local or non-local; our awareness not attached to or contained in our "body"; the world shifting with us as objects and scenes mutate, move, and morph along with every other part of the dream.

Like a river, a dream is far more than a noun. It is an activity, a verb, a process; and in this non-separated, non-dual awareness, we can be the dreamer, the dreamed, and the dream. To primal peoples, sages, shamans, and mystics, this fluid, mutually defining and interacting relationship found in dreams is another way to perceive and assemble the world. And with its shape-shifting boundaries of inner and outer, you and me, self and world, it approximates the way the universe actually works far better than the static and separate "dream" people call "reality" in daily life.

With landscapes more than three-dimensional and horizons vast and infinite, the dream world possesses an ecology that's deeper and richer than the circumscribed expanses of the day. Its panoramas are potentially as real, and in many ways more so, than the unchanging and soulless flatland of physical reality in which we moderns have become imprisoned. Dreaming encompasses a far larger, not a lesser, universe than the one we are used to.

Today, most people live in the smallest psychic space of any humans in history. We've lost connection to the great cycles of the seasons, sun, moon, and stars. We find ourselves unable to listen to or value the wisdom of our bodies, feelings, or imagination. And we've become strangers to or threatened by alternative reality states and other modes of perception sought by people throughout the millennia. In other cultures, shamanic, mystical, and non-ordinary states were highly valued and sought for the wisdom, healing, and inspiration available there. And in those more soul-oriented cultures, methods for inducing *dreaming* — through plant medicines, fasting, ordeals, religious trance, etc. — were highly developed.

To paraphrase Jung, humans have four modes of perception, four ways to let in the universe and engage with the world. He called these avenues *sensing*, *feeling*, *thinking*, and *imagination*. Our current system of education trains us in only one of them — thinking, thinking, thinking — and this faculty has become the foundation and paradigm of knowledge. This constriction of focus is like buying a stool with one leg. You can use it all you want, but you'll always be out of balance.

In the dreaming universe, the windows of the imagination are flung open. Images, associations, and possibilities refuse to stay in line. They proliferate, run wild, and overlap. In the halls of science, you study water in a beaker, but in a dream, you are the ocean itself. And there, you must learn how to flow, dissolve, swim, and surrender, for if you stay in your head you will drown.

Dreams are not *opposed* to reality, though they've been defined so in the paradigm we've inherited. Our myths and stories, *our dreams* — and the possibilities and relationships allowed in and excluded from them — *determine what our "reality" is*. We should cease arguing over whether our dreams are true, since the reality and truth we experience is a result of our dreams, and instead ask whether our dreams are worthy. Are they good, broad, and deep enough? Do they locate us within the grand dramas and cycles of life? Do they create a sense of gratitude and wonder? Do they connect us with the past and future, with our ancestors and children? Are our dreams inspiring, enlivening, guiding, and sustaining... or draining? Do they deserve our allegiance? Are they dreams worth living?

In the world of dreaming, "inner" and "outer" shift, and mutually define and penetrate each other. It's an oxymoron to "know oneself" as a separate entity, for the separate self doesn't exist. In this field of possibilities and potentials — many currently undiscovered and unexplored — I will not "find myself" in isolation, for the world outside can change, catalyze, or evoke in me that which has yet to come forth. In dreams, relationships are all-important. All aspects are relative — they exist in relationship to each other. When everything is related, the many forms of being are all relatives, and we are no longer alone. As we rediscover and reclaim our capacity for dreaming, we can belong to and be part of the family of life again.

In the Dreamtime, creation is present, palpable, and happening now, not just a historical event. In this numinous realm, the self is multidimensional — a verb more than a noun, an act more than an "it" — and reality lives, senses, reacts, and responds. In this world of great forces, the unknown dwarfs the known. The universe and landscape are alive; magic and mystery abound; the possibilities are endless. And if we wish to explore, experience, and learn, curiosity and wonder are far better guides than facts.

MYTH: THE POWER OF STORIES

The ills and issues of people today are not just a consequence of problems in their personal histories or difficulties in daily or psychological life: work, relationships, money, or bad parenting. They also result from mythic dismemberment — being cut off from the great cycles and stories that have guided humanity through the millennia.

Myth's function is to bring together the great and the small, the eternal and the transitory. For millennia, myths taught that people, nature, and "reality" were multi-layered and multidimensional. They connected people to the great web of life, and to roles and tasks that were archetypal. Having deep relationships with these important, but now ignored, aspects of existence results in feelings of belonging and a realization that we can, and do, make a difference. By reconnecting to something larger, healing can take place.

For thousands of years, men and women came together, told stories, faced danger, hunted, gathered, and did what had to be done to protect and serve what they loved. Together they celebrated the joys and grieved the losses that came with these responsibilities.

Today the greatest dangers are no longer "out there" in the physical universe. The current mythic landscape of isolation and disconnection — from the feminine; from our bodies, feelings, and dreams; from nature and the earth — is where most ills and issues of modern individuals take root and play out. The real darkness lies inside the human soul, spawning dysfunction and danger throughout the world. And in these times, we need courage, good companionship, and mythic guidance no less than ever.

Myth and rites of passage have been central to human culture as far back as we have records. Which is primary? Were myths developed and told, with rituals developed to enact the stories and teachings articulated in the myths? Or did rites evolve first, with myths then articulated to fit, support, and round out the experience of people who participated in those ceremonies? Whatever the answer, myth and ritual arise together in human societies. And certain images — of seasonal changes, heroic adventures, and rites of passage — appear over and over and serve as metaphors for changes that are core to the human experience of growth and maturation.

These images, expressed in stories and enacted throughout history in ceremonies and rites, attuned and linked the human world to the multitude of forms and movements in the larger web of life:

- To the cosmos: the sun, moon, and stars; the turning of the earth and the seasons;
- To the elements: the great powers of the earth, air, fire, and water;
- To the past and future: our ancestors and those still to come;
- To our relatives: the plants, animals, and other species — all those children born from the (mother) earth and (father) sun.

On vision quests we work with many stories:

a. The grand "mythologem" of the hero's journey,

b. The life stories (functional or not) the participants bring with them,

c. The account or chronicle of the solo time itself, and

d. Other tales — from past participants or our own lives; from different cultures, traditional folktales, and myths — that may prove instructive or helpful.

In some sense, every myth is a story, but for many people immersed in our current cultural consensus, there's a great deal of confusion about what myths and stories are, and what they aren't.

A common use of the word *myth* — for example, in the statement "that's a myth" — implies that a myth is something unreal, synonymous with a lie. In other circumstances, the word *myth* is used to denote (and denigrate) someone else's belief system. But people making these judgments are usually unaware that they have their myths as well. The modern point of view that we're living in a world or time free of myth is itself a myth. Rather than signifying something unreal or false, it is our myths, usually unconscious, that determine what gets labeled real or unreal in the conceptual universe we live in.

All myths are projections. And all myths are metaphors. Myths are projections in that they arise from archetypal forces (universal patterns) in the human psyche. Those "constellations of energy" need to be brought forth to be shared and communicated. This bringing out, this projection, casts them into form as ritual patterns that appear across cultures, as petroglyphs and paintings on cave walls, and as stories that survive for millennia. This creation of an outward form and representation originating from an inner condition — as in all creativity — is called projection.

To say that myth is metaphor conveys that the stories (paintings, songs, rituals, etc.) are not literally true. But concurrently, those tales convey and reveal a truth or perspective that's larger, deeper, and more multidimensional and nuanced than what the rational, logical, and literal language of the neocortex is capable of describing.

Aphrodite, taken literally, looks like a pain-in-the-ass, high-maintenance drama queen. But as a representative of sexuality and desire — the alluring pull, the primal urge in all life to mate and procreate, along with its capacity to undermine and destroy valued forms of social relationship — her whims, fancies, and jealousies become more profound, and her alliances and conflicts with other gods instructive.

The story of Jesus, taken literally, makes as much sense as Santa Claus. However, the dying and resurrected god — a theme present in many myths throughout the world — evokes the cosmic cycle of death and rebirth as winter becomes spring. It can also represent the process of transformation as one form passes away in the creation of another; the mysterious relationship of spirit and matter; and questions of identity, when what's timeless and eternal manifests in a life that's form-bound, dualistic, and temporary.

There may be no answer to the age-old question, "Am I a man dreaming he's a butterfly or a butterfly dreaming he's a man?" Yet, it's important to ask. Reality is always more than you think it is. Asking the question implies an openness to other possibilities, an acceptance of an ultimate mystery. The most important question around myth and story is, ultimately, *whether you're aware you're telling them or not*. Are you open to possibilities other than the dream or story you're identified with? "God loves the wicked who know they're wicked far more than he loves the righteous who know they're righteous."[11] Can we, pointing out another person's myths or "stories," be aware that the judgments behind the finger we point are based on stories we're telling ourselves?

There is no reality without myth, no reality without stories. Myth and story determine the ground upon which we stand. They determine the definition of "me." They determine what our "reality" is. Stories, like masks, express and reveal truths that could not be stated otherwise, while simultaneously having the potential to conceal other truths. And of course, as myths tell us in so many ways, it is not the stories themselves, but the stories we're unaware of – our shadow – that gets us into trouble. *"God loves the wicked who know they're wicked (who recognize their shadow), far more than he loves the righteous who know they're righteous."*

There's nothing wrong with a "story" per se. In fact, a good story may reveal more about someone than hours of description. As people become more self-aware and emotionally literate, they become more conscious of, and articulate about, the possible origins of their assumptions, beliefs, and feelings.

Do my feelings arise out of a social situation, such as an agreement being broken? Do they arise from an internal discomfort, such as a need not being met? Or do they arise from my response to a story I tell myself, one which may (or may not) have much in common with current reality? Whenever feelings arise from an internal story, not only are our feelings self-created but the story — if it is not checked out — disconnects us from whoever or whatever we are in relationship with.

Stories themselves are not the issue — it's the unconscious use of stories that mask and avoid feelings, or the use of them to disconnect rather than dialogue with another, that's a problem. After all, consider the following statements:

- Unconditional love is ultimately what heals.
- You have to grieve your losses if you're to ever get past them.
- You can't run away from your problems.
- The more you live in the present, the happier your life will be.

These statements may all be true. But they are all "stories." And, as Campbell notes about myth (that myth determines what is labeled "real" and "unreal"), the sayings or stories listed above create a reality that is powerful and useful for many people. We all tell stories. The question we need to ask is whether the stories we tell make us more open, powerful, grateful, and connected to life and each other... or not. Of course, the assumption that it's better to be open, grateful, and connected is a story of its own.

RITUAL AND CEREMONY

There's a far more detailed discussion of this subject in Section IV: Ritual and Ceremony, including specifics for performing many of the rituals that could be done on a vision quest. What follows is a brief summary of the main points without describing the myriad components of the actual practices involved.

Ritual is the language of "the old brain," those neurological structures that developed and functioned long before the evolution of the neocortex, or conscious brain. Verbal language is primarily an activity of the neocortex, but verbal language has minimal effect on the older, more foundational aspects of our brain's physiology. The activities involved in ritual and ceremony — making offerings of tobacco, cornmeal, blood; arranging stones in circles; calling in the directions, etc. — make little logical or linear sense. But something deeper than our rational minds "gets it" and responds. The limbic system and the reptile brain understand.

Why enact ritual? Though we identify with them, our conscious minds are not very powerful. If your conscious identity and rational mind is a person in a rowboat, the unconscious is the wide, heaving ocean. Who do you think is really in charge? Our conscious minds can filter and process forty bits of information per second. During that same second, our subconscious minds sift through 40 million. If we're hoping to make changes that make a difference, we should remember that ritual and ceremony will be listened and responded to by the one who's actually in charge.

Ritual and ceremony are defined differently, though in actual life they can overlap. *Ritual is transformative;* it makes a change. Rituals and the changes they make can be small or large, but the transformative nature of the event defines it as a ritual. A puberty ritual turns boys into men. Fasting changes our consciousness. Smudging, prayer, and invocation change secular space into sacred space.

Ceremony is not transformative; it is *confirmatory*. Ceremony can mark, announce, confirm, or anchor a change that has previously taken place. The inauguration of a president is a ceremony. The election is the ritual that makes someone president. The inauguration marks, validates, and makes the change in status visible to all, but it did not create the transition. Puberty ceremonies for girls are similar, in that it's not the ceremony that makes them women — nature or the earth has accomplished that. But the ceremonies publicly celebrate and validate what has already happened.

There is no absolutely correct way to do ritual or ceremony. There may be appropriate and inappropriate ways to do specific ceremonies — a Catholic mass or a Lakota sweat lodge, for example — but the test of a good ritual or ceremony is its effectiveness. When Buddhism spread to Tibet, it met a highly shamanic culture. Tibetan Buddhism is colorful, artistic, layered, and complex. In Japan, Buddhism became Zen — stark, simple, and basic. Which one is right? To be effective, a good ceremony must fit the environment — the psychic landscape of those who participate in it. The important question is, "Does it work?"

Rituals and ceremonies can be made for ourselves, our families, or an auditorium of strangers. Rituals can be conducted for born-again Christians, neo-pagans, or Orthodox Jews. The intent might be to descend, ascend, transcend, or simply come more into the present. Simple, elaborate, short, drawn-out, costumed, casual... "energy flows where attention goes." There is no pat answer or right way. What's important is whether the process captures our attention; whether it gathers, focuses, and moves the energy.

ADDITIONAL THEMES

ARCHETYPES

The vision quest process fits the heroic journey archetype. But unless you majored in psychology in college, you may not really know what an archetype is. The word *archetype*, associated with Carl Jung, founder of archetypal psychology, is defined as a pattern fundamental to the human psyche. These patterns, mostly below the level of our awareness, form the invisible foundation from which humans perceive and engage with the world. They are the background that frames, determines, and puts in context the entire foreground that we pay attention to. These patterns, inherent in the unconscious parts of our psyches, result in certain things just "making sense" to virtually everyone.

An example is patterns of three and four. We accept, mostly without question, that there are four directions (east, west, north, and south), four seasons (spring, summer, autumn, and winter), four elements (earth, air, fire and water), even four times of the day (morning, afternoon, evening, and night). But though these divisions by four make sense to almost everyone, there's no logical, rational reason for time or direction to be divided this way.

If you stood in a wide-open space, such as a flat plain or ship on the ocean, and slowly rotated to scan the horizon, there would be no obvious reason to divide the circle you've perceived into four quadrants or directions. If you baked a pie for dinner guests, you'd likely divide the pie based on the number of guests, in four, six, or ten pieces. It makes sense for the pieces to match the number of guests. But, when speaking about the "circles of life" — directions, seasons, times of the day, or elements — we always divide our pie into four. This division results from a pattern within the human psyche, an archetype, and it makes sense because of the way we're built, not because of the way the world objectively is. Perceiving through this archetype, we see the world in its terms — divided by four.

Patterns of three abound as well. We divide time into past, present, and future. Our stories have beginnings, middles, and ends. Astrological signs are cardinal, fixed, or mutable. The great gods of Hindu mythology are Brahma, Vishnu, and Shiva (creator, maintainer, and destroyer). The Bible talks about the holy trinity. These all demonstrate the importance of patterns of three. Birth, life, death... Again, these patterns are not part of any objective world or physical universe, but represent the universe as perceived through the human psyche. Archetypes represent the deep patterns within us, mostly unconscious, that structure and define the way we perceive and see the world.

Strong evidence for the existence of archetypes comes from the worlds of dream and myth. The previously mentioned universality of certain themes, such as the heroic journey, is found not just in every culture but in virtually every myth. The recurrence of these mythic themes and images can only be explained by the existence of underlying patterns or blueprints in the human psyche.

From this point of view, the myths and stories that last — the legends that have staying power and have weathered millennia — do so because they express archetypal themes in a faithful and compelling way. This faithfulness in representing the archetypal blueprints — from the abduction of Persephone to Superman and Star Wars — gives them their strength and an almost universal appeal.

Just as some constellations in the sky stand out more than others, some patterns or constellations in the psyche may be stronger, and hence easier to see, than others. The hero's journey is universal, while other images, such as the dying and resurrected god, the warrior, the wise man (woman) or sage (crone), the innocent youth, the frightening dragon or monster, the sex god or goddess, and the adventurer, are also common and widespread.

In any culture or cosmology, the pantheon of gods and goddesses will represent archetypal forces. Within these cultural images, there will be some ordering or hierarchy related to the importance of archetypes. Thus, there are major and lesser stories; greater (Zeus) and lesser (Janus) gods; and different classes of deities (Olympians, Furies, Satyrs, nymphs).

Participants on vision quests often talk about issues and concerns that are both personal and archetypal. Some of these (this is by no means an exhaustive list) could be:

- Hero, warrior, or sovereign (king or queen);
- Sage, magician (shaman), ally, or spirit guide;monster, dragon, devil, or destroyer (Kali);
- Innocent youth (virgin, youngest brother or sister, inner or magical child);
- The source (sacred mountain, world tree, heavenly realm, or the center of the earth);
- Lover, soul companion, or temptress; or saboteur (judge or critic), dark lord, Judas, trickster, or betrayer.

ARCHETYPES OF FOUR IN THE MEDICINE WHEEL

In the teachings of the medicine wheel, we have four...

Directions	South	West	North	East
Elements	Water	Earth	Air	Fire
Seasons	Summer	Fall	Winter	Spring
Modes	Sensing	Feeling	Thinking	Intuition
Times	Midday	Evening	Night	Morning
Shields	Childhood	Adolescence	Adulthood	Elder

In this metaphor — one whole circle divided into four — *wholeness requires each of the four quadrants to be represented fully and completely*. Cold temperatures for an afternoon do not make a winter. Using the metaphor of a four-legged stool, each leg needs to be solid, strong, and the same length as the others; otherwise, the stool is unbalanced and dysfunctional. Seeing these divisions by four as metaphors for a balance of different "expressions of energy" can help us determine which energies or expressions are underdeveloped and inaccessible, which are compulsive or overbearing, and what needs to be done to achieve balance.

FOUR SEASONS

The four seasons — summer, fall, winter, and spring — are woven into the four shields medicine wheel teachings. These teachings illustrate the interplay of oneness and diversity as the circle or cycle (oneness) moves through the directions and phases of its revolution. The cycles — of a day, year, or human life — interpenetrate and build on one another. Their images and metaphors cross-pollinate in the medicine wheel teachings, for these forces/powers are both in the world "out there" and in the psyche. Indeed, the teachings grow from traditions in which inner and outer, self and world, were not separate. Self is embedded in the world, world in self — these are just different points of view. What follows is a brief elaboration of the teachings applied to the yearly cycle.

Summer

In summer, the sun is high in the sky — like noon of the day — and directly south. Birds, insects, fish... the earth pulses with life, vitality, and sensuality. It's a time when things grow rapidly. Life is active and expansive, like childhood. Times of cold and contraction are far away; carefree ease envelopes us. The medicine wheel teachings of the south speak to this energy of expansive growth; to childhood; to physical, sensual, earthy life; to safety, security, material reality; to emotional expression; to the lessons of trust and innocence.

Fall

Summer wanes; the sun moves lower in the sky. We move into the west shield, the direction of the setting sun. Birds migrate south; leaves turn color and fall off the trees. Sap, the energy of life, moves away from the periphery. It migrates down stalks and stems, returning below ground to the roots. Like leaves falling off trees, this is a time of separation — the time of adolescence. The child pulls away from the parents. Like sap returning to roots, the gaze turns inward; introspection intensifies. The lessons of the west speak to the creation of the separate self; finding one's values, passions, and inner life; the balance of pulling away and connection. Fall initiates the descent, exploring the shadowlands, the land of dreams, shamanic journeys, the realms of the soul.

Winter

Winter is nighttime of the year; the direction is north. The land is cold, barren, and stark. Life has fled to warmer climes. That which remains slumbers in dens, huddles together in shelters, or endures underground. Animals live on layers of fat built up over summer and fall; squirrels and mice hunt out nuts and seeds stashed away in secret hollows. Winter is the shield of adulthood, a time when we live on what has been grown in summer (childhood) and harvested through the fall (adolescence). Resources are limited; we examine what we have. Our choices have consequences. We must generate clarity of vision, wisdom, the right use of attention and energy, and then act. We learn about the giveaway. As adults, what must we do to feed "the people?" What choices will support the greater whole — the inner child, the wise elder, or the world?

Spring

The earth continues to rotate and move through space. Warmth returns; the sun moves higher in the sky. Night gives way to morning. Colors, shapes — the whole visible world — emerge from blackness. Barren fields are soon filled with flowers, leaves, grass, and a riot of color. Seeds take root and plants burst from the ground. Spring brings transformation, the sudden, irrational appearance of what was, a short time ago, invisible. Spring represents the rising sun, illumination, an obliteration of boundaries; an in-flooding of something greater — insight, enlightenment, vision; life outside the box. Spring evokes the spirit, what's infinite, boundless, and eternal, the source behind and emerging through all forms.

FOUR WINDOWS

Four windows is a term created by Stephen Gallegos in his book *The Personal Totem Pole*.[12] These windows refer to Jung's classification of "modes of knowing," the ways human beings can perceive, learn about, and grasp the world. Jung called these four modes *sensing*, *feeling*, *thinking*, and *intuition/imagination*. To fully understand these modes and their implications is a huge undertaking, but a few relevant ideas and ramifications can be mentioned here.

Western culture places an inordinate amount of attention on one mode, thinking, while giving little to no attention to the others. We attend kindergarten, grade school, high school, college, and more. Resources are invested, and twelve to twenty years are devoted to training the mind and refining the thinking process. During this training, we are expected to sit still, ignore the body and its urges, stay focused, and not give in to our daydreams or imaginations. And no one asks or pays attention to how we feel about all this.

Jung considered each of the other modes to be *different, but equal* to thinking in terms of their potential development and contribution to a full and integrated life. Yet they're by and large ignored in our education. Imagine these as four children, one overfed, obese, entitled, and self-absorbed while the others are ignored, criticized, and on the verge of starvation. How functional and happy a family would this be?

Given this imbalance and overemphasis on thinking, a great deal of healing on a vision quest may have to do with simply getting out of our heads (severance) and evoking, affirming, and accessing those other modes of knowing (incorporation). Those other modes of knowing can be accessed by bringing focus and awareness to

- The body, through being in, and connected to, the sensuous landscape of the living earth;
- Our emotions and the world of feeling, via prayer, death lodges, truth mandalas, journaling, and ritual processes of various sorts; and
- The realm of imagination and intuition, through dream work, gazing, medicine walks, allurements, attunement practices, etc.

COUNCIL

There are many possible forms of council — closing council, talking staff council, fishbowl councils, dream council, etc. — that could be part of any particular program, but an underlying thread ties all of them together. The core concepts of council are related to the teachings of the medicine wheel.

The medicine wheel is a circle, and we all — men, women, young, old, human, animal — are part of the circle of life. Each point on a circle is equidistant from the center, so there are no priests or special, holier-than-thou members in our village. Everyone's connection to (and expression of) the source, though different, is equal.

Every position on the wheel is a part of a larger whole. Each position is unique; each voice has something useful to be said. A yearly cycle passes through four seasons. The day expresses itself in morning, mid-day, evening, and night. Each part of the cycle, or circle, is necessary for life's completion. None can be bypassed or ignored. Standing in a circle, the view from the south, looking north, is far different than the view from the west, looking east. All forms and seeming oppositions of life — young/old, male/female, rich/poor, well-read/illiterate, white/colored, married/single, gay/straight, successful/struggling — have their perspectives, teachings, and challenges, as well as their unique and particular truths. Wholeness requires them all.

Council is based on these teachings. In council, all are invited to speak, and all are equal. No one's voice is more important than another's; no particular view is anointed as "right." People may pass if they have nothing to add, but everyone is welcome and encouraged to be heard. Councils can have different ground rules or guidelines. They might be of the once-around-and-done variety, or they could have successive rounds until everyone feels finished. They can proceed by passing the talking stick around (usually to the left) or in a "popcorn" (as-moved) style.

Whatever the particular style, council usually proceeds with no interruptions and no cross-talk. When someone speaks, his or her viewpoint is respected and listened to. Self-importance[13] and other forms of inequality are discouraged. (If the council is of the popcorn variety and someone speaks repeatedly before others have had their turn, a facilitator may need to address this.) A council is designed to get the full wisdom of the circle, and that requires each point of view speaking its truth and being heard. Winter follows fall, not spring. Every voice must be heard in its turn.

The results of a council are usually satisfying to all concerned. In the West we're trained to bow down to authority, to stay silent, to hand our voices over to experts. Years of training — "children should be seen and not heard"... all desks facing forward and focused on the teacher... eating when the bell rings... obeying the boss under threat of firing — have made us subservient or — in reaction — aggressive. It's sometimes hard to speak up or disagree, even to a doctor when it's about your own body.

But council eliminates hierarchy, authority, and obedience. It invites, welcomes, and requires us to step up, find our voice, and speak. Even when the intention of a council is to find a solution to some dilemma, and none appears, the experience of speaking and being attended and listened to can be satisfying, and, to some, deeply healing.

DEATH AS AN ALLY

[On vision quests we cross a threshold. We leave behind the human world in order to meet the unknown, primal reality, the mystery. An exploration of life's great transformative moments, death and birth, may be useful to speak of, or (as in the case of the death lodge) plan ceremonies around.]

Birth and death are the two great transformations in life. In rites of passage, each birth is a death and vice versa. Every beginning, every start of something new, is also the end of some past position, paradigm, or state of being. Crossing any threshold leaves one space behind as we step into the next, and the significant movements of life may be seen as a series of death and rebirth rituals. Child to adult, single to married, childless to parent, worker to retired (elder), married to divorced: each beginning is an ending; each ending the start of something new.

However, at times of literal birth and death, one of those spaces is unclear. At birth, we begin to learn about what we've entered into but have little memory of what was left behind. In death, we're aware of what we're about to leave behind but ignorant of what (if anything) lies ahead. Death's approach puts us at the threshold of a great heroic journey. We stand at the precipice, ready to leave home in some ultimate way, fearful of the monsters (loss) awaiting us, with no sense of direction, destination, allies, or companions to help us on the way.

In Carlos Castaneda's writings, Don Juan taught that death was always "over your left shoulder." This was meant to make Carlos aware of reality: ignorant of when death would come, he could die anytime. Living with this awareness cut through the widespread denial of death and the idea there will always be time — later — to work things out. In this way, the presence of death becomes an ally to a warrior, an ally to whoever wants to live fully and impeccably. Death may arrive via a plane crash, a terrorist attack, ice on a winter road, cancer, a moment I'm not looking while rounding a curve. Knowing that I may have little or no time makes priorities come into focus. If there could be little or no time to do it all or get to it later, what are the things that are really important?

Death encourages us to live impeccably. If I die tonight, do I want my daughter's (lover's, friend's) last memory of me to be of me acting like that? Do I want to be filled with these resentments when I'm about to dissolve into the mystery? Or, conversely, do I want resentment to be the last taste in the mouth as my friend remembers me? All those untied threads, conflicts unresolved, promises or agreements not kept, plans never pursued... am I free to meet my maker with all that on my mind?

Awareness of death impels us to do it now, to leave nothing pending, unexpressed, or unresolved. If we do this, we can be free and unburdened when "he" comes. And if by chance, death doesn't arrive for a decade or more, those years will have a sense of lightness and freedom, our basket empty of regrets, our shoulders unbowed and unburdened by anything unsaid, undone, or incomplete.

THE OTHER STORY

The "other story" begins with the insight that we always see the world through a lens. This is both necessary and the source of many a potential problem. For example, if we want to look at the rings of Saturn, it's necessary that we look through a telescope. But that won't help us see pathogens in our blood or what we might trip over down by our feet. Each lens — telescope, microscope, wide-angle — has gifts, a power to bring certain things into focus. Each is useful for its intended purpose but useless or even dangerous in other circumstances.

Likewise, as we turn our attention to our personal or collective history — our past and the wounds we've received — we may be looking through a certain lens. Today, many people adopt a psychological lens, one developed over the past hundred years, starting with Freud. Generally speaking, the psychological lens focuses on our neuroses, deficiencies, and what caused them (Mom, Dad, trauma, etc.). It then attempts to give guidance or remedies to address those issues and concerns. It tells a story that we are wounded, that our direction has been set or altered by the past, and that, within limits, here's what we can and should do about it.

This lens can be useful, but it's not the only one. In other systems, peoples' fates were set before, or outside of, personal history, and the narrative of life had far more to do with the destination — where they were going — than with where they came from. In this story, there's a force or soul entity, sometimes called daemon or genius, that acts and asserts its will and direction through a life. In these terms, Van Gogh and Mozart expressing their genius and gifts in new and unique ways had little to do with whether their mothers breastfed them or read them fairy tales.

We'll never have access to the inner workings of Mozart's and Van Gogh's psyches, but we can try on and use lenses other than the psychological. Looking at the night sky with its two-thousand stars, one could connect the dots and make any picture or pattern one wants. Any "constellation of reality" will focus on some relationships and ignore many possible others. The psychological "constellation" is useful in some types of personal work, but other constellations are possible.

The "other story" takes the point of view that "you are exactly where you should and need to be, and life — the universe — has conspired and helped to get you here." This story encourages people to look at their lives and see the patterns of blessings that exist alongside are just as much a reality as any pattern of wounding. Here, the focus shifts to helpers — allies, mentors, friends; books, movies, songs, artists; unexpected events, surprise meetings or gatherings; perhaps the vision quest experience itself — that have brought energy, insight, and direction to peoples' lives, and helped them arrive at where they are now. That shift of focus may also shift peoples' attitudes from complaint to gratitude, from cynicism to faith, and it holds open the possibility that we are blessed, belong here, and are not alone.

This other story does not deny the truth or the power of the psychological lens, a lens that has helped and given depth to many a healing journey. But it does offer another point of view that has the power to bring different things into focus. It offers possibilities; gifts for the heart, mind, and imagination that aren't contained in some of the usual ways we've been conditioned to look at the world.

PARADISE LOST

Many myths fit the theme of paradise lost. Three elements make up this theme:

1. Long ago, "once upon a time," things were wonderful. We were close to our dreams and original nature; people and animals could speak together. God walked in the garden with us in the evening; lions laid down with lambs; etc.
2. Something bad happened. Adam ate the apple; Mud Boy became jealous of his sister; Hades abducted Persephone.
3. As a result, the situation changed for the worse, and that's why things are the way they are now. And these stories sometimes imply there are ways of atonement — tasks to accomplish and a righting of wrongs that will allow us to return to the way it was.

The Garden of Eden is an obvious example. The story of Persephone is another. And many Native American or African tales follow this script. These stories can be interpreted in a literal or evolutionary way, implying there was an actual earlier time — usually before "civilization" — when people lived more in harmony with themselves and nature. Encounters with some primal, nature-based peoples (not all, certainly) can often seem to support this interpretation.

These myths can also be interpreted psychologically in terms of:

- **The birth process.** Every human floats in amniotic fluid. It's warm and comforting, like paradise. All our needs are met. Then birth happens, and we're thrust into a harsh world.
- **Self-consciousness.** As children, we act on impulse, in harmony with our instincts and nature. But eventually we become self-aware. We feel our separateness, and we are no longer at one with the world and our environment.
- **Puberty.** The innocence of childhood ends as we are flooded with hormones that produce aggression, lust, and socially unacceptable urges. We experience the call to separate from parents to create an autonomous, individual identity, as well as the need to discover and test our (and others') limits.

Whatever the ultimate origin of these stories, their widespread appearance tells us they speak to something compelling in the human experience. This mythic theme is clearly broader-based than any memory of parent-child or social conflict, and the theme's commonality may make it useful in framing or giving context to the issues to be explored and brought to the quest experience.

Sharing this theme can help participants access the feeling of wounding and/or loss. All feelings of hurt or loss imply an earlier, happier time, and the situation *now* is unfavorably compared to how one felt *then*. In addition to sadness and loss — prevalent in all versions — some versions, like the Garden of Eden, also contain characters (God) who express judgment, anger, and pathology. Confrontations with these critical, angry voices — these negative versions of "god" — could also play a part in peoples' quest experiences.

PRAYER

Prayer is an offering to the unknown. Many people, for good reason, have a general aversion to ritual, prayer in particular, because they were force-fed religion in one context or another. But in its most basic form, prayer constitutes an energetic opening to the unknown. It's a way to establish a connection between the self and all that lies outside those boundaries and definitions that make up the sense of "me."

Prayer involves speech. When I pray, I speak from what's known. I speak from everything that makes up my sense of self. That includes my language, memories, values, and whatever stories I tell that define me. I speak from what I know — from the "I" — as a man of a certain age, with particular experiences, hopes, dreams, interests, and longings. But what I am speaking *to* lies outside all that. I speak to that "something," that Great Mystery from, or through which, all life and awareness emerges.

DATE: / /

when Vision Quest done, what do
GOALS I want to come away with?

- optimism, enthusiasm about aging
+ living the rest of my life

- ↑ ability to cope w/ sickness, disease
↓ mobility, need for help,
- make the most of abilities
I have left

- How do I want to die?
long disease
Cancer
CVA, MI

? death w/ dignity

what are my fears?
my regrets

DATE: / /

If the assertion we use only ten percent of our brains is true, we could consider prayer as a heartfelt attempt on the part of the ten percent to initiate communication (by words) with the 90 percent, that far-larger and mysterious part of us that is doing we know not what. Like any skill, prayer can be done well or poorly. Speaking from the heart is central to good prayer, and any attempt to diminish the unknown; to define and delimit it; to turn it into the known, such as seeing God as a man with a gray beard, is a mockery and caricature of the real meaning of prayer — a caricature that's practiced by many major religions.

There's a saying that there are only two prayers. The first is "help me... help me... help me!" And the other is "thank you... thank you... thank you!"

In cultures with shamanic perspectives, prayer is about the present, not the future. Prayer is not, "I hope to win the lottery." In a shamanic universe, you pray for something that exists right now. For example, if I were praying to be a better father, I would engage myself fully in the act, seeing, feeling, sensing, and imagining myself being that father with my daughter. By itself, the sentence, "I want to be a better father," is a string of words about a wish for tomorrow. It stays on the surface.

In the shamanic universe, this better father already exists. It is a possibility, a promise, a reality in another parallel world not that far away. Therefore, my prayer is active. It's a power, a practice by which I invest energy in that potential already present. And through that investment, I make the likelihood of that possibility blooming into this reality greater. In a real prayer — as in carving prayer arrows or making prayer ties — "I" see, sense, come to know, and feed the better father that exists already, and thus it blossoms, manifests, and grows within me.

SACRED SPACE

Sacred space could be contrasted with profane or mundane space. In Western culture, where the material and the daily world — "reality" — has been divorced from the world of soul and spirit, most interactions are focused around the values of secular society. These values commonly highlight concerns that are egocentric (attention, status, fame, power); economic (money, work, career); or social (family, romance, friendship, entertainment).

For most practical purposes, "sacred space" can be seen as synonymous with ritual space. In most instances, sacred space is created by ritual — smudging, invocation, prayer — in which other powers, energies, and intentions are invited into the room, into the field we create.

Creating sacred space is a conscious invitation to enter an arena that's more mysterious, to explore matters of healing, balance, spirit, and soul. In creating sacred space, we bring our attention ("energy flows where attention goes") — usually by ritual acts — to matters that are more profound. And the activities performed within this space are meant to support and facilitate moving past what's social and superficial in order to engage with those deeper concerns.

WOUNDING AND SHAMANIC INITIATIONS

"What the modern man most suffers from... is the wounding without the transformation. He suffers the... burden of role definition that confines rather than liberates. He suffers the skewers of the soul without the godly vision. He is asked to be a man when no one can define it except in the most trivial of terms. He is asked to move from boyhood to manhood without any rites of passage, with no wise elders to receive and instruct him, and no positive sense of what such manhood might feel like. His wounds are not transformative; they do not bring deeper consciousness; they do not lead him to a richer life. They senselessly, repeatedly, stun him into a numbing of the soul before the body has had the good sense to die."[14]

INITIATIONS

Traditional tales of heroic and shamanic journeys are often similar, and stories of shamanic initiation could be conceptualized as a specialized case of the heroic journey. In many reports, the initiate enters a non-ordinary realm where he is destroyed or dismembered. He may get torn apart by wolves, drowned and his flesh devoured by fish, or hacked apart and tossed in a kettle. After this dissolution, the initiate will — in some strange way — get knit back together and return to the world imbued with mysterious and unusual powers not exhibited before. These journeys are transformative. The old self — dismantled and reassembled — is inhabited or taken over by larger forces and arrives back in normal life with "medicine" — abilities heretofore unavailable. Shamanic initiations, as a specialized aspect of the heroic journey, can represent aspects of our personal quest for wholeness.

MAKING WOUNDS SACRED

This physical response of the body to being wounded has analogies to the psyche: damage, the trauma of loss, the threat of invasion. In children especially, the psyche is undefended and fragile, and wounding can have consequences that last a lifetime. Scar tissue, shock, numbing, and shutting down in the body have corresponding psychic expressions. This damage can express itself on multiple levels — fears, body armor, dissociation, behavioral traits, depression, etc. — that are deep and hard to access.

Wounding can be part of initiatory rites in primal cultures. Initiations often included trials, tests, and ordeals as well as sacred teachings. A young boy might be cut or scarred, or have his front tooth knocked out by an elder to connect him with a forest god who also lost a tooth. These wounds create changes in the body and make strong impressions that are not forgotten. But, due to their context and circumstances, they differ greatly from childhood traumas. They take place in a community, are shared with others, and are undergone with the assistance of allies and elders. They're also rooted in rich mythologies that provide meaning, connect them to larger forces, and, along with instructions, define their place in the tribe and universe.

Wounding, from the ego's point of view, is a violation, and the solution is a strong defense and better boundaries. But from another perspective, wounds are openings in which the vulnerable self within makes intense and intimate contact with what's outside. Through this opening, the world can enter us, and what's within us can also flow out into the world. Most people today don't have elders or initiatory rites in their lives, and their wounds have only resulted in damage and disconnection. But the process of making wounds sacred can still happen through revisiting, re-experiencing, and re-framing the wounding process, along with appropriate teachings in circles of supportive allies.

Through entering our wounds — no longer covering and protecting these "sacred sites" — we can create healing and practice sacred medicine. There, with help and courage, we can find or take back what we may have lost (our voice, for example); cast out poisons we may have ingested; and, through this process, find meaning in our lives and the choices we've made.

Entering realms of primal experience with open eyes and an open heart can change us. Our stories become heroic rather than tragic. How one enters the darkness and fully experiences that deep core — whether through vision quests, therapy, transformative breath work, or something else, galvanized by inner pressure or external circumstances — is a matter of fate, technique, or preference. The wound is the opening, and, by entering it consciously, we can reclaim lost parts of ourselves. We see where we have come from and the options open to us. We claim our present, our path, and our journey. And, in doing so, we may find, indeed, that our wound has given us gifts.

Our wounds become sacred when these inaugural "openings" cease to be areas characterized by feelings of fear, shame, or victimhood and unconsciously surrounded by defense and protection mechanisms. No longer are they defined as tragedies or injustices, insults to the perfectly comfortable life we think we should have had. Through giving up passivity and victimization, and by owning our journey and actual life experiences, these former obstacles can be transformed into sources of strength. By venturing into even the darkest parts of our lives with acceptance and a fierce, open heart, the archetype of the hero can be constellated in us.

As we grow and heal, our suffering can become a portal, an opening to our souls, our spiritual journeys, and a wider dream of our lives. Through it, we may find courage, our calling, and compassion, this willingness to embrace our own experience forming a door through which we let in the world and connect with others.

WOUNDED HEALERS

Shamanic initiations are commonly seen as a death-rebirth process. In them, shamans undergo ordeals — death, decay, and dismemberment — and are somehow put back together in new and more powerful ways. Though this may seem utter nonsense from a Western, rational, or medical point of view, if the dismemberment is conceived in terms of one's identity, energy body, or psyche — those intangible, nonphysical "entities" that influence and may even determine one's physical self — it seems to make sense.

The wounded healer archetype refers to those who have truly embodied and lived through the process of making their wounds sacred. In many shamanic cultures, one learns to heal by taking on the affliction and finding, though one's own experience, how to survive and return to wholeness. In this way, the disease, ailment, or trauma in question becomes a means for acquiring power and accessing gifts. In this context, illness presents us with a choice of intentions: shall I choose to be a victim of this, or face it as an explorer, a warrior, a learner?

INDICATIONS OF UNRESOLVED WOUNDS

Wounds may be expressed, acted out in active or passive ways. The general list below indicates woundedness in some of its active and passive expressions:

Active	**Passive**
Anger	Self-pity
Loss of vitality	Fear of failure
Aggression	Self-aggrandizement
Inadequacy	Emptiness
Combativeness	Cynicism
Detachment	Helplessness
Manipulation	Repression
Lack of love	Lack of encouragement

SECTION VI:
OTHER RITUALS AND EXERCISES

Action Commitments **139**

Burning Our Inheritance **139**

Claiming Our Gifts and Power **140**

Dance of Life **141**

Dance with Death **141**

Dream Work **143**
- Dream Council 143
- Dream Inductions 143

Eulogies **144**

Flowering Tree Ceremony **144**

Goal Setting **145**

Invocations **146**

Letter from the Death Bed **146**

Mission Statements **147**

Opening and Closing Rituals **148**

Presenting Your Ego to a Tree **149**

Smudging **149**

Truth Mandala **150**

SECTION VI:
OTHER RITUALS AND EXERCISES

The rituals and exercises that follow could be included in a vision quest program. Some, like smudging, might seem central to the whole process, while others (the truth mandala, for example) may be among the most important experiences of the solo. One could prove useful as part of the preparation or return, while others seem more optional or tangential. Some are better performed by the whole group, while others are clearly more appropriate for individuals. These are all possible additions to the vision quest process. None of these are required or unquestionably essential. But, as when cooking rice and beans, supplementing the core elements with spices and other ingredients can enhance and seriously affect one's satisfaction with the meal.

ACTION COMMITMENTS

Action commitments do not refer to specific exercises, but to a collection of undertakings people can pledge to do and be accountable for. One concern with any program of self-help or spiritual growth is that it can be a "special event," disconnected from the fabric of daily life. It is easy to go away for a weekend or week and, in the company of like-minded people, feel powerful, strong, and understood. But then one returns home — "on the other side of the trees," as we say — and that strong container of support turns into a tattered basket.

Once we lived in tribes and villages. In that context, the elders who taught and took us out on vision quests; the mentors who initiated us into medicine societies; and the friends or siblings with whom we hunted, gathered, or shared ceremony were part of our daily lives. People who knew and understood us, who were willing to listen to our dreams or support our longings, were always close by. This is not the world we inhabit today, so creating continuity and finding that supportive container on the "other side of the trees" becomes a special concern.

Action commitments attempt to bridge that discontinuity. At the close of a quest program, people can be given (or choose), tasks — something they pledge to do — and someone to communicate with and be accountable to regarding that task. These could be specific actions in their daily lives or a commitment to communicate with other participants. Maintaining connection and developing continuity is a worthwhile objective, and, as in all programs separate from work, family, and the flow of daily life, one of the hardest to achieve.

BURNING OUR INHERITANCE

Note: The following ritual is particularly difficult to describe in gender-neutral language. Since it involves stepping back into previous generations, not only does it have the usual issues of "he and she" and "him and her," but "father/mother" and "grandmother/father" are added to the mix. If one is working with all men or all women, the problem is simplified: men step back into Father's and Grandfather's worlds; women into Mother's and Grandmother's. In a mixed group, one can use the terms parents *and* grandparents*, but it helps to suggest that women translate those into Mother and Grandmother (Mother's mother) while men do the same for Father and Grandfather. Otherwise,* grandparents *could refer to four different people.*

This is a simple ritual, taking place around a fire, that can be, for some, quite powerful. The ritual involves three elements: severance — the burning of the past, the inheritance handed down from previous generations; incorporation — claiming the parts of that inheritance you do want to carry forward; and confirmation — announcing those intentions and commitments to a community.

People stand in a circle around a fire. Two sticks or logs are placed before each. The leader speaks, asking each person to take one full step back, and, as they do so, step back into the world of their parents. When everyone has moved back, the facilitator says, "Imagine your parent's (father's or mother's) world at the time of his or her birth: your father's (or mother's) parents, their living situation, and what was happening in the world at that time. Imagine your parent growing — the house, family, brothers and sisters — and what it was like to grow up there. How was your parent nurtured, or not, and what were they told? What did they learn about the job, the responsibilities of being a man or woman? What did they learn about God, duty, their place in the world; and what constituted success or a "good" life? How were they treated by their parents? What modes of expression were denied or unknown to them? What were their possibilities, and what horizons were they unable or forbidden to go beyond? What did they learn about women, men, sex, marriage, and family — his role and hers — and did they question the role and place carved out for them?" (etc.)

After the people "inhabit" the world of their parents, the leader asks them to step back again into the world of their grandparents, guiding them through a similar, imaginative journey as they take on and embody the world, lessons, attitudes, and goals their grandfathers or grandmothers were taught to carry through life. This could be done again — stepping into the era of great grandparents — but often people do not know many (or any) details about that world or person.

After people have inhabited their grandparent's world, they begin the journey back. Guided by the leader, they are told to, by holding their arms in front of them as if they were carrying a log, take possession of the sum total of the attitudes, beliefs, and life situation they (as the grandfather or grandmother) were given, and to step forward, placing the bundle upon or in the hands of the child (the participant's father or mother) who followed them. Then, standing in the place of their parents, people step forward once more and bring that "bundle" to be placed in the hands of themselves, the man or woman standing here in the present.

Participants are told to feel the weight and the quality of the world — beliefs, attitudes, etc. — that their fathers or mothers have given to them, and what they are grateful for and what they don't want. After a pause, they are told to pick up one of the pieces of wood at their feet. One by one, people step forward and, naming the parts of their parent's/grandparent's world that they don't want, and will not, carry forward, they offer it to the fire to burn. When everyone has done this, they are directed to pick up the other stick, this time thinking of what they've received that they do want to carry on. Stepping forward again, they name and claim these qualities and commitments, before offering them to the fire to be transformed into light and warmth.

CLAIMING OUR GIFTS AND POWER

This ceremony can help anchor and ground the lessons of the quest, and it could be used as part of the return/reintegration process. Doing it around a fire adds to its impact.

Participants are invited to come forth, take a staff or other "sacred object," and, standing before their companions, claim their gifts and power.

Over the course of the vision quest, many have challenged their old stories and authorities, delved into the darkness of their psyches, and allowed the formerly unknown to express itself and be witnessed. They may have explored, discovered, shared, and learned much about community, authority, feeling, truth, passion, dreams, and themselves. This ceremony is a chance to claim and own it, a time to speak of and commit to it while being witnessed and affirmed by those who have shared the joys and sorrows of the journey with them.

Ritual is transformative. Ceremony is confirmative. Claiming our gifts and power is a confirmation in which we are seen, heard, affirmed, validated, and celebrated by our community, the community with which we have undertaken this challenging and rewarding journey. For some people, it can be as difficult to own their gold as owning the shadow is for others. It's important to encourage each person to "be an adult," to step up and "take it," the discomfort and responsibility of power that comes with laying claim to and ownership of their deeper and truer selves.

DANCE OF LIFE

The dance of life can be done as a group exercise, pre- and post-quest, or individually during the solo. It calls in the powers of the seven directions — east, south, west, north, above, below, and within — through a form of ritual movement. This is traditionally done in the morning, inside a medicine wheel or circle if one is available, after each group member (or the individual) speaks his or her day greeting or morning prayer.

It's almost impossible to verbally describe the form of a ritual dance in this space — it must be experienced and participated in to be learned. The sense of separation at the root of all our problems cannot be addressed or healed without reweaving the strands of the web that have been frayed. This dance calls in the directions and connects each individual (and the group) with the wider universe, the larger field that surrounds us and supports all life.

DANCE WITH DEATH

The dance with death, sometimes referred to as "a warrior's last battle," is done at night around a fire. Consequently, there are logistical concerns that may need to be addressed, depending on the time of year, weather, firewood available, etc. In addition, since the "dance" requires the participants to fall and lie on the ground for 10 to 15 minutes, the condition of the ground — wet, rocky, muddy, rife with cactus — may also need to be taken into consideration, and adjustments made. Also, since this dance requires a musical accompaniment, a sound system may need to be provided.

(I have done this in the desert using candles placed in small paper (lunch) bags as a substitute for fire, and music played through a car stereo, doors open and speakers facing outward.) After the fire has been started and sustains itself, the ritual is introduced and described:

This ritual is inspired by the writings of Carlos Castaneda. Reportedly, his teacher, Don Juan, would oftentimes bring Carlos's attention to his mortality by saying, "Death is just over your left shoulder." In so doing, Don Juan attempted to remind Carlos to live impeccably, to rearrange his priorities in order to give his attention and energy to what's truly important. For when death arrives, what's not worthy of you — even if you have invested your whole life in it — will be obliterated in the force of mortality's numinous presence.

Death's proximity simplifies our choices: to avoid, flee, shrivel up in fear... to cringe, complain, hide, and play the victim, or to make a warrior's choice, and — for whatever time you have left — engage life with your whole being and live like you have never lived before. Don Juan claimed that those who act with an awareness of death's approach, becoming impeccable and ceasing their destructive and energy-wasting habits and routines, will be rewarded with a gift. In their final moments, death will pause, letting the warrior dance his or her last dance, a dance of goodbye and a dance of power before disappearing from this world.

INSTRUCTIONS FOR PARTICIPANTS

There will be four movements, four musical pieces, each lasting three to four minutes. In the first movement, you dance to honor or celebrate "all the battles you've fought." You dance for what you've learned, the work you've done, the schools you attended. You dance for marriages, children, trips taken, crafts learned, businesses started — all you've attempted and done — whether they were successes or failures, victories or defeats. You dance to celebrate the fact you entered this life and grappled with its joys and challenges.

The music changes. This marks the second movement, where you dance your goodbye to the Earth, to all the places that you've loved and that have touched you. Flowers, trees, starry skies, ocean shores; mountains you've climbed; gardens you've planted; lakes you've canoed or swum in... You won't see them again, so shout out your goodbyes to the seasons, the morning sun, the places you longed for but never visited. Goodbye to it all.

In the third movement, you bid goodbye to all the people you've loved — brothers, sisters, children, parents, and all those you vowed never to leave. Imagine them standing at the edge of the darkness around you. These are your last moments. Dance for them; show and shout your love, your goodbyes to dear friends, old lovers, pets, life companions, and the mothers or fathers of your children. Leave nothing unsaid!

Once again, the music shifts. All are gone except him — Death — and he's coming closer. This will be your last dance, these your last moments as he moves closer and closer. At some point, you'll hear a voice counting down from 20 to zero (start this with about 60 seconds left) as Death approaches ever closer. (Facilitator shouts out the count!) When the count reaches zero, Death arrives, and he touches you. At that point, fall to the ground, wherever you happen to be.

....

When the dancers have fallen to the ground, the leader speaks for four to five minutes about all of it fading away, using phrases like "all your plans, all you hoped to do, drifting from your grasp." "The words you wish you said; the love you didn't express... there's no more time." "Friends, family, cherished dreams, fading from your sight, drifting out of reach." During this part, it's helpful to have a musical accompaniment here that's moody and melancholy to fit the feeling of life, loves, dreams, and friendships drifting away.

After a few minutes, the "fallen warriors," having experienced life draining away, hear a change (both in music and message). "But wait a minute! Death is smiling. He was pleased by your dance, and because you have danced so well, he is offering you a gift: a few more moments, a little more time — a minute, a month, a day, a decade of life on this beautiful earth; another chance to feel the cool ground beneath you; another night to open your eyes and see the stars in the heavens above."

"As you slowly return to this world — on this night, in this field, on the Earth — treat this time as the gift it is. Feel the cool breeze on your cheek. Hear the songs of the crickets and call of the owl. Notice the trees towering around us. Death will soon be back to collect his due, so use this time to cherish those dreams or say the words you've left unsaid (etc.). When you're ready, make your way back to the fire and the circle of companions here with you. Look into their eyes as someone who knows you will die, who knows your time is short, who knows this time we share together is precious and will all too soon be over."

INSTRUCTOR NOTES

Doing this well requires creating a musical accompaniment that includes:

1. The initial four pieces that comprise the movements of the dance;
2. A selection of cuts that are melancholy, for playing during the time the dancers have fallen and life is slipping away;
3. A short transition piece as Death changes his mind; and
4. Music for the return to life, which could be inspiring, tender, and/or somewhat celebratory.

The leader of the ritual needs to be familiar with and aware of the timing of the pieces, especially for the countdown in movement 4 as well as the period when life is slipping away. In movement 4, it's useful to wear a stopwatch, know the length of the piece, and start the count a minute from the end, the numbers shouted out about three seconds apart, the watch available to slow or speed the count as needed. And the fourth movement of the dance is best accompanied by a musical piece that comes to a dramatic resolution as death arrives.

The leader can encourage the dancers and remind them of the instructions. For example, at the beginning of the first musical piece, shout out, "For all the battles you've fought, for all you've done no matter how it turned out!" Do something similar at the beginning of each movement. During the movements themselves, encouragement can be helpful. For example, in the third movement, saying goodbye to the people, shout out, "They're watching you! Tell them your feelings! Let them see you dance!" etc.

DREAM WORK

(A lengthy discussion on the subject of dreaming appears in Section V: Themes Within Vision Quests.)

DREAM COUNCIL

Calling a dream council requires having a dream or dreams to work with. If more than one dream is present in the group, several options present themselves: working with all dreams sequentially; hearing all dreams, then using the council to address them all at once; or choosing among the dreams and working with one or two. With the last option, the selection process could be based on the relative perceived power of the dreams, whether the dreams seem full or partial (a fragment), or whether the dream reporters want to share (and work with) the dreams.

Once the dream or dreams are chosen, begin with a full telling by the dreaming narrator. Encourage the person to describe the dream fully — to the best of his or her ability — in the present tense. When this has been completed, pass a talking staff around the circle, having each person report on the dream, beginning with, "If this were my dream, what it would say to me is... " until everyone has spoken. The dream reporter goes last and begins his or her impressions with the same statement. It can be useful to pass the talking staff again once everyone has spoken since interpretations shared by other participants often resonate and stir up feelings and new insights in those who spoke previously.

If there's time, and it seems useful, some other dream techniques, such as telling the story from the point of view of the "non-I" characters, may suggest themselves here. At the start of a dream council, it is always helpful to remind people that the dream is for the whole group, not just the dream reporter, and that whatever anyone sees or hears in the dream is *true for them*, and not necessarily a statement about the person who "had" the dream.

DREAM INDUCTIONS

A dream induction is some form of activity to promote, support, or encourage the appearance of dreams. It may be, and most often is, a form of guided imagery, and it could be done as a whole group before bedtime or be a suggestion for each person to enact before sleep. Both have advantages and disadvantages. If done as a whole-group activity, some may remain awake for hours, snacking or having conversations, and the dream induction may be a thing of the past by bedtime. If suggested as an individual activity, many, if other interests intervene, may forget.

Energy flows where attention goes. Suggestions to induce dreaming may help dreams manifest. Here are some examples:

- Place paper and pen by the side of the bed where they are easy to access in the night.
- In the morning, linger on awakening, which may help fragments or wisps of dreams to reconstitute themselves.
- Relax and settle into one's body before sleep and upon awakening.
- Scan one's psyche before sleep and ask, "What's really important right now?"
- Ask for dreams before closing one's eyes. One could ask for a particular dream on a desired topic, or simply ask an entity — God, Psyche, or the Dreaming Universe, for example — for help or guidance.

If a dream induction is done for the whole group, limit the total time and relaxation instructions. It's probably late, and people will drift off easily. Use evocative imagery.

One favorite is to imagine approaching a well. When you arrive, pick up a stone. Hold it in your hands. Examine it; feel its weight. Looking intensely at it and speak, telling it, "I want to remember my dreams tonight." Extend your hands and drop it into the well. Listen to the splash. This image contains many elements:

- The conscious world (above ground) and the unconscious realm underneath (with water),
- What's solid (stone) and liquid,
- The seen and unseen worlds,the senses (seeing and holding the rock, hearing the splash), and intention ("I want to remember... ") and letting go.

EULOGIES

It can be a useful exercise for participants to write eulogies for themselves, addressing the question, "If you died now, what would you want to be said about you at your funeral?" This question invites death into the circle, and it encourages people to take a broader, more detached view of themselves, a view most people on a quest are looking for. The imminence of death also encourages clarity, sobriety, and a willingness to look at things as they are; to honestly assess one's strengths and weaknesses — or "character defects" as they say in AA — and see them in their entirety. To clearly assess that sum total, we need a little distance from ourselves.

In the exercise, distance is created by taking the point of view that *someone else* will be reading and speaking this eulogy after the subject has died. This speaker is a "friendly other," not the Critic — a close, but objective, friend. He or she is familiar with the hopes, dreams, fears, and challenges — the heart — of the dying person. This close other knows the inner life of the dying, but also views him or her from outside, aware of those places where the inner and the outer lives matched... or did not.

The writers-readers know the core values, commitments, successes, and failures of the person. They see the thread, the irreducible residue, the story of this life, and the eulogies tell this story: what's completed, what remains, and what's left undone. They speak both *of* the person and *for* him or her, conveying what the deceased would deem important to say if they could be here to say farewell themselves.

Remind people that the eulogy is to be written *as if they died now*, not in 30 years after they've discovered a cure for cancer and brokered peace in the Middle East. (Someone did this once.) The eulogy is an assessment and remembrance of their life as it is *at this moment*, not a fairy tale of the good little princes and princesses becoming gods.

When the eulogies are written they may (sooner or later) be spoken to the hills, burned in a fire, shared with the group, or offered to the mystery in some way.

FLOWERING TREE CEREMONY

The written instructions (below) can be passed out and gone over with the group. If each person has the instructions present, questions (other than "how much time should we take?") will likely be minimal. If there is any need for emphasis, it probably should be on taking the relationship with the tree (or other parts of the landscape) seriously, again accentuating the need for a new myth where we're not more important than all the other parts of creation.

If the landscape you're in lacks trees, the instructions can be adjusted, substituting a large boulder, for example, or modified to simply create a circle. One would then sit in the center and at the circumference, facing toward and away from the directions themselves.

INSTRUCTIONS

The tree is an archetypal symbol. Standing at "the center of the world," its roots penetrate deep into the underworld and the past. The trunk emerges into this world and the present, and the crown reaches toward heaven. Through this connection of root and crown, earth and sky, life flowers, bearing seeds and fruit. And as the fruit falls from the tree, we are reminded of our own lives — the letting go, the giveaway, the transcendence of our own ego and death. The ceremony offers our selves to ourselves.

Be guided to a tree. Let your awareness become fully present. Create feelings of communion. Make an offering (tobacco, prayer, affection, etc.). Sit with your back against the tree, and

- Facing south, ask, "What must I give away to understand the experience of my emotions?" Wait. Then move, again with your back to the tree, and

- Face north and ask, "What must I give away to clarify my mind?" Wait. Moving once again,
- Face west and ask, "What must I give away to heal my body?" Wait. And finally,
- Face east and ask, "What must I give away to find my path with heart?" Wait.

Your back no longer leaning against the tree, face it from a short distance away, and, moving around the cardinal directions, ask:

- From the south, facing north (toward the tree), "Who am I?"
- From the north of the tree, facing south, "What is my true direction?"
- From west of the tree, facing east: "Where do I come from?"
- From the east, facing the tree/west: "Where am I going?"

When finished, circle around the tree. Bring your full attention to its presence. Give thanks or an offering, and perform some kind of closing ceremony to finish.

Record your answers. They can and will change over time.

GOAL SETTING

In a contemporary-day vision quest, the issues of The Return — how to bring this rich and intense experience home to the "other side of the mountains" — are always crucial. Working with peoples' goals, intentions, and commitments could be part of the incorporation process. The exercise below can be useful in bringing what could be abstract and subjective into a series of concrete action steps to take when they arrive home.

On a sheet of paper, write the words *Do*, *Have*, and *Be* at the top of the page.

Make a list of everything you want to do, have, or be in the next two years (or five years, or one year). The labeling is unimportant. One could *have* a regular exercise program, *be* in better shape, or *do* a five-mile run four times a week. Making this list may take 20 to 30 minutes.

Go down the list and in front of each item, label it *A, B,* or *C*.

Put *A* in front of each item that would make a major qualitative difference in your life if it were to happen, or that you would grieve if it didn't eventually happen.

Label the statement *B* if it would really improve your life or bring you great pleasure, but without it you could still live without a great deal of regret.

Label it *C* if it would be nice, but in the final analysis, not really necessary.

On a new sheet of paper, make a list of all the items or statements labeled *A* on the previous page.

Go down the list of the *A* items, and mark them in order of importance (*A-1*, *A-2*, *A-3*, etc.) The thing you labeled *A-1* is the one that, if you were to achieve it, or if it were to come to pass, would most significantly impact and improve your life. What you label *A-2* is the next most significant, etc.

Next, take a new sheet of paper, and at the top of it write *A-1*. At the top of another new sheet of paper, write *A-2*. On another sheet, *A-3*...

On the sheet labeled *A-1*, list everything that would have to happen for *A-1* to come to pass. Include all the details; for example, "research possible schools," "take X amount of time off work," "save Y dollars," "book plane tickets," "learn Spanish," etc., depending on what the goal is.

Then go down the list and mark them 1, 2, 3, etc., the numbers indicating the order in which these things would have to happen to ensure *A-1* comes to pass.

At this point you will have determined the thing that would most change your life for the better, and you will have a plan — a series of steps, listed in order — for how to bring it about. Most people have never done this in their entire lives.

Do the same for *A-2* and *A-3*. Or these could be done later if there's limited time.

INVOCATIONS

To invoke means to call on or summon. This can be for a blessing, help, inspiration, etc. An invocation is a solemn prayer, a plea to some larger force — gods, saints, allies, ancestors, the spirit of the mountains, etc. — for aid in some endeavor. Traditionally, invocations marked the beginning of church services, or, via ritual or other means in pagan times, called in powers relevant to the task at hand.

Invocations can take many forms. These could include smudging, prayer, chanting, candles, creating designs or spaces with circles, pentacles, etc. But whatever their form, they happen within sacred space, or are part of creating that sacred space. An invocation includes the form (smudging, prayer, chant, etc.), the naming of whom or what is addressed, and the request.

Many opening circles begin with an invocation. People stand. Perhaps a smudge bowl is lit, smoke is wafted over the body, and the first prayer begins: "Great Mystery, Spirit-in-all-Things, thank you for... " After that, the bowl is passed around; each person smudges and has an opportunity to speak. In so doing, we call on larger forces, naming them and asking for their help — "Mother-Father God... spirit of the summer... powers of the night... Grandmother Moon... my grandfather, Silas... the animal powers... medicine teachers... etc."

The names, entities, or powers called on can be many. By speaking to them we satisfy the requirements of creating sacred space — the calling in of forces and presences beyond our human, socially created circle. We connect to larger energies at play in the world, energies that support and sustain all life, energies that may have created us. By giving them our attention, acknowledgment, and respect, our prayers open a conversation and create a portal through which energy and attention may pass in both directions.

LETTER FROM THE DEATH BED

Writing a letter from your death bed to your self-of-today helps to get in touch with your core wisdom — your soul — by imagining and becoming the wise older man or woman, who then offers advice to the you of today. Various processes, such as the goals exercise, reach forward in time, hoping to project some passion, desire, or energy (felt now) into the plans or visions of tomorrow. This exercise moves in the opposite direction.

People are told that they will imagine, embody, and become the person they will be years from now when they sit in their death bed. This exercise is not focused on how the person will die, which could be quick and dramatic with little time for thought. The image we seek is peaceful and content, as elders reflectively looking back on their journey with the accumulated wisdom from all those years of experience. This image could be five or 50 years away, depending on the age and condition of the people in the circle.

In this imaginary journey, each person becomes that elder, wise with years of experience yet to be had by the person they are now. From this perspective, the elder writes a letter to the person he or she is today. He or she offers advice, encouragement, support, and caution — whatever that wise elder within would say to help the person who is living within the concerns and conditions of the present day. The letters may be kept private or shared with the rest of the group.

This exercise fits well within the theme of The Return. Accessing our wise elder energy is one way of giving voice to our soul's purpose or mission. As an elder on the death bed, each person is free of the concerns and demands of daily existence. There are no questions about whether to remodel the kitchen, buy a car, or change careers. On one's death bed, the wise elder can sense those threads woven through life that have brought continuity and definition, the threads that create the story of a life.

As these elders reach back to today — to the people sitting in our circle who may have both a mission and a partner who wants that new kitchen; to the people connected to their souls who have to return and live on that "other side of the mountain" — they can offer advice about the importance of holding to one's vision. They can speak about the gifts that are (and aren't) important to give, and the direction they need to take from here if they're to feel satisfied with their journey and life.

MISSION STATEMENTS

A Vision without a Task is just a pipe dream.
A Task without a Vision is just drudgery
But a Vision with a Task can move the world.[15]

Mission statements could be useful in preparing for the return. Mission statements say "this is who I am" in the realm of the soul. These statements include the element of vision and the element of task, and they announce how vision (the connection to the imaginal, archetypal, eternal realm) will be enacted or expressed in the current or concrete conditions we experience today.

Vision is a statement of harmony between you and your soul, you and your purpose or higher power. A statement like "my purpose is to bring music into the world" speaks to vision, to *what* you are here for. Task is more specific. It refers to the *how*, the expression of vision in the context of the culture and life one inhabits. "Bringing music into the world" is vision, but being a conductor of the Boston Symphony Orchestra, teaching a children's choir, or playing washtub bass in a jug band are very different ways of expression, different forms that vision can take.

Working with vision and task through the medium of a mission statement, it's important that the vision be broad enough and the task be specific enough. Imagine sitting on a mountain or in a wide valley. Vision happens in those moments when your eyes are pulled to the horizon. Touched by the vastness and sensing the unknown that stretches beyond your field of view, you're drawn out of yourself as your awareness expands into a larger picture.

"I want to grow enough food to feed my family" is a noble goal, but too small to be called a vision. The man or woman who wants to grow food to feed his or her family is speaking from the "I," the ego or conscious self. Vision connects a person to a larger story, a frame of reference greater than this self. As such, a vision may not be something *you have*, but something greater that *has you*. Living or enacting it will stretch, pull, or push you forward, and tug at you like a current you can't avoid. It beckons beyond the fences of daily life like a great dream you must realize or grow into.

A task must be both in accord with one's vision — "bringing music into the world through drinking two cups of coffee a day" won't do it — and specific enough to provide direction and be practical. The statement "I create a world of peace through speaking the truth" is close to a mission statement. The vision, the purpose — "creating a world of peace" — is a larger framework and is stated. The requirement of "what" is met.

But "speaking the truth" needs to be more specific to be useful. Speaking the truth: how, when, where, and about what? Will you be speaking the truth to the military–industrial complex, to drug addicts, to your wife or husband... or to your neighbor's spouse whom you have fantasies about? Will you speak the truth about capitalism, baseball, obesity, rising hospital costs, or your abusive childhood? Will you speak the truth in a therapist's office, through writing articles in a newspaper, or by running for political office?

A good mission statement connects earth and sky. The sky is grand, expansive, transcendent. It's home to hawk and eagle, a place of vision and light. But by itself, the sky is aloof, distant, and above it all. It's airy and ungrounded. Earth is imminent and right here, solid, grounded, and foundational. It's the realm of form, the body, rootedness; a place of death and rebirth. Task brings vision down to earth. As the Native American teacher Sun Bear said, "If your vision doesn't grow corn, I don't want to hear about it."[16]

Most people who realize a vision and create a mission statement find the articulation of purpose aligns deeply with their core self. It may feel joyful, like remembering a passionate involvement you've had forever with roots in childhood. Joseph Campbell advised that if you want to find it, "follow your bliss." Related to this is that in the four directions teachings of the medicine wheel, the second lesson of the north (becoming an adult) has to do with the giveaway. The giveaway asks, "What gifts do you have to give to your people?"

This big question is really two questions. The first, "What are my gifts?" is not just a report of talents or capability. It asks, "Who are you? What brings you alive? What is it that, when you're doing it, feels totally right, like your best and fullest?" Your gift (and mission) are not about martyrdom, about giving up who you are (for example, your love of music) to save the starving in East Africa. The real giveaway involves embodying yourself fully... for your people. If your gift — who you are — is to be a shaman, musician, or poet, *that's what you give* to your people! If your core passion involves writing, dance, or architecture, that's what you give to your people! The giveaway involves fully inhabiting your life, for your people!

Therein lies the second question: "Who are your people?" Where and to whom will you give this gift? To your partner and kids, to anyone in recovery, to those on a spiritual path? To war veterans, to children who've suffered trauma, to men, or to those seeking economic justice? To Gaia or animals on the verge of extinction? The question "Who are your people?" — like the relationship of task to vision — brings the path of the heart into the actual steps you'll take tomorrow. It brings the landscape and narrative of the soul into work, family, and community.

A full appreciation of mission — the melding of vision and task — can bring us into the Warrior Archetype. At the center of this archetype is a commitment to something larger and outside of the self. The self and its needs for comfort, convenience, or affirmation are not the center of one's concerns. Warriors' loyalties lie elsewhere, and, given those commitments and loyalties, they are willing to mold, change, and discipline themselves to serve that mission by achieving the tasks at hand.

OPENING AND CLOSING RITUALS

An opening ritual is a symbolic act that marks a beginning. It can be quite simple. Walking along a path, one can draw a line in the sand and say, "When I step over that line, I am leaving behind *X* and stepping into *Y*. It can take many forms: a movement in space from one room to another, prayers, invocations, lighting of candles, etc.

A group of people gathering for a vision quest involves a different space, set of intentions, and community than most situations in normal life. It may be too much and too difficult to simply drop all concerns from that world "on the other side of the trees" and be fully present in this new one. An opening ritual is a good way to mark and make the transition from one space into another. People have made a literal transition, some flying across the country, taking buses, or driving hundreds of miles. But it is that other transition — from mundane to sacred space — that we are more concerned with.

A good opening ritual will address both aspects: the leaving behind and the moving into. A simple starting point could be asking people to stand. The smudge bowl is lit and passed around. Each person wafts the smoke over themselves, symbolically cleansing their energy fields from everything not aligned with our collective intentions. In so doing, they're asked to leave behind the worries and concerns that have followed them into this new space. People then speak, addressing the Great Mystery, God, the Spirit-in-All-Things, and expressing gratitude for the blessings and gifts they've received, invoking and asking help from ancestors, guides, and the Earth itself, powers beyond those they are aware of now. By doing so, they cast their attention, voices, and intentions into sacred space, toward something greater than themselves.

Closing rituals also mark a leaving behind and an entrance into. Only this time the door to the sacred space is shut as we move homeward toward the dream of daily existence.

In various programs, we find it useful to close with a Final Council. In it, each person is aware we're ending and this is their final chance to speak from the heart to the whole group together. When the council is complete, everyone stands, as we did at the beginning, coming together in a huddle, making physical contact. Wishes or blessings for those facing challenges in the near future; words of wisdom to carry away together; hopes for what's coming; words affirming our bonds and mutual caring... are offered and shared in the hope that, as the circle is broken, we remember we have companions and are not alone.

PRESENTING YOUR EGO TO A TREE

This exercise can be great fun, as well as quite revealing. It begins by having people go onto the land and wander (separately) until they find a tree that "speaks to them," a tree they feel connected to in some way. (In a desert, this could be a boulder.)

Once they find the tree, participants stand a few feet from its trunk and proceed, for at least five minutes, to "present their ego to the tree." This must be done powerfully and energetically, and it should last the full five minutes, no matter how awkward it may feel. Once someone has presented his ego to the tree, he stops, remains silent for 15 to 20 seconds, and then asks the tree, "Is there anything you'd like to say to me about all this?"

"Presenting your ego" — what does that mean? In simple terms, your ego is what you do to get attention from people. It's your "shtick," the "face" you show to the world because you think it will get a response that you want. For example, one person's shtick might be, "Look how smart and funny I am!" Perhaps she was good in school and learned to make everyone laugh so her classmates wouldn't envy or resent her. And it worked so well that she continues it, in some form, to this day.

Another person's ego or shtick might be letting everyone know how tough, unflappable, or competent he is. But a shtick doesn't have to be positive. Some version of "let me tell you what a difficult life I've had" is used by many people to elicit support and sympathy, or to avoid making choices and taking responsibility. Whatever it is, once you recognize it, you must speak aloud for at least five minutes, telling that tree how smart, funny, or tough you are, or what a tough life you've had. When finished, after a short period of silence, you ask the tree to respond, to let you know what it thinks of this.

This exercise doesn't have to be "serious." Let it be fun. When presenting one's ego it can be helpful to ham it up, to exaggerate. The point is to not hold back, to put it out there. The learning can take place during the presentation itself. You hear a voice — "What a crock of shit" — as you express this shtick that you do consistently whenever people are around. Or insight can come in the tree's response, as you hear a comment or observation that is wise, deep, and soulful.

SMUDGING

Smudging is a ritual found, in various forms, throughout the world. It involves the burning of herbs — usually associated with some medicinal properties — that have effects on the physical or psychic space in which they are burned. It's often associated with Native Americans, who burned sage for cleansing and purification, cedar for clarity and balance, or sweet grass for openness and harmonious energy.

But the practice is not limited to North America. Copal is a well-known plant whose resin is used for smudging in Central and South America. Frankincense was widely used throughout Europe. The scientific name given to sage, the most widely used smudge in North America, was Artemisia, because it was sacred to Artemis and burned in her temples in ancient Grece. And many Catholic rituals began with processions, at the head of which a smoldering smudge or incense pot was swung back and forth to clear the space.

Practically, there are many options. Sage comes in both the broadleaf (white) variety often burned in a bowl or leaf-by-leaf and the common variety (*Artemisia vulgaris*). Common sage can be stripped from the stalk, crushed into powder, and burned in an abalone shell. Or it can be wrapped into cylinders (commonly with cedar) to make the popular smudge sticks. Sweetgrass is most often woven into long braids. Cedar, in small sprigs, is very flammable and goes up like a torch. It can be lit, then quickly blown out, and the sprig will smolder.

Smudging can be used to cleanse or bless an individual, room, or designated space — even an entire house — and the methods will vary accordingly. The smoke from the burning leaf, stick, or smudge bowl may be wafted over someone or throughout an area, or the smoke may be fanned and spread with a feather or wing. In general, unless you've been immersed in a particular tradition, it's better to give attention to the spirit or intention of the ritual (cleansing, blessing, or prayer) rather than worry about the details or letter of whatever method you're using.

Smudging can also be a vehicle for prayer. Much like in the use of a pipe, smoke spreads, scatters, and disperses throughout a space — it is carried to "the four corners of the world." Thus, the smoke created by smudging can be viewed as carrying prayers out into the universe.

Smudging is commonly used at the start of a gathering, meeting, or ritual. Since it cleanses and blesses, it prepares participants for whatever is to follow, and the ritual of smudging marks a change. Done with reverence, silence, and prayerfulness, the group is moved from a secular, social, and psychologically scattered environment into a focused and sacred space.

TRUTH MANDALA

The truth mandala[17] is a ritual for accessing and exploring the world of feelings, our inner lives. This ritual can be powerful and effective when used with groups, though on a vision quest it's a solo activity. It can be used as a way to address particular issues or relationships or as a general method for evoking, expressing, and learning about the deeper currents in our psyches.

First, a large circle is created — a border of stones, branches, rope, a line in the sand. It's then divided into four sizeable quadrants by two lines through the center perpendicular to each other. Each quadrant represents a difficult emotion. There is a quadrant for *Fear*, one for *Anger*, and one for *Grief* (sorrow, or loss.) The last quadrant is called Emptiness , and it represents a lack of feeling, which could be experienced as numbness, apathy, or confusion — generally a damping down of, or disconnection from, emotion.

An object, something distinct, is placed in each quadrant to help identify and mark it. For example, a thick stick could be placed in the anger quadrant and could be used to pound on the ground when angry. A stone might represent fear: the hardness and contraction this emotion brings to the heart. Bones or dead leaves could mark the grief quadrant, representing the loss of something vital or important. A bowl, empty or turned over, could mark the field of emptiness.

A flat stone or smaller circle is usually placed in the center.

INDIVIDUAL INSTRUCTIONS

Decide that the truth mandala will last some predetermined amount of time, making sure there's enough, or it can be considered finished when there's nothing more to express. Allow periods of waiting — times for emotions to ebb and flow, come and go.

When ready, step in. If you enter the quadrant of anger, speak or express — out loud — all you are angry about. It could be past or present, personal or political, small or large. It might be about your angry father, your critical brother, or the spouse who left you without child support. It could be about politics, the extinction of species, or those who pollute the earth.

When finished, or just moved, enter another quadrant to express your fear, grief, or loss. Move around the circle as you are drawn. Return to quadrants you have previously stepped out of as memories or new feelings surface. Just begin. Speak your truth about love, dashed dreams; rivers and rainforests; your friends, father, or future. Oftentimes, speaking the words stimulates the feelings. Feel free to cry, scream, pound, or wail.

You can proceed from any quadrant to any other. There are no requirements to visit every quadrant and no prohibitions against stepping back into a section you've previously stepped out of. It's common to go from anger to grief, then back to anger... to fear, then emptiness, and back to anger again.

As the time for ending approaches, having fully expressed your truth, move to the center and sense the power and hope inherent in your capacity for feeling. Acknowledge that our pain alerts us when something is wrong, toxic, or out of balance. Affirm the courage it took to speak these truths, to feel these emotions. Recognize that anger, fear, and sorrow are like an immune system, rooting out toxins and mobilizing the possibility, energy, and opportunity to change.

Affirm the hope represented by the fact that at least one person in the world — you — is willing to hear the truth, to eschew denial, and to face the reality of his or her emotions. There is someone who doesn't need to hide or medicate the anger, grief, fear, and emptiness he or she lives with. Say "Yes!" to your longing to live, truly live, even amidst all the suffering and injustice.

In closing, people may want to thank the earth for listening, and for creating the eyes, ears, senses, and heart that can sense and feel all this. Some may want to smudge, clear the energy, and, having experienced powerful emotions, take a break before moving on to whatever is next.

SECTION VII:
THE RETURN

The Promise and the Challenge....153
Facing Challenges: The Odyssey....155
The Promise: Finding Fertile Soil....156

Practical Steps on the Path Home....157
Stone Pile Communications....157
Writing a Letter of Intent....157
Calling a Council of Allies....157
Changing Physical Space and Time....158

Vision and... "Reality"....158
Stopping the Train....159
The Circle of Purpose....160
Worthy Opponents....161

SECTION VII:
THE RETURN

As mentioned in Section I, in earlier times the incorporation process might continue through months (and years) as the sacred dream experience was woven into the fabric of daily life. But today's small groups have limited time, and participants will soon be heading back to a home, community, and daily life likely to be, at best, partially supportive, and, at worst, indifferent or hostile.

Since ongoing incorporation and integration is largely unavailable within small, temporary groups that quest together, people must be prepared to return to a daily existence mostly deficient in the qualities and assistance traditionally critical to completing a vision quest. The task of The Return is to bridge these two worlds, to bring something from the imaginal, liminal, soul-filled realm back to the world of daily life.

This may be far more challenging and difficult than four days alone without food.

Many myths of the heroic journey show the return to be dangerous. Danger means there are outer forces (people, vested interests, situations) and inner investments of energy (habits, beliefs, ways of seeing the world) that oppose any major change of orientation. Those guiding modern-day quests must address and allow for this fact. Suggestions, teachings, and tools for going back to daily life need to be provided. The final days provide a last opportunity to affirm and anchor the gains that have been made, and to offer perspectives, practical advice, and resources to continue the journey "on the other side of the mountains."

What follows is a sample talk — as if it were being given to a group about to depart — that contains teachings, tools, and perspectives that may be helpful for those about to go back. Borrow or add to this as you see fit.

THE PROMISE AND THE CHALLENGE

You have gone to the mountain, desert, or forest. You have fasted, endured, celebrated, and prayed, and now it's time to return home. Many have loved ones and sources of support waiting and anticipating their coming back with excitement. Others face confusion, situations and relationships that don't work, and major changes that need to be made, and after the clarity of their solo time they may dread or wish to put off returning. But this next step must be made.

The following poems speak about both the promise and the challenge of the return. The promise, ultimately, is that daily life contains the garden and soil where we will plant the seeds of our vision. There, the possibility of enacting and manifesting our soul's calling will play out. We must follow through, tend and nurture this garden, and watch it grow and develop. Of course, we face the danger of forgetting and losing touch with what we have gained.

This poem, by Mary Oliver, is called "The Return." Theseus, the youthful Athenian hero, volunteers to face the Minotaur, a monstrous half man, half beast, who lurks in a bewildering labyrinth. Even after battling and defeating the monster, Theseus still must find his way out. Fortunately, Ariadne, daughter of the king of Crete, has fallen in love with him, and, before he enters presents him with a ball of string, making him promise to unravel it as he traverses the dark passageways. He speaks:

The deed took all my heart.
I did not think of you,
Not till the thing was done.
I put my sword away,
And then no more the cold
And perfect fury ran
Along my narrow bones,
And then no more the black
And dripping corridors
Held anywhere the shape
That I had come to slay.
Then, for the first time,
I saw in the cave's belly
The dark and clotted webs,
The green sucking pools,
The rank and crumbling walls,
The maze of passages.

And I thought then
Of the far earth,
Of the spring sun
And slow wind,
And a young girl.
And I looked then
At the white thread.

Hunting the Minotaur
I was no common man
And had no need of love.
I trailed the shining thread
Behind me, for a vow,
And did not think of you.
It lay there, like a sign,
Coiled on the bull's great hoof
And leading back into the world.
Half blind with weariness
I touched the thread and wept.
O, it was frail as air.

I turned then
With the white spool
Through the cold rocks,
Through the black rocks,
Through the long webs,
And the mist fell,
And the webs clung,
And the rocks tumbled,
And the earth shook.

And the thread held.

After heroic challenges and inner struggles, we must return to a life that's usually far less epic, far more ordinary. We return to daily life because of those bonds that are not chains. These are bonds of love, family, friendship, human warmth, and belonging. They are strings of responsibility, in the best sense of the word — response-ability — the capacity and potential to make a difference. These threads are necessary to weave a spiritual life. Like Christ who was birthed in a manger, what is primal, archetypal, God-like, or transcendent must be brought to earth.

The next poem was written by Mirabai, a resident of sixteenth-century India. She was born into an aristocratic Brahmin family and, early on, married off to a prince. In some respects, her family represents the "family" from which we all have come, staid, conservative, and representative of the social order. Later, her husband died, and Mirabai left to follow the Bhakti path, traveling from village to village, singing, dancing, and praising Krishna. Her relatives were mortified that a woman of her standing would act this way, bringing dishonor to the family. Many messages were sent: "Come home and behave yourself!" Finally, they dispatched her brother with a burro, commanding him to "put her on this donkey and bring her home."

Mirabai replied with a poem, and it's called "Why Mira Can't Go Back to Her Old House."

The colors of the dark one (Krishna) have penetrated Mira's body,
All the other ones washed out.
Making love with Krishna and eating little,
those are my pearls and my carnelians.
Chanting beads and the forehead streak,
those are my bracelets.
That's enough feminine wiles for me.

My teacher taught me this...
Approve me or disapprove me,
I praise the mountain energy night and day.
I take the path ecstatic human beings have
taken for centuries.
I don't steal anything, nor do I hit anyone.
What will you charge me with?
I have felt the swaying of the elephant's shoulders
and now you want me to climb on a jackass?
Try to be serious!

This represents one challenge in going back. You have experienced hunger and aloneness. You've sensed the motion of the earth as the sun and stars circled above you, felt the "the swaying of the elephant's shoulders" as you plumbed the depths of your soul. Now, you return, and the world says, "climb on a jackass!" The stories are so small, the concerns so petty: "Earn more, buy more! One-day sale only!" Commercials blare and conversations numb as conventional society moves to dumb us down. It sells substitutes for real experience, trying to medicate our emptiness and enroll us in avoidances and addictions. "Tune in to the last episode of Survivor!! Climb on this jackass!" It can be a challenge to go back.

But our hero — You — has heeded the call and adventured into a realm of great and primal forces to face demons, charm enemies, and overcome obstacles. Whatever has been found — whether it appears as a magic potion or a Golden Fleece, whether we call it truth, or vision, or soul — it needs to be brought back into the world we have left.

In some stories, this is the most difficult and dangerous part. In Grimm's fairy tale "The Water of Life," the youngest child succeeds, obtaining the life-giving liquid. But his older brothers deceive and betray him. They steal the transforming fluid in hope of winning favor with the king and, eventually, gaining his throne and possessions. They wish to take what is magical, precious, and sacred and turn it into what is social and profane — wealth and power. This conflict between the old order and the new, between the sacred and the profane, often appears as danger in the return.

FACING CHALLENGES: THE ODYSSEY

The Odyssey is the greatest single story devoted to the return. Odysseus leaves his beloved home, Ithaca, his son, Telemachus, and his wife, Penelope, to fight in the Trojan War. After ten long years, the campaign is finally over, and he aches to go back home. *The Odyssey* chronicles his journey to return to where he belongs and the place he loves — his land, people, wife, and son.

But Poseidon, god of the sea, is angry when Odysseus kills one of his sons, the Cyclops Polyphemus. As Odysseus sails home, Poseidon sends storm after storm against him. He is lost, shipwrecked, stranded; he faces challenge after challenge. He's tempted by Sirens and seduced by Calypso. His men are bewitched and turned into swine.

The journey home takes another ten years, and by the time he finally completes it, all his ships and men have been lost. At long last, he comes within sight of Ithaca's shores, the land he loves. But "wily, cunning," Odysseus is no fool. He lands at a hidden cove down the coast, disguising himself as a beggar to take the measure of the place. He will observe what's happening before announcing he is back.

But the situation at home is not very welcoming. Suitors clutter his court. They assure his wife that he is dead and will never return, pressuring her to remarry. They drink his wine, abuse his servants, loot his stores of grain, and conspire to kill his son, hatching plots to steal his kingdom and take what is rightfully his. Witnessing this deceit, he reveals his identity to a shepherd who has remained loyal, and then sends for his son. He will need allies for what must be done. They make a plan.

Be cautious on your return. Proceed strategically. Odysseus isn't foolish; he doesn't assume everyone will be thrilled to see him. If he disembarked in the main harbor and walked down "Main Street," he would have been killed. He knew he was the rightful ruler of the land, but first he scouted and assessed the situation, determining who his friends were. He revealed his true identity to his allies, made plans for dealing with his enemies, developed a strategy, and prepared well.

It's difficult when returning from a vision quest, or any numinous or transformative experience, to realize that not everyone will support you. No matter how loving or open you are, the world's other inhabitants have their own agendas. Purpose, intention, planning, and protection can be just as important when re-entering the human world as it was walking into the wilderness.

Christ said "Love thy enemy," but he never said they weren't the enemy. Adversaries and adverse situations exist, and anyone trying to steal your throne is your opponent. A throne is a metaphor for power, whether you label it your truth, passion, soul, voice, calling, or vision. Anyone denying that or wishing to take it from you is an "enemy."

Upon your return, don't be naive. There are people with whom you do not want to share your vision; there are situations where sharing your truth will only result in ridicule or hurt. But there are also places, allies, and friends who want to honor what you've accomplished, who want to support and recognize who you are. It's important and necessary to share your experience with those allies, and by doing so, bring it into the daily world, back to your community and your people.

THE PROMISE: FINDING FERTILE SOIL

As mentioned, the traditional question of the north shield teaching — "What gift do I have to bring to my people?" — is really two questions: "What is my vision or gift?" and its complement, "Who are my people?" Consider your gift to be a seed. It might feel small or tentative, an unfamiliar energy you're carrying, but imagine it's like an acorn — newly arrived, but with the potential to grow a magnificent oak like those towering above. If this acorn comes to rest on the pavement, it will be crushed. If it's planted in the desert, it will die.

If an acorn falls to the ground and begins to take root, the young seedling is very tender. A storm or period of drought could destroy it. But when our oak has taken root, grown, and branched out, it has developed the strength to survive storms and times of challenge. A supportive community that validates, mirrors, and affirms your experience upon return from a quest is fertile soil to take root in. Having a small group of allies with whom you've shared this deep experience can provide a taste of what you're seeking before the actual return home to job, family, commitments, and the hectic pace of modern life and can be instrumental in allowing those new commitments, insights, and visions to stay alive.

The acorn is your gift and vision. Upon your actual arrival home, finding that rich, nurturing earth is the first order of business. Ask yourself, "Who will listen to my story; who will acknowledge and support me?" Do you have friends who will remind you of your intentions, ask you, "Have you painted this week?" or "What have you done with your music lately?" Those people are your allies. They constitute fertile soil, and you need to find them.

You may encounter people or situations where you are unsure of the response you'll receive to the truths and commitments of your soul. You'll need to feel your way. Someone at the office knew you were going on a trip and asks questions on your return. Share a little about what you did; if their response is affirming, share more. But if their eyes glaze over, or they start to make jokes, stop. You are not being heard, and encounters like this will not help your vision grow.

In the natural world, every seed is protected by a shell, an impervious barrier that safeguards what's inside until the conditions are right. Moisture, warmth, soft ground... If those conditions are not present, the shell must remain intact; otherwise, what's inside will perish. The shell guards the germ against opening in the wrong place or at the wrong time, in environments and conditions that are harsh, inhospitable, or barren.

Just as you searched for "your spot" in an unfamiliar landscape, upon returning, determine where there is fertile soil and where there is not. Be like Odysseus, cautious in assessing who your allies are. You do not have to be good. It is naive to believe we should be nice and open all the time. Love your enemies, yes, but they *are* your enemies!

In the sacred space of a vision quest, we cultivate a fierce openness to our inner lives and each other. But that openness is rare on the "other side of the mountains," and it's important to protect what is raw, open, and tender from hostile and barren environments. We need to bring the seed — our gift — back home with its shell intact. It must be planted — if it's not, it will die — but only in the nurturing soil of soulful relationships and interactions. The task of the return is to find that soil — in relationships, work, and our connection with the beautiful earth — and hatch, tend, and cultivate our vision so it can grow, flower, and bear fruit to feed and heal a hungry world.

PRACTICAL STEPS ON THE PATH HOME

STONE PILE COMMUNICATIONS

For those on a group quest, the "stone pile letter" is a way to help keep the community going. On the solo, the stone pile is a place you leave a sign of some sort that says "I've been here." Later, your buddy arrives, leaving another sign to mark his or her presence. Stone pile letters begin when a participant volunteers to write about the journey back within a month — the successes and difficulties in living out the vision — and send the letter off to the rest of the group. Then it becomes someone else's turn to "visit the stone pile" by writing a similar letter within the following month and mailing it to everyone. And onward it goes. Technology has made it easy (email, Facebook, Google) to have group communications, and some groups have kept in close contact, or even have reunions, over many years. Some, if they're geographically close, meet for dinner at regular intervals. Others gather for trips to wilderness areas or return to where they all fasted. The stone pile letter can help a group stay connected.

WRITING A LETTER OF INTENT

A letter of intent is often required before participating in a vision quest. It helps to write one for going back. Consider the journey home — what your tasks and purposes are. What are your intentions about how you want to live, what you want to leave behind, and what you wish to embody, enact, and incorporate? Who, or what, are your allies or sources of support? What challenges, fears, or obstacles will you have to face, and what are your plans for doing so? Writing this letter can easily be done in an hour. As you head back to your house or apartment, job, work, relationships, family, etc., how do you want to live and express yourself there? Making a plan or statement about living purposefully will help offset the tendency to go unconscious and once again be ruled by habits, routines, or the desires of others, and it can help jumpstart your efforts to bring your vision more into your life.

CALLING A COUNCIL OF ALLIES

Throughout most of human history, people did not come off the mountain and return to isolated lives. They were members of a village, tribe, or community that supported their quest and vision. Part of the difficult work we face, personally and culturally, is discerning associations on a human-sized scale where soul and spirit can be spoken of and validated. Finding, establishing, and then contributing to "your people" are central to a successful return.

Company is much stronger than willpower. We can make all sorts of resolutions about what we hope or plan to do, but in time our will begins to taper off. But, if you have companions willing to join you, you'll likely be doing that practice months down the road. Getting community support for your vision or having others enrolled in your dream helps you significantly.

People often return home excited to share their quest experience with a partner, close friends, children, etc. This is good, a part of planting our seeds in the world. But it gets tiring to tell this story again and again, or repeatedly respond to inquiries when you are pressed for time or randomly run into friends. It is richer, and far more effective, to call a council of allies.

Within a few weeks of returning, create an occasion, perhaps a barbecue or pot-luck dinner, and invite those who are your confidants and supporters. Gather as many of them as possible for a celebration, during which you'll tell the story of your quest. Share your hopes in coming back. Be honest about any fears of losing your connection to spirit and vision. Ask these people to be your allies, to encourage and help you honor and serve your dream. This is a powerful thing to do. It begins grounding the quest in daily life, creates an immediate support group, and relieves you of the burden of repeating you story endless times. You can tell it once, fully and well, to those you love.

If you have previously written a letter of intent for returning home, you can also share this with your council, asking their assistance in holding you to your commitments and purpose. And calling together this council of allies can reap unexpected benefits. Friendships grow deeper from sharing ceremonies such as this. Many have reported their friends thanking them, the ripples then spreading as these friends are inspired to bring more truth, depth, and purpose into their own lives.

CHANGING PHYSICAL SPACE AND TIME

In a rite of passage, the return phase is called incorporation, and conscious acts or rituals of incorporation are helpful. One concrete way to ground your vision in daily life is by changing your physical space. Imagine a typical house containing a kitchen for cooking, a dining room for eating, a bathroom for bathing, and a bedroom for sleeping. It might also have an office, den, even an "entertainment center." Where is the space devoted to spirit?

We have become conditioned to live in a secular world, and our physical environments are arranged for practical, social, and mundane purposes. These spaces reflect *and influence* our lives and priorities. Visualize the Taj Mahal, the cathedral at Chartres, Zen rock gardens, Machu Picchu... These sacred spaces contain and evoke energy. Look around your living space and see where your attention is drawn and what energy commitments are physically manifested. Ask, "Could this be changed?"

There are many possible ways to do this. You could make an altar. Walls, usually decorated with photos or mass-produced images, could be home to masks, drums, mandalas, or dream-catchers. Elements of your vision quest — walking staffs, stones that spoke to you, hawk or raven feathers... medicine objects of all kinds — may be willing to accompany you home to remind you of your vision. A room used for storage could be cleared, creating a new space to smudge, write, do yoga, paint, journey, or meditate — to engage in whatever practice brings you back to the center of your circle. Welcoming Spirit into your home can have subtle or profound effects on how you view or relate to the world, as well as helping your living space become more alive.

Einstein declared we live in space-time, and the complement to changing our space is changing our commitments of time. Our duration on this earth is limited, and time may be our most valuable resource. Energy flows where attention goes. Who or what do we give our time or attention to? Is this what we want? Ask this question seriously.

There are a multitude of ways to give attention and energy to spiritual life. You could meditate, sing, or paint; run, dance, or pray. Perhaps you love to walk outside. Having a dog is a good excuse to get out. Any of these, done consistently, declare, "Spirit, I give you my time." Making these commitments nonnegotiable or the first thing done in the morning makes your soul's journey a priority. The time required need not be long. Ten minutes of smudging, singing, or gratitude may be enough. Keeping this commitment limited may even be wise. A "little bit of something" that's consistently done is far better than a whole lot of resolution you fail to live up to. Prioritizing this time *and following through* is an investment in a life beyond the ordinary.

VISION AND... "REALITY"

The greatest insights and the most important work sometimes happen after leaving the wilderness. One woman from a religiously conservative part of the country was strongly affected by sitting in council with people who looked her in the eyes, spoke their truth, and openly shared their feelings. Day by day, she opened in response, smiling, laughing, becoming visibly more animated, and allowing more physical contact.

Driving home after the program concluded, she crossed the city limits and burst into tears. Faced with her daily life, she now realized home was a wasteland. It lacked support for who she was or wanted to be; she knew no one with whom she could share what was in her heart and soul. She saw the barren soil and lack of any garden in which to cultivate her longing. Her quest's greatest challenge was not going without food or being alone in the wilderness — it waited at home. Before her lay the difficult work of changing her life.

Like it or not, "vision" does not immediately make you happy. This can be a difficult part of the return. Knowing your truth or having a sense of direction and purpose ultimately results in a wider range of options and possibilities, but it may not feel good. The woman mentioned above acquired an expanded vision and sense of community, a new appreciation of the difference a circle of support could make. But this new awareness meant she could no longer avoid recognizing the wasteland at home.

Any strong experience of truth, community, connection, or possibility makes us more acutely aware of areas in our lives where they don't exist. If the gap between potential or expectations and reality widens, what was once tolerable may now be unacceptable. What was once discounted can't be avoided anymore. Our new vision can, in the short run, make us disturbed and dissatisfied. But simultaneously, we have knowledge of what we want, a sense of direction, and choices we didn't see before. We have more power.

STOPPING THE TRAIN

Imagine you are on a train. Inside this train is a dining car with linen tablecloths, silver plates, crystal, and a fresh rose at each setting. You prepare to sit and have a tasty meal. How wonderful it will be! But an urge comes over you, and you go outside, climb up a ladder, and stand on top of the train. The view is vast, inspiring, but several miles ahead you notice the tracks head straight over the edge of a deep canyon.

You have just had a vision! You have seen something you did not know before. But you no longer have the option to go down, sit in the dining car, and enjoy your meal. There is a loss involved. But there are also new possibilities. You can talk to other people, saying, "Please look where we're going!" You can try to stop the train; you can jump off. You have many choices, decisions, options you hadn't considered before. Your vision has not made you happy, but it offers you new possibilities, directions, and priorities. Likewise, your quest may make you much more aware of what is not working in your life, what is without spirit. In the long term, there's much more potential for happiness and joy, but the short-term effect may feel the opposite.

The man who brought Aikido to the west, Morihei Ueshiba, slight of build and in his eighties, could ward off six large attackers using just a fan. It seemed almost miraculous. His students would ask, "Sensei [teacher], how is it possible for you to stay in balance all of the time?" He would reply, "No, no, no, out of balance all of the time." From his long and consistent practice, he sensed imbalances in minute detail and constantly corrected them, though to others he appeared always centered.

Airplanes flying across the country are mostly on autopilot. Like thermostats controlling temperature, when the plane drifts off course by a certain amount, the autopilot brings it back. New commitments and realizations, or "vision," can function like that autopilot. They become our north star, our rudder and compass. When the storms of daily life, social pressures, and habitual responses blow us off course, vision pulls us back in the right direction. Like Morihei Ueshiba, we become more sensitive to being out of balance, and this awareness of disturbance gives us chances and choices to act and live with more freedom, purpose, and joy.

After contacting deeper realms of the soul and an expanded sense of self, returning to daily life can produce feelings of tension. But whether this is experienced as creative or as psychological tension is in your hands.

Imagine you hold your vision in one hand, your current life circumstances in the other. Your wrists are encircled by a rubber band. The farther you stretch a rubber band, the more tension it's under. If life circumstances and your authentic path are closely aligned, your hands are close to each other and there's little strain. You are on course and feel at peace. But if those life circumstances and your vision are far apart, the elastic band — the circle of your life — will feel taut, filled with anxiety (something could break!) and limitation.

To whatever extent you're able to hold onto and invest your attention and energy in that vision, the tension endemic to that life will be eventually resolved as life circumstances change and move closer to the life you're capable of realizing. But the stress involved in this discrepancy could also be resolved by giving up your vision and hope, becoming resigned, having a drink or two, and watching TV every night. Vast industries are making money by medicating this kind of discomfort and dis-ease.

Summing up, to whatever extent our vision differs from our current circumstances, tension will be present in our lives. But this tension can be viewed as a prompt, a challenge, a reminder of where our work is, seen as an opportunity for passionate engagement with a chance to make a difference. Don Juan, Carlos Castaneda's teacher, said, "Faced with life, we can make ourselves strong, or we can make ourselves weak. The amount of work is the same." Hold to your dreams. Seek and get support in doing so. Your life circumstances will, sooner or later, change.

THE CIRCLE OF PURPOSE

When facing those difficulties, struggles, and obstacles in going back, the ritual of the last night — the Purpose Circle — provides a framework for thinking about this. Each challenge of the return, though different in form, evokes the question, "Can I face this head-on and stay within my purpose circle?" Daily life contains a bigger challenge than that last, long night. Can you stay in your center? Can you stay awake? The stones making the circle represented the allies you have. Your last night you may have prayed for determination to stay awake or protection from cold or animals. You may need every bit of this determination when you face your parents, your lover, the mortgage or the refrigerator.

But you've had practice. Having faced the dark tunnel of the night and passed through death and rebirth, can you enter the daily fray as a spirit living a spiritual life? Your vision quest included many acts of power as you went without food, companionship, and comfort in an unknown and unusual environment. Undertaking a quest was a commitment to live consciously, to stay awake within the dream, to stand at the center of the circle. This commitment must be carried back with us if we're to transform our daily life.

Consider the following example: You enroll in an Aikido class. You do this in response to some intent. Perhaps you've been fearful all your life and want to feel less afraid. Or you want to learn how to handle conflict and not be thrown off balance so easily. You may be doing it for exercise, or from a desire to get more in touch with your body, or because your neighborhood seems dangerous. A dozen different reasons might lead you to this class.

Eventually, you'll be required to step out on the mat. Your opponent will step out as well. You both bow. Your opponent advances, kicking, punching, trying to knock you down. You move, counter, retreat. Perhaps you respond well, or maybe you get thrown. You'll get back up, bow, and do it again. You accept this process, even want and need it, because it helps you develop the skills and attitudes you desire. You engage with, even welcome this aggression in service of your purpose. And it is good.

When finished, you bow again and thank your opponent. The class is over; you make your way home. Opening the door, you see the face of your partner and say, "What's wrong?" She replies, "I'm sorry, I broke the tail light and dented the fender on your car," and you respond, "Jesus Christ, can't I depend on you to do anything?"

You are frustrated, furious. You feel like a victim, but how did you get thrown so easily? A half hour earlier, someone was kicking and tripping you... and it was fine. Now, a dented fender — a blow not even aimed in your direction — knocks you down and drains away your energy. How did you lose your aliveness and vitality so quickly when you walked in the door?

The problem is not with your partner, the car, or the cost of repair — the events and circumstances of your life. Our struggles begin when we cease to be in the center of the circle. Power, purpose, and self-definition have been ceded to the world, and soon everything becomes a blessing or a curse, as we whine, complain, or feel fortunate. One of the most critical tasks of the return is staying connected to your vision and purpose, so those things which threaten to throw you, be they mortgages, college, car payments, work, or relationships, do not turn you into a victim.

The Odyssey took ten long, hard years. But Odysseus didn't give up, drown his sorrow in drink, or complain about the neighborhood. It took perseverance, every ounce of courage, and more than a little help, but he remembered who he was. His purpose was unwavering: to return home and reclaim his throne. Circumstances and the world do not make us victims. We must cooperate to become one: be distracted, forget our dream, and give up the authorship (authority) of our story. Our attention (and our selves) must wander until we're not in our circle anymore.

The fast is over, and you've returned from the desert, mountains, or forest. It may have been rocky, hot, damp, cold, or cloudy. Perhaps you wished the ground was softer, the breeze cooler, the sky clearer. But no one ever shakes their fists at the sky and complains, "I have a right to more sun!" The thought is absurd. You enter the wilderness with purpose and accept what is there. Had it rained, sleeted, or snowed, you would have met the challenge, discovered your endurance, and made something out of it.

But going home, it's so easy to forget. The checkout clerk is grumpy, and we react with resentment, telling ourselves we have a right to not be treated that way. We have no such right. The store clerk (landlord, partner, parent, etc.) is like those clouds that rained on you. She is living in her own head, wrestling with her own demons, barely seeing you at all. Be in the center of *your* purpose circle. Don't take it personally. Take almost nothing personally. Feel frightened, rejected, upset for a moment, but get back to the center of the only space you can really influence.

WORTHY OPPONENTS

In traditional India, a person would seek out a guru he admired and wished to emulate. Perhaps you want to radiate light and unconditional love. You would need a model, an encounter and experience of that possibility, and you would spend time with the guru to be taught, to learn, to somehow absorb that energy.

But you would also need to be shown all the places where you are anything but that. You'd need to see your shadow, resentment, anger, and complaining. Enter the "Upaguru," or worthy opponent, someone to push every button you ever had, someone to bring out all your drama and self-importance. You seek a guru to understand and realize love. But the upaguru will show you all those places where you're not even close.

If you are living with purpose — say, "radiating light and unconditional love" — you accept and surrender to these unwanted "opportunities for growth." You bow and say thanks because you need to see where your work is. The world we return to at the end of the quest may be difficult, but it is rich with upagurus. You will not have to search for them.

Our challenge is to stay within our circle of purpose, and vision is defined as seeing what is really there. When we live with purpose and intention, we also recognize our shadows — what we need to deal with — and rather than avoiding or attacking people who bring up our dark feelings, we can approach, step up and accept the challenge.

Write that letter of intent. Describe your purpose in going back. As you return home, remember. Bring back your purpose circle with you.

It's hard to leave a group you've grown close to and shared so much with. But, it's the love that you've given and shared that makes the parting difficult. This love is a seed that's taken root and grown within us. It's young, tender, precious... and it doesn't have to die when we depart. We can choose to feed it still, choose to carry back the circle of support of our companions and be happy for this tender sorrow. And we can thank The Mystery for vision, for love, and for all those bittersweet blessings of life.

SECTION VIII:
REQUIREMENTS AND RESOURCES

Guide Requirements **163**
Physical-Plane Abilities 163
A Connection to the Land — to Nature 164
A Knowledge of Core Themes and Processes 164
Personal Skills or Qualities 165
Personal Integrity 166

Sample Documents **167**
Preparation Letter (Sample) 167
Flora and Fauna Description (Sample) 169
Equipment List (Sample) 172

Emergency and First Aid Procedures **175**
First Aid Procedures 176
Body Checklist 177

Other Resources **178**
Statement of Wilderness Ethics (Sample) 178
Suggested Readings 179
Poems and Poetry 179
Related Knowledge or Skill Areas 185

SECTION VIII:

REQUIREMENTS AND RESOURCES

GUIDE REQUIREMENTS

Several organizations that offer vision quests to the public — Circles of Air and Stone among them — have training and certification processes to ensure guides working for them are qualified to lead their programs. Certain requirements — camping and wilderness skills or first aid training, for example — will be almost universal, but other differences — the way an organization emphasizes particular themes, or whether guides are granted freedom and encouraged to improvise or are expected to toe the company line — can result in different expectations and definitions about what makes a qualified guide.

I recognize that what gets labeled a "vision quest" can vary widely, and a multi-day excursion into Montana's Bob Marshall Wilderness will require much more, in physical preparation, at least, than an overnight in the woods beyond the field. The following is a brief examination of five core topics, painted with broad brush strokes, that need to be adequately addressed or attended to in order to lead a vision quest well and safely.

PHYSICAL-PLANE ABILITIES

Most vision quests take place in wilderness areas, or in other natural places far away from houses, roads, and traffic noise. Although there are exceptions — a quest in a rural area on a small, private piece of land, for example — this could also mean far away from cell-phone signals, hospitals, or immediate medical help. Though the requirements of any area — and therefore the guides — may vary, those leading vision quests must be competent in and able to meet the requirements of the particular program and place. This could include the following:

BEING IN ADEQUATE PHYSICAL SHAPE

In many California desert quests, participants and guides drive to the base camp. In other parts of the country, getting to base camp requires hiking with a pack, a hike that could be an easy, level mile, or a long uphill trek in thinning air. Whatever it is, a guide must be in adequate shape, not just for the hike in and out of base camp, but also to attend to any participant, possibly far away from base camp, who needs help.

KNOWLEDGE OF, AND COMPETENCE WITH, EQUIPMENT.

Depending on the area, this could include using and repairing water filters and pumps, tying knots and setting up tarps, orienteering and using compasses, dealing with vehicle breakdowns, and being familiar with clothing and rain gear, etc.

AWARENESS OF LOCAL FLORA AND FAUNA, AND ANY RELEVANT CONCERNS AND ISSUES

North America and Europe are fairly safe parts of the world, but no vision quest is without risk. In our Vermont quests, there is very little that poses any sort of danger, although moose and black bears may concern some. Other areas — some of our Southwest sites — are home to mountain lions, lynx, bears, rattlesnakes, scorpions, javelinas, and Gila monsters. Throw in a dash of poison ivy and a sprinkle of cacti, and many could be frightened. The ability to provide participants with a reality check on actual — as opposed to imagined — dangers is helpful, as is giving them information about reducing risks and what do should those encounters occur.

WILDERNESS FIRST AID OR FIRST RESPONDER SKILLS

I have led somewhere around 175 small-group vision quests, and I have yet to need — knock on wood! — any serious medical skill. But it could happen, and I have had many close calls. A guide needs to be prepared for what could happen, not just what's likely to happen. That includes knowing who to call and where to go. Having a list of phone numbers — state police, emergency room, national forest, search and rescue — is important.

But just waiting till someone else gets there is not enough. That could take a long time. As guides, we need to be able to minimize risks, stabilize situations, and have a knowledge base from which to make decisions that could be crucial. Training in either wilderness first aid (WFA) or wilderness first responder (WFR) is essential. These courses — there are too many to list — are offered at different places and times across the country. Google the courses in your area or start here and continue until you find what you need.

Wilderness First Aid: https://www.soloschools.com/

Wilderness First Responder:
https://www.wildmed.com/wilderness-medical-courses/first-response/wilderness-first-responder

A CONNECTION TO THE LAND — TO NATURE

Leading a vision quest requires certain undeniable skills, and if you don't have them, you may not be ready. But skills alone — technical expertise and intellectual knowledge — are not enough. Vision quests are often about healing and becoming whole. That might focus on the inner work of reconnecting to our bodies, senses, self-worth, or original innocence. But the outer work of repairing or reweaving our disconnection from nature and the living earth may be just as important. Often, they go together.

Most people drawn to guiding quests have some kind of love for and deep connection to the spirit of the land. Perhaps we take this for granted; it's hard to imagine anyone leading a vision quest without it. This love and connection could be labeled "spiritual" — a broad, big-picture sense of oneness between the great forces of sun, moon, wind, water, etc., and all that has been created by them. But it could also be more "scientific," a fascination with and appreciation of the infinite and minute detail — soil microorganisms, the structure of the retina, etc. — that allows it all to fit together. Love has many languages. It's just important that it be there.

For many guides, time on and connection to the land is part of their spiritual path. And though there are common elements, this path is not meditation. Most meditative disciplines begin by removing the practitioner from the impact of sensuous and social life. They focus on inner awareness and attend to one thing — the breath, for example — in order to loosen the grip of thoughts, emotions, and the distractions of the outer world. On vision quests, manifestations of the outer world — beautiful sunsets, visitations by lizards, claps of thunder — are not distractions. They are encounters, experiences, invitations to connect and respond. If we truly have emerged from and exist within nature, that connection and relatedness is an inextricable part of discovering who we are.

A KNOWLEDGE OF CORE THEMES AND PROCESSES

If telling someone to "go out into nature; find a place; stay there for four days and nights, don't eat, and then come back" were all that was involved in a vision quest, there would be no need for a guide. (I've actually heard stories of at least one fairly well-known teacher who, other than adding that early return would be a failure, offered little more than that.) But most who guide quests are aware that good preparation and support can be crucial in the power and depth of the experience.

The material presented in the pre- and post-solo phases of the program may need to be tailored to the audience. If the group about to go out consists of a dozen 16- to 19-year-olds, a nuanced exploration of elderhood or the use of words like *archetypes* may be irrelevant or beyond their capacity to comprehend. In fact, hours of sitting around, staying focused, and addressing anything may be a stretch and need to be rethought.

But, assuming you work with diverse groups of adults with a broad cross-section of intentions, goals, and personal histories, you will be well-served to have a basic familiarity and knowledge of the following:

- **Fasting and physical-plane issues.** Since fasting is a part of every vision quest, and people may have fears about it, this is almost a given. But beyond what's relevant to the "average" participant, you will need to respond to people who

- › Are diabetic and have questions about the dosage of insulin if they are not ingesting carbohydrates;
- › Are hypoglycemic and worried about what will happen without carbohydrates and a source of blood sugar; or
- › have histories of eating disorders, like anorexia, and wonder if fasting will trigger old memories and emotions that are toxic and dysfunctional.

- **A general knowledge of vision quest history and lineage.** For most modern people, a vision quest is something outside the box, a novel, even exotic, event. Many will be curious and may ask questions about:
  - › The format and structure of this quest, why it isn't more "Native American," or why a sweat lodge isn't part of it;
  - › Altered states, and whether smoking pot or taking mushrooms is recommended or allowed; and
  - › A zillion other things: People are afraid of the unknown, and a vision quest thrusts us into the unknown. It takes away books, smartphones, comfort, conversations, food, daily routines, and an audience that will applaud or even care about our story. Knowing the questions are coming and where they come from is helpful. Recognizing that anxiety and questions in the face of the unknown are expected and part of the process allows us to let it be... to not feel like we have to make it go away by meticulously answering all the questions.

- **The heroic journey archetype, rites of passage structure, medicine wheel teachings, etc.** These concepts and themes are all part of the preparation process at Circles of Air and Stone. To whatever extent they are part of yours, you should know them well. If not, you should be well-versed in whatever *is* included as part of the pre- or post-quest instructions. The following have all been included in various quests that I'm aware of:
  - › Specific rituals: sweat lodges, pipe ceremonies, fire-walks, shamanic journeys, etc.;
  - › Instruction in meditation, Qigong, tracking, etc. to increase presence or awareness;working with dreams: teaching, training, incubation, interpretation;creating, writing, telling... working with life myths or stories; and
  - › Specific maps of the psyche: four shields, Inca medicine wheel, Enneagram, Myers-Briggs, soul-centric wheel, alchemy, soulmaps, and more.

- **Ritual and ceremony.** A major ritual in itself, a vision quest will likely include many other rituals and ceremonies within it. Required, expected, freely chosen, planned, made up in the moment... stone piles, goodbye circles, death lodges, altars, burnings... the list may be short and simple or long and elaborate, but a guide will need to know the specifics, as well as many possible variations, of rituals that are suggested or recommended by the quest program being offered, as well as the general purposes, principles, and available materials for those who are moved to create rituals and ceremonies of their own. This knowledge base will continue to grow over time. Many possibilities I can now share I'd never considered or heard of until someone came back from their solo having done it.

PERSONAL SKILLS OR QUALITIES

Vision quests have been and could be offered to many particular subgroups. Vision quests for women, men, recovering Catholics, the deaf, French-speakers, the transgendered, war veterans, victims of violence, etc., are all possible, and in those cases, certain specific knowledge, skills, or experience would be required from those who guide. But there are a few general skills and qualities, a lack of which will make guiding and facilitation almost any quest difficult.

THE ABILITY TO SPEAK BEFORE GROUPS

There is a significant amount of instruction involved in preparing people for vision quests, and if you are anxious or get tongue-tied when speaking, this will seriously affect your ability to do what's required. One can practice — taking public-speaking courses or joining Toastmasters may be helpful — but other, more psychological work may be required to quiet the inner critical voices that make this so anxiety-producing.

- In addition, guides do not just give information; sometimes they have to give feedback, say no, or state things people may not want to hear. These situations tend to be more difficult and anxiety-provoking than the former, but they may be no less necessary.

PEOPLE SKILLS

It helps if you are extroverted, enjoy peoples' company, and like to interact with them. But even if you're not, being able to engage, instruct, and direct people without seeming cold or brusque will make that instruction and direction more effective. And becoming "emotionally literate" — able to make "I-statements," speak directly, and share feelings without judgment — will go a long way toward heading off any interpersonal conflicts.

THE ABILITY TO COPE WITH UNPREDICTABLE EVENTS

The unexpected sometimes happens: freak storms, car trouble, washed-out or snowed-in roads, etc. Choices must be made; plans may have to change. The willingness to take responsibility, whether it comes from confidence, commitment to getting the job done, or somewhere else, is something every guide will, sometime, need to exercise or develop.

THE ABILITY TO HOLD SPACE

In the role of guide, we hear and are aware of peoples' emotional difficulties and struggles. We are also responsible for logistics, making sure everyone gets heard, and staying on schedule. Holding space is defined as the ability to witness (without judgment) someone else's emotional state while simultaneously being present to our own. This means we can listen and empathize but not allow one person's needs to take over the group because we also hold the others' needs and the program's needs as well. Sometimes hard to do well or gracefully, it gets easier with practice.

A WEALTH OF PERSONAL EXPERIENCE TO DRAW ON AND SHARE

This, like many things, takes time. After decades, no matter how unique a situation is, you've experienced something like it and you may have a funny story or something useful to communicate. "I don't know" is an honest and fine response until you do.

PERSONAL INTEGRITY

Personal integrity may be the most important quality of a vision quest guide. A simple definition of personal integrity is being who you say you are. Do you walk your talk, practice what you preach? Of course, no one is perfect, but someone guiding others on a journey that requires them to face their fears and access their vulnerability must be someone they can trust, both to bring them back safe and sound and to hold their vulnerabilities and confidences in a respectful and appropriate way. This requires more than just the knowledge and skills to deal with logistics and safety. It requires an inner, or psychological, solidity.

To use a common metaphor, people who quest are often "going out on a limb." When a person goes out on a limb, he or she prays to be supported and wants to know that the branch is solid, that there are no hidden cracks (wounds) that compromise its integrity, that the core is not rotten or eaten away. Guides — those who teach and stay behind at base camp — are a primary source of human support for those undertaking this process, and if they lack solidity or integrity, damage can result.

Walking your talk: are the words you speak, actions you take, and emotions you express in alignment? Do you practice what you preach? We've all heard of gurus who preach celibacy while sleeping with their students, and others who get rich while dismissing material desires. These extremes may never appear during a normal vision quest program, but I've witnessed some huge gaps in integrity in some teachers I know.

A lack of integrity may go unnoticed for a while ("you can fool some of the people some of the time . . .") but eventually it will show up and damage will result. Whether the damage is hurt feelings on the part of participants or actual injury, we damage ourselves by living that way. We cannot control who comes to us to undertake a quest. We could love the group and be sad to see them leave, or we might be happy to have them go. That is out of our control.

But doing our best is within our control. We can ask if we did, again and again. It's good to answer yes.

SAMPLE DOCUMENTS

The sample documents and presentations below are not meant to be taken as any kind of prescription about what wilderness or vision quest guides should do. Rather, they are here to provide examples and to offer suggestions and ideas as you create your own programs with their particular emphases and forms. As mentioned in the introduction to Ritual, what makes a good ritual is whatever works *for you*! Consider these sample documents, presentations, and suggestions in that light. Find, use, and create what works for you.

PREPARATION LETTER (SAMPLE)

To all those undertaking a fasting quest: I honor your desire to participate in this process, your courage and commitment to face yourself alone on this earth, and the calling to discover and unfold deeper and greater aspects of yourself. Most people never take the time, and should they have it, find ways to avoid truly meeting themselves. So, I honor you.

It is important that you read [describe your preparation materials here] as soon as possible. Good preparation makes a difference in the depth and quality of a vision quest, and your preparation takes place on many levels — physical, logistical, mental, and psychological. The specific and practical information on ritual, ceremony, flora and fauna, equipment, etc. is all valuable, but a quest can also reorient our energy and attention away from the concerns of daily life and toward deeper questions of purpose and unattended features of our inner landscapes. The following suggestions can help in this process:

Keep a journal, if you don't already do so. Committing to a vision quest starts the process of preparing emotionally and spiritually. But issues that present themselves at the beginning often change as this process unfolds. Preparation should include refining and honing one's purpose as the time to fast approaches. Issues that arise spontaneously in one's life, as well as dreams, insights, and significant encounters with people or animals can all contribute to this focusing. Keeping a journal can be an invaluable aid in this process.

Write a letter of intent. A letter of intent will not only help you organize your thoughts and deepen your focus, it will help us prepare to help you. Some questions you might consider in a letter of intent include the following:

1. Issues of *severance*: "What parts of my life do I wish to bury, say goodbye to, or leave behind? What attitudes, stances, situations, and habits no longer serve me?"
2. Issues of *incorporation*: "What do I wish to call into my life? What do I want to integrate, take on, or accept? Are there aspects of a new life that call to me?"
3. Questions of the *threshold*, the passage: "What are the monsters in my life? What do I really fear? What are the big obstacles, inner and outer, to my growth? What stops me from letting go of what I wish to sever from, from taking on what I wish to manifest? What are my allies and sources of strength, and what tools do I have to call on them?"

Undertake a medicine walk. A description of a medicine walk is included in your preparation packet. In simple terms, a medicine walk is a one-day journey in a natural place of your own choosing. During the day you follow your intuition, going wherever and doing whatever you are drawn to do without a preconceived plan. This should be undertaken about a month before the actual vision quest. This walk can be an allegory of your life story, and many core issues that are to be addressed in the vision quest may make their appearances. Taking this walk and recording what happened, what spoke to you, the feelings that arose, any animals that appeared, and what all this "said to you" can be extremely helpful.

Answer or write about important questions. "If I went on a vision quest seeking only one thing, what would it be?" Or, "If I had to reduce all my yearnings/feelings//purposes to one question to be answered or one thing to be gained, what would it be?" How is that one desire or question in play in the many specifics of my daily life?

Form a council of allies during the final weeks before the program begins. This group, large or small, is a gathering of people with whom you will share your hopes for and the intentions and purpose of your quest, and whom you will ask for support. They take on the role once performed by the village or clan. They're your community. You can also meet with them after your quest, to share your journey.

When your council gathers, speak to your intent: Share whatever questions you are taking out; what you are beginning, ending, or marking; your hopes and dreams. You might perform simple ceremonies with your council, such as giving items to each person that are symbolic of your quest or telling each person about his or her importance to you. You could ask this council to hold vigil for you during your fasting time or pray for you on the last night. Ask your council for the support you need. Their love and encouragement will feed you during your fast, and your journey will nurture them in return.

These are all suggestions. They've been helpful to many, but they're not exhaustive. We encourage you to discover and do whatever contributes to your preparation, for this process involves realizing and claiming your own authority. We look forward to hearing from and meeting you, and we'll do our best to help you in any way we can.

FLORA AND FAUNA DESCRIPTION (SAMPLE)

This description of physical-plane concerns and flora and fauna in the Aldo Leopold Wilderness is meant to be an example. It may be useful as a model, and you may choose to hand out something like this (or send it beforehand) to participants.

It's impossible to answer in a few short pages all conceivable questions about the varied landscapes in which one might undertake a quest. Even in one area, such as the Southwest, concerns about rainfall, temperature, lightning, fire danger, or flooding vary according to the season, altitude, and current weather patterns. Get familiar with your area and do your best.

FLORA (PLANTS)

Concerns about flora are relatively minor in the Aldo Leopold Wilderness. There are only two plants one needs to pay attention to: cacti and poison ivy. Three basic types of cacti common to the Southwest, barrel, cholla, and prickly pear, all exist here. While in theory avoiding cacti should be easy, they can sometimes be hidden in the grass, hard to see, or close enough to a trail that you brush against them. And of course, people do not always pay attention when walking, leaning back, or lying down, and getting stuck with spines, especially in the foot when not wearing heavy boots, is not an unusual occurrence.

Of the three main cacti varieties, the barrel family (beehive, fishhook, hedgehog, etc.) are usually the least troublesome. Generally small and close to the ground, their spines are usually dense and tightly woven around the plant. In some varieties (fishhook, for example) the spines curve inward and don't resemble ice picks pointing out. Although sharp and able to penetrate lightweight shoes, barrel cacti are less likely to cause harm with a minor impact.

The prickly pear family — beavertail, pancake, porcupine, desert — are very common throughout the Southwest. They are easily recognized by their grey-to-green flattened lobes that are shaped like Mickey Mouse ears. Different varieties range in size from 15 inches to 6-feet high. The majority found in the Aldo Leopold area are of the smaller proportions. Most have sharp spines that can range from one to three inches, but some are relatively spineless. However, those with minimal large spines are usually covered with glochids, golden tufts of numerous small (one-quarter-inch) spines that are hard to remove from the skin.

Cholla cacti are tall (growing up to five feet or more) stick-figured plants with sharp spines. They can be quite bothersome because their "branches" are segmented, and when you brush against them, a whole segment can break off and attach itself to your skin. In addition, like porcupine quills, many chollas have barbed spines. Once they penetrate the flesh they are designed to move inward, and they're hard to remove. Also, when cholla die and their segments fall to the ground, the gray, drying tufts of spines can last a good while and be difficult to see among grasses and other plants.

Poison ivy exists in the Aldo Leopold Wilderness. It possesses the shiny, three-leafed signature of its cousins back east, but unlike them, it grows on a long woody stalk and can reach a height of up to six feet. It particularly loves rocky hillsides that get sun and generally doesn't stray out into the grassy meadows or graveled and sandy flats of the river valleys. If you are allergic, learn to identify it and stay away.

FAUNA (ANIMALS)

The Aldo Leopold Wilderness is home to a wide range of animals. Deer, mule deer, and elk are common. Hawks, vultures, kestrels, and an occasional eagle hunt the hillsides and valley, while along the rivers, ducks, herons, and beavers are not unusual to see. However, this section is restricted to a discussion of those animals that might be a cause of safety concerns.

LARGE MAMMALS

Black bears are common, although their coat may range from black through brown, or even a golden or cinnamon hue. Bears in the wild are shy and will avoid humans if possible. They are mainly nocturnal, but are often out in the daytime, and their dens are usually in areas with thick cover — steep, wooded canyons, for example. Although actual encounters are rare, signs of their presence — scat, torn-apart stumps, turned-over boulders, scratched trees, and torn-apart burrows — can be fairly common.

Wild black bears will generally avoid humans and, upon encountering them, will usually flee. The main exception (and danger) is getting close to, or between, a mother and her cub. The protectiveness of mother bears is legendary, and they can be quite aggressive if they decide you're a threat to their young.

If you encounter a bear and your only concern is safety, you should look slightly askance (some male bears can take a stare as a challenge) and slowly back away from the area. Do not turn your back or run — to do so is to act like prey. While bears are more vegetarian than most carnivores, they are still hunters and very fast over short distances. And if for some reason (highly unlikely) you are attacked by a bear and have nothing to protect yourself with, quickly get down on the ground and curl into a tight ball with your fingers laced behind your neck. This will protect your vital organs.

Mountain lions are found throughout the Aldo Leopold Wilderness Area. A full-grown mountain lion can be 8 feet long and stand 30 inches high. Tawny, straw-colored to reddish above and lighter to white below, they are mostly nocturnal, but are sometimes out during the day. Generally solitary, territorial hunters, they may cover 20 miles in a night. They are usually shy with humans, but attacks, sometimes fatal, have occurred. Reported attacks are often on small individuals who are trail running in the mountains — a classic acting-like-prey situation.

In an encounter with a mountain lion, if your primary concern is safety, do not run away! Stand your ground. Raise your arms up over your head, making your outline and shape look larger. Speak confidently, even a little aggressively, like you are powerful and not to be messed with. And remember, you are a full-grown animal too, one of the most dangerous on the planet. Let the cat know it!

Lynx and bobcats are also native and common to this area. Their habits are similar to mountain lions, but they are much smaller (shorter and less than three feet long) and hence much less potentially dangerous.

Javelina (wild pigs) or collared peccary are quite common throughout this area. A full-grown adult can reach a height of two feet and be almost three feet long, with a large, pig-like head and shoulders. Their bodies are grizzled gray with black and white hairs, and they have tusks that protrude from their jaws. They often roam in large family packs and are usually quite docile, but families with young can charge humans who are acting aggressively. If this happens, quickly climb a tree or large boulder. Those tusks are sharp and dangerous, but javelina are hoofed creatures and will be unable to follow you when you climb.

STINGING AND BITING ANIMALS

Rattlesnakes are fairly common over a wide range of the Southwest, and among the nine most-common species, there are often different races within the species. For example, the Western rattlesnake, one of the most common, may have blotches and bands that vary from beige to black to pinkish depending on the area and soil color of the landscape in which they live. Although separate species are often hard to distinguish, the wide triangular heads, narrow necks, and rattles on the tail make their broader category quite obvious.

All species of southwest rattlesnakes are poisonous, and their bites, though rare, are extremely painful, though not usually fatal. Since most rattlesnake venom is a blood, and not a neurotoxin, the severity of the bite is related to the volume of venom in comparison to the volume of blood in the victim. It usually requires a large snake and a small child, or someone with a preexisting infirmity, to produce a fatality. In over 50% of bites, there is no injection of venom, but a live bite can cause muscle and flesh damage around the bite area, as well as nausea and sickness. Most rattlesnakes can sense ground vibration and will avoid approaching footsteps, although if you get too close, the snake will rattle to warn you of its presence. In that case, stop in order to allow it space to withdraw, or step away yourself.

If someone does get bitten by a rattlesnake, getting medical care as soon as possible, if it is nearby, is recommended. But in wilderness settings, that is often impossible. In that case, the victim should avoid moving, as muscle movement and blood pumping can help spread the venom throughout the body. She should stay warm, calm, and at rest, trying to keep the body part affected as immobile as possible. Sickness and pain over the course of the next 24 hours can be expected.

Snakes are all cold-blooded; they do not maintain a constant, warm, body temperature as mammals do. They need sunshine and/or warm weather in order to be out and about. As the weather gets cold, they become sluggish and could easily fall prey to other animals, so they seek shelter in the ground when cold evenings approach. Knowing this may prove helpful if you are concerned about them. Even if day temperatures are warm, if evening temperatures drop into the 60s and below, the snakes will soon disappear, and one need not worry about stepping on them in the dark. And cold nights are to be expected on spring quests in the Aldo Leopold Wilderness.

Scorpions. There are two genii or classes of scorpions in the American Southwest, and both are found in the Aldo Leopold Wilderness. The first, the giant hairy scorpion (seriously!), can grow to a length of four inches. While the legs and tail may be sand-colored, the main part of the body is darker and can appear black. Like most scorpions, they are mainly nocturnal, and therefore seldom seen. I have seen two in 25 years of leading quests in this area. While they may look ugly or frightening, their sting is akin to that of a bee and not usually considered dangerous.

Scorpions of the second genus, Bark Scorpions, are smaller (usually no more than one-and-a-half inches long) and lighter in color. Tan, beige, or even slightly translucent, they live under rocks, debris, and dead tree bark. Their sting is highly venomous and can be life-threatening to small children. It's very painful and can induce sickness in adults.

The **Gila monster** is a large, venomous lizard. Fat, sausage-like, and up to 22 inches long, it lives in southwest New Mexico and southern Arizona. It has blotches of black, which may be mixed with pink, orange, or yellow. It's fairly rare and primarily nocturnal. (Over a twenty-year period, only one has been seen in this area by participants out questing.) Usually slow-moving, it can lunge quickly. It has a powerful bite, is hard to dislodge, and has poisonous venom in its lower jaw. An attack is not fatal but it is very painful, and it may require medical help to remove the jaw.

The **desert tarantula** is a large arachnid with a hairy body and legs. Up to three inches in size and mostly nocturnal, it can bite and release irritating abdominal hairs if roughly handled. Generally, it's not considered very dangerous.

EQUIPMENT LIST (SAMPLE)

The general equipment list in your preparation manual is adequate, but it can be modified to better fit the particular needs of the quest you are participating in. The following are my thoughts on what's required to undertake a vision fast in a manner that will both keep you safe and allow your attention to be focused on your purposes in coming here, rather than on concerns about safety or comfort.

We will be spending time at two different locations. For the first three days and the days following your solo, we will be camping with cars and vehicles nearby. On the fourth day, we will hike in (about 1.75 miles) to a base camp, from which you will search for your place of power, your "home" in which you will fast during days five through eight. On the ninth day, we will all hike out and return to our preparation camp. In packing, therefore, you should consider the pre- and post-fasting time as well as the solo. During this time, you will be eating, so stoves, food, etc. will be a consideration. We will bring a small backpacking stove, but if you have your own it may be helpful. The cars can be used as closets for gear, so you have the option of being a little more lavish in terms of clothes and comfort during this phase.

TENT

People often bring a tent for the time before and after the solo period and take out a tarp for their time alone. While a tent provides a little more protection, it also creates an experience of being "inside," and cuts off some access to nature. Therefore, we recommend bringing a tarp for the solo. A tarp will provide you with shelter should it rain, and people often sleep out in the open under the stars whenever it is clear (which is most of the time in New Mexico). Instruction on setting up a tarp will be provided during your preparation.

The weight of the tent is not of major concern, since we'll be within walking distance of our vehicles during preparation, and you do not have to backpack the tent into the wilderness. If space and weight are concerns in regard to packing — for example, if you are traveling by plane — you could consider just bringing the tarp.

TARP

An 8' x 10' or 9' x 10' tarp is quite adequate. Larger sizes provide roomier shelter but add more weight. High-quality tarps made of coated rip-stop nylon are available in camping and outdoor gear stores. They are strong and fold up small, but are expensive, around $45. Plastic tarps (commonly bright blue or green, but sometimes brown or camouflage) are adequate, and they may be found in department or hardware store for about $8. They are bulkier and noisier in the wind, but if you think this may be the only time you'll ever use this, it may make more sense to go with economy.

ROPE

You will need rope for stringing the tarp. Fifty feet may be adequate; 100 feet is more than enough. Your rope should be nylon and thin (not clothesline size), preferably about ⅛-inch in diameter. It is sometimes called paracord.

BACKPACK

Your backpack should be comfortable, adequately sized, and in good condition, but this is not a hiking expedition. We will be hiking in about 1.75 miles to our base camp, mostly downhill. It will take us slightly longer on the way out.

SLEEPING BAG

Your sleeping bag should be rated, at a minimum, to 20°F. You may not need that much insulation, but you'll wish you had it if it gets cold, and more is better. The average temperatures for this time of year in the area are a high of 75°F during the day and lows around 40°F at night. We may get the average, or it may be warmer. But consider the possibility it could be 10 or 15 degrees colder, some nights dipping into the mid-20s.

Down bags are lightest and compress into the smallest space for packing, but they are expensive and can lose their insulating ability when wet. Synthetic bags are a bit bulkier and heavier, but they're cheaper and keep most their insulating quality when wet. Cotton or flannel bags are not recommended.

Your feelings of warmth and comfort when sleeping will be increased by having a good insulating pad between you and the ground, and a good warm hat, since your face and head will not be fully inside the bag.

INSULATING PAD FOR SLEEPING ON

The ground can be hard, and a good pad can make your nights more pleasant and comfortable. In addition, the ground is cold, and the portion of your sleeping bag that's beneath you will get compressed by your weight. The insulating value of your pad can make the difference between rest and an endurance test. Most pads are either some form of foam (Ensolite, Ridgerest, etc.) or a foam/air combination, such as the popular Thermarest pads. They vary in cost, thickness, weight, and compressibility. They can also have other uses. (Thermarest sells a nylon "frame" that can turn the pad into a chair with back support.) Here again, your needs and resources may determine whether you decide to go "Lexus" or "Toyota."

People often bring a **ground cloth**. Oftentimes the insulating pad is shorter than you are, resulting in your lower legs and sleeping bag resting on the bare ground. If the ground is damp, the sleeping bag can absorb moisture from it. A simple piece of three-by-seven-foot plastic is fine, or a couple of garbage bags will do in a pinch.

CLOTHES

For all-purpose clothes for cold or wet weather, synthetics are lightweight and work as well as or better than wool. These go by a variety of names — polypropylene, Thermax, Capilene, Synchilla, MTS, fleece, polar fleece, etc. — and they are essentially woven plastic. Therefore, they absorb very little moisture and will keep you warm even when wet. Cotton clothes, though comfortable, absorb large amounts of water, be it rain or perspiration, and once they are wet, they are difficult to dry. If they are on your body, the heat to dry them will come from you. If you do bring cotton clothes (blue jeans, long underwear, T-shirts, etc.) it is important to have good rain gear so they will not get soaked in a downpour.

GOOD BOOTS

Light hiking boots are appropriate for this terrain. The trail down to the area you will be fasting in is steep, 1.75 miles long, and there are many loose rocks. *Boots with ankle support are necessary.* If you have weak ankles and need, or want, more support, a thicker boot may be right for you. The preparation and post-quest phases consist of many group meetings and time sitting in council, and other lighter footwear is appropriate for that time. The solo area is near a river, and people often hike along the river or cross it several times during their quests. Sandals or old sneakers are useful for walking in the river, and they can serve as lighter footwear for other times.

For cold and/or wet weather:

- Good raincoat or rain poncho
- Hat (fleece, wool, or knit), gloves
- Socks (at least one pair should be thick and warm)long underwear — long johns for your legs, and long-sleeved for your torso
- Warm jacket — this may be fleece, down, or whatever you have. Some cold-weather jackets are heavy and will take up half your pack, so consider size.
- Neck warmer (gaiter) or scarf. We lose a lot of heat from around the collar, and these items are small, light, and very effective.

For warm weather:

- Shorts
- Light shirt
- Something for your head — a bandana may be adequate, but if you tend to burn (and the sun is strong in the high desert) — a hat that shades your face will be welcome

WATER FILTER OR PURIFICATION TABLETS

Solo time takes place in a beautiful valley with access to a river. There is also a spring, sometimes running year-round, but in drought years not, that produces good drinkable water. Possibilities for drinking water during your solo are hiking to the spring and filling/refilling your water bottles, taking water from the river and purifying it with iodine or other purification tabs, or using a water filter or pump/filter. Water filters and water purification tabs are available in most backpacking and camping stores.

EMERGENCY KIT

See the list included in your preparation materials.

OTHER EQUIPMENT

- Small day pack
- Clasp knife: a simple folding pocket knife is adequate. Swiss Army knives are excellent.
- Flashlight and extra batteries, or candle lantern
- Large garbage bags (two to six) — these have many possible uses
- Journal, pen or pencil
- Matches made waterproof. Matches kept in a zip lock bag are perfectly fine. Don't be fooled by so-called waterproof matches. Their tips are coated in wax, so the sulfur maintains its integrity, but they are more of a pain than a help. The wax often smears on the striker, so contact and spark do not get made. The heads often break off. And though the matches are protected against water, the box is cardboard and will fall apart if it gets wet and you'll have nothing to strike the match on. Just keep the box and matches dry and you'll be fine. Some bring a disposable lighter for insurance.
- Cup and utensils (These can be metal or plastic. There are Lexan polycarbonate cups, bowls, forks, and spoons that are cheap, almost indestructible, and lighter than metal.)
- Trowel, for digging a pit toilet

PERSONAL ITEMS

Toilet paper and toiletries — toothbrush, paste, floss, biodegradable soap, hairbrush, towel, washcloth, razor, etc. Some of these may be left at base camp during your solo.

OPTIONAL ITEMS

- Musical instrument
- Sacred or ritual objects
- Comfortable clothes for pre- and post-quest time
- Camp stove, pots
- Sunscreen, sunglasses, lip balm
- Needle and thread

EMERGENCY AND FIRST AID PROCEDURES

Emergency procedures become relevant when someone hasn't appeared at the stone pile (see description of stone pile in Section III) and his stone pile partner then finds him injured.

The possible dangers when alone in the wilderness are many, but the likely dangers are far fewer and most of them self-inflicted. Over the years, many hours have been spent talking about rattlesnakes, bears, or mountain lions, reassuring people or giving them a reality check, when what's ordinary and non-exotic — tripping, slipping on a log, or falling when climbing — is infinitely more probable. But there's little to be said about the ordinary. Tripping and falling can happen just as easily at home.

The dangers that are relevant to the landscape and time of year should be addressed as part of the preparation process. Many of these are listed in the physical-plane outline in Section III, but every site may have its own particular set of concerns. As well as animals and the aforementioned falling, these can include lightning, heat exhaustion or stroke, hypothermia, flash flooding, sunburn or sunstroke, dehydration, and exposure to all sorts of environmental conditions due to the vagaries of weather. Most of these will never happen.

But participants need to be given basic information that addresses the "what if?" so they will know what to do and how to seek help should an emergency occur. This needs to be clear, direct, and not too complicated. We cannot assume or expect that those fasting have EMT training or even knowledge of basic first aid. Real help in the form of search-and-rescue or medical professionals may be hours away.

The documents below — First Aid Procedures and Body Checklist — are taken from the final pages of *The Trail to the Sacred Mountain* by Steven Foster and Meredith Little. These have been copied and handed out to participants by many quest organizations in the past. They may prove useful in many situations, but they are based on basic first aid, whose operative mandate is "keep them alive until the ambulance gets there." In the wilderness and on most vision quests, the ambulance won't be arriving anytime soon. For example, if you are the morning person and your buddy didn't come to the stone pile yesterday afternoon because of a clogged airway or excessive bleeding, the instructions below (highlighted in bold) will do you little good. If you can resuscitate your buddy in that situation, you've found your gift!

You may want to use or adapt the documents below or create your own. The requirements in each situation will be unique, and the statement "rules are for fools" is relevant. Assess the situation, use good judgment, and make your best response. A good flow chart for help in making those judgments can be found in Chapter 8, "Safety and Emergency Procedures," of *The Backpacker's Field Manual* by Rick Curtis.

FIRST AID PROCEDURES

(adapted from *Trail to the Sacred Mountain*)

- Make sure the site is safe before you go to your buddy. **DO NOT MOVE YOUR BUDDY.**
- Talk to your buddy and determine if she is conscious. If not, try to wake her (shake gently/shout).
- **Check for and treat any excessive BLEEDING** by applying direct pressure and elevating the wound (except for a head wound).
- **If your buddy is CONSCIOUS:** find out what happened, what injuries and symptoms are present, relax, be loving and supportive, and reassure your buddy (verbal assurance and support are often what your buddy needs most). Observe his level of mental awareness. Treat him for shock. Give water and food (unless stomach injuries are suspected).
- **If your buddy is UNCONSCIOUS: check AIRWAY** — tilt the head back, listen for breathing, and observe the rise and fall of the chest. If there is no breath, tilt the head back to clear the airway (unless you suspect a neck injury). Check the PULSE (carotid on side of neck). If there's a pulse, but no breathing after this, give rescue breathing and continue until breathing resumes, until you're relieved, or until you've tried for one-half hour at least. Check the environment for clues as to what happened. If there is NO PULSE and you believe the pulse may have ceased four minutes ago or less, give CPR if you're certified to do so.
- **Check for and treat symptoms of SHOCK** (discoloration, coolness, paleness, nausea, rapid pulse, thirst). Normalize body temperature (provide warmth or shade as necessary); give water, food (unless stomach injuries are suspected), and reassurance if your buddy is conscious. Elevate her feet six inches if you are sure there are no spinal or neck injuries.
- **Check your buddy's entire body without moving it** — feel for swelling. Note discoloration, high or low body temperature, skin color, unusual odors, discharges, dislocations, etc. (USE BODY CHECKLIST.)
- **Write down observations of your buddy's condition** and the accident scene, as well as anything he told you about his symptoms.
- **Assess the situation** — determine the location. Can a helicopter land there? Report back to base camp. Leave a trail so that guides can find your buddy.

BODY CHECKLIST

HEAD AND SKULL

Injury to the cervical spine (neck)? ____________

Deformities? ____________

Skin color? ____________

Skin texture? ____________

Temperature? ____________

EYES

Contact lenses? ____________

Pupils dilated or unequal? ____________

Non-reactive? ____________

MOUTH

Unusual odors? ____________

Local injury? ____________

NOSE

Blood? ____________

Foreign objects? ____________

Discharge? ____________

EARS

Blood? ____________

Foreign objects? ____________

CHEST

Penetrating injuries? ____________

Bruises? ____________

Breathing difficulties? ____________

ABDOMEN

External injuries? ____________

Rigidity? ____________

Distension or swelling? ____________

Bruising? ____________

Presence of urine or feces? ____________

Irregularity of genitals? ____________

Pelvic fracture? ____________

BACK AND SHOULDERS

External injury/deformity? ____________

Tenderness on touching vertebrae? ____________

Bruising? ____________

ARMS

Skin color? ____________

Temperature? ____________

Tingling? ____________

Tenderness/bruising? ____________

Texture? ____________

Numbness? ____________

Deformity? ____________

LEGS AND FEET

Skin color? ____________

Temperature? ____________

Tingling? ____________

Texture? ____________

Numbness? ____________

Deformity? ____________

OTHER RESOURCES

STATEMENT OF WILDERNESS ETHICS

(This statement may be copied or printed and given to participants.)

Wilderness ethics arise from the recognition and acknowledgment of a two-way relationship, a relationship of reciprocity between humans and the living earth. We respect Nature as the Source of life and recognize that she, in all her myriad forms, is our wisest teacher and a mirror of the soul. The principles stated below result from an attitude of reverence and appreciation for Nature. These principles guide all programs offered by Circles of Air and Stone.

We recognize that each wilderness area is unique and fragile and that the rocks, waters, plants, animals, and all other facets of an ecosystem have a long and complex relationship to their place. This recognition compels us to protect and preserve these places as we immerse ourselves in their beauties, mysteries, and stories.

We believe a good relationship between humans and nature is essential for wholeness. We honor, appreciate, and respect the healing, aesthetic, and spiritual qualities of the natural world. Therefore, we move with care and mindfulness in the places we visit, learning from the plant, animal, and mineral or elemental beings we discover while leaving them undisturbed. To the best of our ability, we restore the land we have spent time on and leave it in a pristine and natural state.

Our purpose includes creating a harmonious relationship with the land, and we do so by loving, protecting, and defending it. To respect both the ecosystem and the rights of humans who follow us to these places, we follow the accepted practices of "leave-no-trace camping" as they have been defined for each region. These practices are followed in regard to building fires; eliminating waste; disposing of trash or garbage; making and using trails and stream and spring setbacks; protecting wildlife, caring for historical and archaeological sites, and properly using vehicles.

As participants in what could be called "spiritually oriented events," we pay attention to the impact of ceremonial practices, such as the creation of altars, medicine wheels, purpose circles, and other temporary disturbances of the land; the use of fire in ritual; and the making and placing of prayer ties or arrows, stone piles, etc. At the end of our time in the wilderness, we dismantle any modifications we have made and restore the land to its original condition.

Our hope and intent are to develop and maintain a sacred relationship with the earth and to treat other humans and the natural world with respect, compassion, and integrity in a spirit of cooperation.

SUGGESTED READINGS

There are many good books that are relevant to the vision quest process. But some seem core, almost necessary, while others have a more tangential relevance. I will try to keep this list to the core; my apologies to any authors or books I've overlooked or forgotten.

FOR A BROAD OVERVIEW

- *The Hero with a Thousand Faces*, by Joseph Campbell, is the classic cross-cultural study of the hero's journey, the "mono-myth" shared by all cultures concerning the human struggle to find or create an identity that can sustain us through the stages of life and bring us into harmony with our community and the cosmos.
- *Letters to the River: A Guide to a Dream Worth Living,* by Sparrow Hart, addresses how the lenses through which we perceive affect the world and reality we live in, for better or worse. And it explores alternative ways to engage with the more-than-human world — the "family of things" — and the sense of connection and intimacy that results.
- *The Roaring of the Sacred River*, by Steven Foster and Meredith Little, looks at the nuts and bolts of self-healing in the wilderness. It includes case histories of guide candidates and the practical aspects of being a wilderness guide.
- *Soulcraft*, by Bill Plotkin, is an introduction and overview of nature-based practices that facilitate an encounter with soul, including dreamwork, vision fasts, council, shadow work, and poetry.

THE CLASSICS

- *Black Elk Speaks*, by John G. Neihardt, is the acclaimed story of a Lakota visionary and healer, Black Elk. His profound and arresting religious visions about the unity of humanity and the world around us have made this a venerated spiritual classic.
- *The Rites of Passage*, by Arnold Van Gennep, a seminal work on rites of passage across world cultures, explains and elaborates on how the ceremonies that accompany key turning points of human life have a common symbolic structure and differ only in detail from one culture to another.
- *The Sacred and the Profane*, by Mircea Eliade, is an exhaustive exploration of the sacred as it has manifested in space, time, nature, cosmos, and life itself, including an expansive view of the human experience as connected, consciously or unconsciously, to it.

POEMS AND POETRY

Poetry is a language that speaks to the soul, and good poems can evoke emotional responses and deepen conversations — about preparation, intention, and purpose, fear, the return, etc. — relevant to the vision quest in ways prose and logical explanations cannot.

If a picture is worth a thousand words, a good poem is worth a chapter of prose. Poets have always been visionaries, explorers of the depths, people drawn to what lies under the surface of things. They open doorways; see beyond what's temporary, arbitrary, or shallow; and seek what's alive, eternal, or enduring. The social concerns of the day (fame, power, success, material things) rarely hold the poet's interest, and the poet inhabits a landscape where words like courage, honesty, love, beauty, honor, and purpose are enduring, vivid, and real.

The few poems copied and commented on below are ones I've used many times to illustrate or introduce various aspects of the quest, but you may have your own favorites that emphasize certain points or perspectives you want to share. Go with what works and feels alive to you, and besides the particular message in any poem, just introducing participants to poetry may be an important gift that they bring home with them.

I use "The Wild Geese," by Mary Oliver, early on to introduce the vision quest process and to emphasize the lesson of making this *your own* quest. The first line of it, starting with "You do not have to be good," helps convey the message that a vision quest is *not about being good;* it has nothing to do with denying, ignoring, punishing, or compensating for the parts of oneself that don't fit some preconceived standard or external idea of what a spiritual event or experience should be; a vision quest is about being real — deeply, powerfully, and intensely real.

The concluding lines of the poem speak of the promise if one can be real. The world calls to you "like the wild geese, harsh and exciting." It does not summon us with harps playing in fields of unicorns and butterflies. The call is "harsh and exciting" because the natural world is not nice. Trees are toppled by strong winds; floods tear apart banks and send rocks and bushes downstream. Animals are hunting and devouring each other in the midst of this beautiful, creative, and fertile field we call nature. The promise in this poem is that if we meet nature on its "harsh and exciting" terms, if we bring our own harsh and exciting inner life, our own raw energy — grief, longing, anger, and sadness — to the encounter, we will be welcomed back into the family of all things. It tells us to be real, to be who we are on a vision quest.

The Wild Geese

You do not have to be good.
You do not have to walk on your knees
For a hundred miles through the desert, repenting.
You only have to let the soft animal of your body
love what it loves.
Tell me about despair, yours, and I will tell you mine.
Meanwhile the world goes on.
Meanwhile the sun and the clear pebbles of the rain
are moving across the landscapes,
over the prairies and the deep trees,
the mountain and the rivers.
Meanwhile the wild geese, high in the clean blue air,
are heading home again.
Whoever you are, no matter how lonely,
the world offers itself to your imagination,
calls to you like the wild geese, harsh and exciting —
over and over announcing your place
in the family of things.

— *from* Dream Work *(1986)*

The following poem, "Praises of This Place," is an excellent introduction to the telling of stories. When the process has been explained and people are ready to share about their solo times, I recite this poem right before the first person speaks. The relevance of the last four lines, "When you are ready, join the conversation — it still needs the strong and delicate sound of your own voice," should be obvious.

Praises of This Place

If not now
when? Who will sing
the praises of this place
if not you?
Can you make love
with limp excuses?
Just one word
in your own voice would cock the heads of robins,
but today they listen only to worms.
Every morning
a thousand birds
give the world a chorus of themselves
without hesitation or regret.
All through the day
the trees and sky
speak in the hushed voices of lovers,
and in the night
the grasses sigh in the warm hands
of the evening breeze
while fireflies flash their honest love
to the distant stars passing overhead.
When you are ready,
join the conversation —
it still needs the strong and delicate
sound of your own voice.

— Thomas Griffin

I use two poems, "The Return" and "Why Mira Can't Go Back to Her Old House," to introduce the last day's conversation about the return. Mythologically, the return may be celebratory or dangerous (as to the last, see *The Odyssey*), and the return to daily life from a quest may likewise be filled with joy or sorrows. These two poems speak to those sorrows ("Why Mira") and joys ("The Return").

I begin the first with some background about the poet, Mirabai: She was born in thirteenth-century India to a prestigious Brahmin family, and early on, married off in an arranged marriage. Her husband later died, and Mirabai left home to seek God, joining and traveling with the Krishna sect. A scandal to her proper family, they tried to force her return, but she ignored their messages and letters. Finally, her brother was dispatched along with instructions: "Put that girl on a donkey and bring her home."

She wrote the following poem in response to her family. The first two lines refer to the process of dyeing fabric. One color, Krishna's ("the dark one"), has stayed, while all the others bleached out.

At the end, she compares the depth and power of her life and experience — "the swaying of the elephant's shoulders" — to the shallowness of ordinary life and her family's social concerns — "a jackass." The obvious comparison between the concerns and power of the quest experience and the superficiality of everyday life questers are about to go back to — "One day sale; don't miss it!"... "Tune in for the final episode of the Bachelorette!" — can be quite daunting at this time.

Why Mira Can't Go Back to Her Old House

The colors of the dark one have penetrated Mira's body,
All the other ones washed out.
Making love with Krishna and eating little,
those are my pearls and my carnelians.
Chanting beads and the forehead streak,
those are my bracelets.
That's enough feminine wiles for me.

My teacher taught me this...
Approve me or disapprove me,
I praise the mountain energy night and day.
I take the path ecstatic human beings have taken for centuries.
I don't steal anything, nor do I hit anyone.
What will you charge me with?
I have felt the swaying of the elephant's shoulders
and now you want me to climb on a jackass.
Try to be serious!

— *Mirabai*

Another Mary Oliver poem, "The Return," speaks to the joys of going back. (I've not reproduced the poem here, but it can be easily Googled and downloaded.) The speaker is the Athenian hero, Theseus, who, intending to kill the Minotaur, volunteered to be sent to Crete and sacrificed. Ariadne, the daughter of Crete's King Minos, is smitten with him. She gives him a ball of string, making him promise to unwind it as he traverses the labyrinth where the Minotaur lives, a maze of passages impossible to find one's way out of. In the poem, he speaks about the string (after killing the Minotaur), the thread representing those positive bonds — of love, community, a place to live out our dreams — that tie us to our people and community.

The poems I've listed below I've found useful to introduce, highlight, or dramatize a particular theme or subject. This is only a small sample — I use many others — and the choice of what to include or eliminate was difficult and a little arbitrary.

- "Singing Images of Fire" — translation by Jane Hirschfield
- "Sweet Darkness" — David Whyte
- "Lost" — David Wagoner
- "The Holy Longing" — Johann Wolfgang von Goethe
- "As if This Were Your Last" — Thomas Griffin
- "When I Was the Forest" — Meister Eckhart
- "The Splendid Torch" — George Bernard Shaw

Singing Images of Fire

A hand moves, and the fire's whirling takes different shapes:
All things change when we do.
The first word, "Ah," blossoms into all others.
Each of them true.

— Kukai (774-835),
translation by Jane Hirshfield

Sweet Darkness

When your eyes are tired
The world is tired also.

When your vision has gone
No part of the world can find you.
Time to go into the dark
Where the night has eyes
To recognize its own.

There you can be sure
You are not beyond love.
The dark will be your womb tonight.
The night will give you a horizon
Further than you can see.

You must learn one thing:
The world was made to be free in.

Give up all the other worlds except the one to which you belong.

Sometimes it takes darkness and the sweet
Confinement of your aloneness
To learn

Anything or anyone
That does not bring you alive
is too small for you.

— David Whyte,
in The House of Belonging

Lost

Stand still. The trees ahead and bushes beside you
Are not lost. Wherever you are is called Here,
And you must treat it as a powerful stranger,
Must ask permission to know it and be known.
The forest breathes. Listen. It answers,
I have made this place around you.
If you leave it, you may come back again, saying Here.
No two trees are the same to Raven.
No two branches are the same to Wren.
If what a tree or a bush does is lost on you,
You are surely lost. Stand still. The forest knows
Where you are. You must let it find you.

— David Wagoner,
in Traveling Light

The Holy Longing

Tell a wise person or else keep silent,
for those who do not understand will mock it right away.
I praise what is truly alive, what longs to be burned to death.
In the calm waters of the love nights
where you were begotten,
where you have begotten,
a strange silence comes over you
as you watch the silent candle burning.

Now you are no longer caught in the obsession with darkness,
and a desire for higher lovemaking sweeps you upward.
Distance does not make you falter...
Now, arriving in magic, flying,
and finally, insane for the light,
you are the butterfly, and you are gone.

And so long as you have not experienced this —
to die and so to grow —
you are only a troubled guest on the dark earth.

— Goethe,
translated by Robert Bly

As if This Were Your Last

One night as I lay in bed
I asked my heart what it wanted
thumping so wildly

about to leap free from
inside my chest.

This is a fine day to die
it said, live as if
this were your last.

So I made a pact with her —
this bloody mother of my life

and every morning this prayer
pulls up the red-soaked dawn —

Strum your bloody strings
I said, pound the sturdy pulse of my life

and I will walk fearlessly
into the dark arms of death

having lived and loved so well
fed fully these moments
all you have given me.

— Thomas Griffin

When I Was the Forest

When I was the stream, when I was the
forest, when I was still the field,
when I was every hoof, foot,
fin and wing, when I
was the sky
itself,

no one ever asked me did I have a purpose, no one ever
wondered was there anything I might need,
for there was nothing
I could not
love.

It was when I left all we once were that
the agony began, the fear and questions came;
and I wept; I wept. And tears
I had never known
before.

So I returned to the river, I returned to
the mountains. I asked for their hand in marriage again,
I begged — I begged to wed every object
and creature.
And when they accepted,
God was ever present in my arms.
And He did not say,
"Where have you
been?"

For then I knew my soul — every soul —
had always held
Him.

— Meister Eckhart

The Splendid Torch

This is the true joy in life, the being used for a purpose recognized by yourself as a mighty one; the being a force of nature instead of a feverish, selfish little clod of ailments and grievances complaining that the world will not devote itself to making you happy.

I am of the opinion that my life belongs to the whole community, and as long as I live it is my privilege to do for it whatever I can.

I want to be thoroughly used up when I die, for the harder I work the more I live. I rejoice in life for its own sake. Life is no "brief candle" for me. It is a sort of splendid torch which I have got hold of for the moment, and I want to make it burn as brightly as possible before handing it on to future generations.

— George Bernard Shaw

OTHER CLASSICS

The poets below have all spoken evocatively about the deeper concerns of life. Their works explore nature, love, the workings of the spirit, promises to the self — the landscape of the soul. Each has a body of work that is extensive; each is worth exploring.

BARDS OF THE SOUL

- Mary Oliver, David Whyte
- Goethe, Ranier Maria Rilke
- The Sufis — Rumi; Hafiz; Kabir... David Whyte

THE LATIN POETS

- Antonio Machado, Octavio Paz, William Carlos Williams

AND MANY OTHERS

- Wendell Berry, D.H. Lawrence
- Chief Seattle, Chief Joseph
- Meister Eckhart, Tich Nhat Hahn

RELATED KNOWLEDGE OR SKILL AREAS

There are certain core elements that are basic to any vision quest: nature, solitude, and fasting. These core elements make up the solo part of the experience. But many other days are dedicated to the preparation for and integration of the experience, and much of this time is spent in some form of group context.

Given that, what a participant remembers as being core, important, or transformative five years after the experience could be the time spent solo on the land, or it could be the connections and bonding that took place in the non-solo part of the program. In that regard, the short list of skills, talents, and abilities below, while not crucial to the vision quest proper, may contribute to feelings of connection and enjoyment that participants may remember long after the experience is over:

- **Storytelling.** The ability to share stories — whether great myths or experiences of past participants — can be a rich and important part of the teaching and mirroring processes. Stories are engaging, can be evocative, and help people see beyond their personal concerns and current definitions of themselves while reassuring them they are part of the community of those who've gone before.
- **Music.** Music, like storytelling, engages and captivates people. Music touches the "old brain," that area of our being that's emotional, sensual, and passionate, a place deeper than our rational, conscious selves. Drumming circles, sing-alongs (especially if someone has brought a guitar), or chanting have been part of many community circles of those going on vision quests, and the connection and bonding brought about is an unexpected gift.
- **Singing**, mentioned under "Medicine Names, Songs, and Animals" in Section 4, Ritual and Ceremony, can also be an effective way to connect with the spirit, the landscape, and one's own inner joy. In addition, various "medicine songs" may provide an avenue for deep prayer.
- **Wilderness skills.** Orienteering, tracking, fire-making, and other "primitive" skills, while not part of the purpose of a vision quest, may, for those who have lost most contact with nature and the land, be an engaging way to open a doorway to what's been lost.

SECTION IX:
FINAL WORDS

GRATITUDE

It's been 38 years since that naïve, enthusiastic young man I was made his ascent to Harney Peak. Many other journeys have been taken; many more miles have been walked. In 1987 I founded Circles of Air and Stone and started guiding vision quests, and for over two decades I've led eight to nine small-group quests each year.

I'm grateful for that and, realizing no one does anything alone, I want to express my appreciation for the guides and teachers who shared their knowledge and taught me along the way. No one is perfect; everyone who carries the light also casts a shadow. I have seen pieces of those shadows in each of my teachers as well as in myself. But guiding quests has been a passion and a path with heart, and the teachers I mention below — engaged in the joys and sorrows of life — have taught me with their hearts as much as with their knowledge and experience.

- First and foremost, Steven Foster and Meredith Little, who, from 1981 until two years before Steven's death in 2003, founded and directed the School of Lost Borders in Big Pine, California. Having read their *Book of the Vision Quest*, I found myself — several years and half a dozen quests after my initial experience atop Harney Peak — in their home to learn the particular form of guiding quests they'd developed over a decade. I wasn't disappointed. I spent two months in their generous presence. They opened their home, hearts, and lives to this stranger, as they have done with so many others over the years. When groups arrived to undergo quests, I assisted and learned. They introduced me to coffee (a special thanks!) and on mornings without programs, I'd join in collecting wood or weeding the garden. They shared their way of guiding, but perhaps more importantly, I learned that people who wrote good books could *be* just as good in their lives. They were the first teachers I'd had who never tried to be anything but human. They walked their talk. By the time I left I was ready, certified, and blessed. Three months later, back in Vermont, I was leading my first quest.
- Sun Bear. I met Sun Bear in 1979. Over the next few years, I participated in several of his Medicine Wheel Gatherings and even became an apprentice. Through him, I met many other teachers, like Wallace Black Elk and Brant Secunda, and was introduced to a spectrum of traditions I hadn't encountered before. This time was a rich stew of knowledge and experience with prayer lodges, vision quests, pipe ceremonies, medicine wheels, etc. But more importantly, I learned to practice starting each day with prayer — lighting the smudge bowl, speaking to the mystery, and expressing my gratitude for the blessings of this life. I have now done that for almost forty years. It has made a difference.
- Wallace Black Elk, who, along with his wife, Grace Spotted Eagle, shared their passion and commitment to a life devoted to the Spirit. I witnessed the grounding and stabilizing influence provided when peoples' most important relationship was with something greater than themselves. With tears, anger, humor, and dignity, they also showed that vulnerability and power need not be opposites. Grandson of Black Elk himself, Wallace's particular medicine was the sweat, or prayer lodge, which he offered generously. But, as often happens, the teachings that come from *who people are* were as, or more, important than what they did.
- I'm also grateful for the wisdom of Joseph Campbell, a man I never met, though I've spent hundreds of hours watching and listening to his talks and lectures. I've also read most of his books, using many as a reference in designing and crafting workshops. Brilliant, and exuding a quiet joy, he put words to what I knew in my heart but had not yet learned to say — words affirming and validating archetypal forces, the collective unconscious, or, as I've come to call it, that Spirit-that-Moves-Through-All-Things.

In the late 1960s, I attended college at Stanford as the winds of change blew hard across the land. Black power, feminism, LSD, hippies, and the Vietnam War formed the real curriculum, whatever traditional classes might have been attended. Though I was enrolled in a "good school," the big, unavoidable lesson was that I wanted no part of the life that school was preparing me for. But becoming clear on what I didn't want, alas, provided little direction or picture of what I did.

Thankfully, along came Carlos Castaneda. In his *Teachings of Don Juan, a Yaqui Way of Knowledge*, and in the many books that followed, I glimpsed another possibility. I sensed — if I could just mold myself and my life — a potential to see the world through a different lens, to live in a more magical universe. This would not be an easy task, but those books gave me hope. They encouraged me to let go, inspired me to explore outside what was known and acceptable. They challenged and emboldened me to begin a journey without a certified map or predetermined destination, and offered a code, of sorts, to live by.

MY VISION

I have undertaken approximately 35 vision quests since that first experience in 1980. Certain themes have recurred, but each has been unique. There is no way I could sum it up and say, "This is what I have learned." Nor would I want to.

In 1987, the first time I trained with Steven Foster and Meredith Little, I went on a quest dedicated to one specific question: "Should I become a vision quest guide? Is this path for me?" I think every potential guide should commit to a quest addressing this issue, seeking confirmation from the Spirit, from something larger than our conscious selves. Anyone — I certainly did — could have motivations related to self-importance, to the ego's desire to be perceived as a certain kind of person. "By what authority do you do this work?" is a question vision quest guides may sometimes have to answer. Where does your power, legitimacy, or confirmation come from? Authority... author... authenticity — what story, or whose, is being told and served in the act of guiding quests?

On that quest, my confirmation was fairly immediate, a fairly unexplainable event "out of the blue" — it literally fell out of a cloudless sky as I reached the entrance of my chosen canyon. I was here to connect earth and sky, to bring the rich teachings of shamanism and primal peoples — the earth tradition — together with those of the sky, the spaciousness and clarity found in Buddhism, and the archetypal energies represented by the heavenly gods in Greek, Christian, and other mythologies.

This message continued to unfold and flesh out over the succeeding days. My task (or delivery system) was to bring forth and translate ancient wisdom teachings into modern forms, and to do this through guiding quests and other adventures of the spirit. In addition, this poem, along with the name of our organization, arrived as an expression of that vision and mission:

Circles of Air, Circles of Stone...
The Earth circles, and night follows day.
We bury our seeds; we bury our bones;
While sacred birds circle and prey.

Circles of Air are fashioned by hawks soaring on thermals and tracing spirals up in the sky. Sky symbolizes heaven, the realm of the infinite, and sky teachings point us towards what's archetypal and transpersonal... to the perennial wisdom associated with the great spiritual paths.

Circles of Stone — like Stonehenge, kivas, and the medicine wheels found throughout North America — point us to the earth and her traditions. Solid, grounded, and rooted, earth teachings bring us to *this* life and tell us that it is possible — and important — to embody something grand and magnificent within it.

The earth circles, and night follows day. In nature, everything is connected. All seeming polarities, like summer and winter, yin and yang, are contained within a circle. To be whole, we cannot just follow the light and pay attention to what's familiar and comfortable. We must honor the darkness; see our shadow as well.

We bury our seeds; we bury our bones. Life is marked by passages, by beginnings and endings. We plant, and we bury. Our lives are received from and must be given back to the earth. New seedlings are fed by decomposition and decay. Joy and sorrow walk hand in hand; every beginning marks an ending (and vice versa). These passages need to be honored, not avoided, and it's by giving back, not by getting what we want, that we sustain life.

While sacred birds circle and prey. Pray... or prey? Elegant, majestic, and seemingly weightless as they soar toward the heavens, those birds are hunting, their sharp eyes and breathtaking vision focused on (and ready to devour) the earthly life below. As above, so below: embodying a sensuous, physical life on the ground is what fuels and makes possible that exhilarating climb to the sky.

For millennia, westerners have been taught to look to the heavens. In doing so, our bodies, emotions, and the feminine qualities of sensuous, living nature were forgotten. But the word *human* comes from *humus* — to be of the earth. Christ, born in a manger, amidst the straw and the animals, once said, "My kingdom is expressed all throughout the earth, and people do not see it." Gazing skyward, we miss what's right at our feet: a spiritual path right here, a recognition we're standing on holy ground.

I've written this book to help those of you who want — through leading vision quests — to help bring our people back into good relationship with the earth that created us. We've all evolved and grown from this living planet, and the recognition of a presence and power woven all throughout the natural world constitutes the primal human spiritual experience, the foundation upon which the structures of most religious beliefs have been built.

Primal cultures referred to this living presence as the Great Mystery. It was the source and origin of everything — all facts, forms, and expressions of existence — the wellspring out of which emerged all that could be experienced and known. This Great Mystery was a focus of reverence, the matrix, mother, background to, and context within which we live, learn, and perceive.

To experience the Great Mystery was to know the Creator. To experience means to be intimate with, and developing a relationship of appreciation, gratitude, and respect with this Unknown was the primary task of life. Creating, nurturing, and sustaining this relationship led to a sense of belonging, of finding one's place in the universe and having a home. Discovering Nature and our inner nature are intimately related, and developing this relationship results in deep feelings of peace and an experience of wonder, purpose, and connectedness with all parts of creation.

People in the twenty-first century have inherited cultural belief systems of separation and disconnection, and they suffer the wounds, pain, and dysfunctions that result from those stories. Healing and becoming whole is both personal and cultural, and I believe healing the pain of our personal histories must happen in the context of a new story or "dream" that connects us to our deepest truths, and to the gifts we're meant to carry and bring forth to the earth community.

As we've heard, a famous quote goes:

A vision without a task is but a dream.
A task without a vision is drudgery.
A vision with a task is the hope of the world.

This means that spiritual realizations must be incorporated — embodied — to become real. The new story requires bringing vision and task — earth and sky — together. Rather than transcendence, we seek embodiment and expression, the bringing forth of our uniqueness, power, and radiance to give back, feed, and befriend the world. Rich encounters with the "other world" should thrust us into more profound confrontations and engagements with this one, demanding we become deeper, wiser, and far more human as we approach the divine.

This will require developing an expanded sense of self, a heart big enough for the paradoxes and polarities, and strong enough to accept the joys and sorrows, insights and disillusionments, springtimes and falls. The unavoidable difficulties that deepen our encounters with our souls must be honored if heaven is to be found here and now, enacted within life. We are in Earth School. Escaping to another world, at the expense of this one, avoids half the curriculum. We must be engaged in both to be whole. Sun Bear, my former teacher, said, "If your vision doesn't grow corn, I don't want to hear about it."

Becoming fully human involves embracing our wounds, our personal history, and the magnificence of what nature has created within us while leading functional and soulful lives that make a difference in our communities. Illumination isn't an endpoint. After we're born again, we have to grow up and learn to act like adults if we're to find ourselves back in the Garden again.

Leading vision quests can be a calling, a spiritual path, a path with heart. To you who are committed to "taking people to the mountain," I honor the courage it takes to choose a sometimes-difficult path. I also honor the wisdom involved in avoiding those well-worn, rutted tracks that are hard to break out of and might kill your soul. Leading quests is important work and a sacred task. Helping people embrace their shadows and discover their passion, purpose, and voice, while developing a relationship with something greater than the self they currently know, *is* a dream worth living.

I celebrate and believe in this work. I've witnessed the power that comes from transforming struggles into heroic adventures, and the joy that results from doing so. I want to bless you — all who read this — on your journeys toward meaningful lives, lives where you can give your unique gifts and make a difference. Carry the torch forward! It will bring warmth to your heart and the hearts of those you love. And it will be a beacon of light to those who are lost and searching for the way home.

— *Sparrow Hart*
May 2018

NOTES

Made in the USA
Middletown, DE
28 June 2022